YALE AGRARIAN STUDIES SERIES

James C. Scott, Series Editor

The Agrarian Studies Series at Yale University Press seeks to publish outstanding and original interdisciplinary work on agriculture and rural society—for any period, in any location. Works of daring that question existing paradigms and fill abstract categories with the lived experience of rural people are especially encouraged.

—James C. Scott, *Series Editor*

James C. Scott, *Seeing Like a State: How Certain Schemes to Improve the Human Condition Have Failed*
Steve Striffler, *Chicken: The Dangerous Transformation of America's Favorite Food*
James C. Scott, *The Art of Not Being Governed: An Anarchist History of Upland Southeast Asia*
Timothy Pachirat, *Every Twelve Seconds: Industrialized Slaughter and the Politics of Sight*
James C. Scott, *Against the Grain: A Deep History of the Earliest States*
Hannah Holleman, *Dust Bowls of Empire: Imperialism, Environmental Politics, and the Injustice of "Green" Capitalism*
Johnhenry Gonzalez, *Maroon Nation: A History of Revolutionary Haiti*
Christian C. Lentz, *Contested Territory: Điện Biên Phủ and the Making of Northwest Vietnam*
Dan Allosso, *Peppermint Kings: A Rural American History*
Jamie Kreiner, *Legions of Pigs in the Early Medieval West*
Christian Lund, *Nine-Tenths of the Law: Enduring Dispossession in Indonesia*
Shaila Seshia Galvin, *Becoming Organic: Nature and Agriculture in the Indian Himalaya*
Michael Dove, *Bitter Shade: The Ecological Challenge of Human Consciousness*
Japhy Wilson, *Reality of Dreams: Post-Neoliberal Utopias in the Ecuadorian Amazon*
Aniket Aga, *Genetically Modified Democracy: Transgenic Crops in Contemporary India*
Ruth Mostern, *The Yellow River: A Natural and Unnatural History*
Brian Lander, *The King's Harvest: A Political Ecology of China from the First Farmers to the First Empire*
Jo Guldi, *The Long Land War: The Global Struggle for Occupancy Rights*
Andrew S. Mathews, *Trees Are Shape Shifters: How Cultivation, Climate Change, and Disaster Create Landscapes*
Francesca Bray, Barbara Hahn, John Bosco Lourdusamy, and Tiago Saraiva, *Moving Crops and the Scales of History*
Deborah Valenze, *The Invention of Scarcity: Malthus and the Margins of History*
Brooks Lamb, *Love for the Land: Lessons from Farmers Who Persist in Place*

For a complete list of titles in the Yale Agrarian Studies Series, visit https://yalebooks.yale.edu/search-results/?series=yle10-yale-agrarian-studies-series.

The Invention of Scarcity

Malthus and the Margins of History

DEBORAH VALENZE

Yale UNIVERSITY PRESS

New Haven and London

Published with assistance from the Annie Burr Lewis Fund.

Published with assistance from the foundation established in memory of James Wesley Cooper of the Class of 1865, Yale College.

Yale University Press books may be purchased in quantity for educational, business, or promotional use. For information, please e-mail sales.press@yale.edu (U.S. office) or sales@yaleup.co.uk (U.K. office).

Set in Minion type by IDS Infotech Ltd.
Printed in the United States of America.

Library of Congress Control Number: 2022942177
ISBN 978-0-300-24613-1 (hardcover : alk. paper)

A catalogue record for this book is available from the British Library.

This paper meets the requirements of ANSI/NISO Z39.48-1992 (Permanence of Paper).

10 9 8 7 6 5 4 3 2 1

For Ruth L. Smith

Contents

Contents

Preface

We live in an era preoccupied with issues of social justice, global inequality, and environmental degradation, making this a good time to talk about the historical roots of scarcity in relation to food. For the past decade, I've taught a course on the history of European food that begins with two propositions: everyone needs to eat and everyone once worked at procuring food. The story necessarily shifts over the millennia to property ownership and land use, then over the centuries to agricultural improvement, industrialism, the modern market, and hunger in a world of plenty. Missing from required reading in these contexts is an explicit historical analysis of how food became a transactional variable like anything else, most noticeably for those who could least afford it and often for those whose ancestors might have produced it. Contemporary production of food, caught up in a complex system of marketing, encourages modern consumers to disregard such fundamental questions.

To my mind, Malthus stands at the center of this, though his role has never emerged in a straightforward way from his own writings. Scholars in charge of his legacy generally recognize that Malthus held outdated ideas about economic growth, but they nevertheless value his insights into economic life and sexual reproduction. Most well-educated people believe that Malthus was a "Malthusian" in favor of limits to individual reproduction, yet correcting that misunderstanding only deflects attention away from more important prior questions about who governs available resources, their use, and their distribution. As one of the founding theorists of neoliberal economics, Malthus played an important part in ordering our thinking about these issues. The ecological trap implicit in his story poses a timely question for a new generation: we need to look at what he had to say whenever he actually talked about food.

I have pondered Malthus on multiple occasions during my own career as a student, a teacher, and a scholar, wrestling against the perplexing power of his formula. Only recently did a fissure appear in his historical armor when I had a crucial insight while reading his diary of travels to northern Norway. I had just completed a book on the history of milk when I encountered his meticulous chronicle of reindeer dairying by the Sami people and I had a hunch that those pages offered a clue to the larger issues embedded in his famous *Essay on the Principle of Population.* Though Malthus had devoted considerable energy to this exercise of observation, the people of Lapland figured nowhere in his definitive revision of the *Essay* in 1803. It was clear that the northern herders posed "a problem of translation," to borrow a phrase from Dipesh Chakrabarty, as an anomalous feature of human life outside European civilization. Here was an unexpected way to pry open the constraining conventional context of political economy, which left no room for alternatives to a very specific standard of food production.

I am not the first to question Malthus's narrow gauge for humanity, yet historians have stood back from asking how much Malthus actually knew about the rural world. When presented with practical evidence, he tended to hold fast to theoretical positions and dismiss matters that failed to correspond to his own model of social and economic life. His inattention to the productive work of women (including within the dairy) led to obvious problems in understanding the survival strategies of ordinary families and the interplay between rural and commercial society. I devoted a chapter to that fact in a book on women workers in Britain, going as far as to label the key transitional phase of industrialism as "the Age of Malthus," when the work of women was subsumed under the larger project of creating a civilized female sex in the early nineteenth century. Now I realize that the *Essay's* narrow comprehension of rural inhabitants (by far the majority of the European population during his lifetime) and his peculiarly negative view of pastoral life deserve deeper analysis: they point to assumptions about the longer history of humanity and our basic interactions with the environment. Malthus was committed to an eighteenth-century model of social progress—what I identify as stadial theory in what follows—that rendered "backward" rural producers, along with pastoral peoples, as vestiges of the past and obstructions in the path of progress. I soon became aware of an equally influential system of human classification embedded in that body of thought, which Malthus helped to cement into place at the beginning of the nineteenth century. His narrow gauge carried important implications for the history of agriculture, particularly for those occupying the margins of rural society and, significantly, colonial spaces that would be deemed marginal in nature by western European nations later in history.

In order to pursue a new view of Malthus, I have adopted an interdisciplinary and synthetic approach to a wide array of subject matter in British, European, and environmental history. Scholarly research has grown increasingly specialized and narrow over the past few decades, particularly in the empirically grounded methodologies favored by British historians. Larger arguments are often only implicit in the work of junior scholars, who may worry about securing employment and acceptance in their fields before treading on academic minefields. In the course of researching this book, I was struck by how many important findings lay untapped and thus unfulfilled, as it were, either because they spoke to a narrow subspeciality or because times had changed and the general direction of research had left evidence and ideas undiscussed. In many ways, then, my argument rests on the shoulders of several generations of scholars who came before me.

By necessity, this book begins with a consideration of the general argument of Malthus, including its persuasive power as a hieroglyph for scarcity. Relying on grain agriculture as a universal measure of food and civilization, Malthus offered a dire forecast for food production alongside humankind's propensity to reproduce. The explanation for the origins of these two constructs lies in the context in which Malthus wrote his *Essay.* Chapter 2 examines biographical details contributing to Malthus's profound rebellion against Enlightenment optimism and centuries-long customary benevolence shown the poor in Britain. Malthus reacted against his father's infatuation with Rousseau, a fact that merits closer examination and that provides insight into the contrary orientation of his writing. The dramatic tenor of the *Essay* was hardly new to eighteenth-century readers of Gibbon and the Ancients. But as chapter 3 shows, Malthus used these very sources as a basis for his own origin story about the connection forged between civilization and cultivation posed against the savage existence of barbarians. Within this depiction lay an important dynamic of power. Writ large as a struggle against nature, Malthus aligned his arguments with mainstream agricultural production of wheat, or corn, and its physical realities in the English countryside. Given what we know about marginal forms of rural life that were eclipsed and overruled by agricultural improvement, this chapter establishes a way to think about such oppositions in relation to property ownership, land use, and marginality.

Malthus mined the texts of political economy in order to fashion his own portrait of the way in which Indigenous populations related to the environment, analyzed in chapter 4. The "ignoble savage" of the New World provided him with a foil reminiscent of Rousseau, but with a sleight of hand, Malthus rendered the concept just as pertinent to the laboring classes of Britain. Their lazy inattention to the commands of nature proved that the staff of life demanded urgent defense, represented by the British plan for civilization. As primitive human beings, savages reminded the cognizant reader of categories of humanity destined to inferiority. Buoyed up by the case for wheat cultivation, Malthus adeptly negated other paths to agricultural modernity. To place this strategy in its proper context, an interlude following chapter 4 gives a brief history of the centrality of bread to European culture. Chapter 5 moves beyond the prescribed formula of modern agriculture in order to see the dominance of grain agriculture within a longer trend, the Great Domestication, as a framework for cultivation on a global scale in the late eighteenth and early nineteenth centuries. All these threads, though distinct, are intertwined within the story of how Malthus's *Essay* aligned social attitudes with the emergence of a new era of economic thought.

Two final chapters examine lifeworlds outside the model of modern western European economies. Chapter 6 takes the fundamental test for property ownership used by the British—the act of employing the land beneficially through cultivation—and measures its capacities within a wholly different ecosystem. Malthus searched the Scandinavian settings he visited for familiar paternalist arrangements of British agriculture and social relations, which he seemed to have found in isolated settlements here and there. What he missed seeing is worth our consideration. His voyeuristic visit to a Sami settlement, like the ponderings of John Locke over America, revealed their territory to be an amalgam of place, time, and a familiar ethnic imaginary. Malthus viewed the Sami people from a conceptual distance and felt no compunction about applying a measure of superiority to them. A more anthropological approach to humans and animals in their relationship to the environment uncovers the limitations of the aspiring political economist. While Malthus believed that Indigenous peoples carried on a brutish, parasitic relationship to their environment, my account aims to turn the tables: his refusal to eat the products of the region and his wish to shoot a valued bird of prey shed light on the closed categories of history and humanity he brought to the task of population theory.

History cannot be undone, yet chapter 7 attempts to unravel historical developments in order to imagine different designs with possible alternative outcomes. To this end, I have used the detailed work of agricultural economist Ester Boserup and rural historian Joan Thirsk, whose perceptiveness enabled them to make arguments for diverse approaches to agriculture. Their findings went against the grain of contemporary work in their respective fields, development studies and agricultural history, yet they pursued their points at great length. Both women argued that in rural development, a great deal of evidence was dismissed without a hearing in the court of history. In light of the inadequacies of monoculture and trade policies that extinguished the small landholder and producer, they illuminated alternative pathways for rural inhabitants in Europe and the Global South. Such options may have been more sensitive to soils, climate, and livestock, as well as the autonomy of people rooted in a variety of settings. "Sustainability" was not a term in use when they did their fieldwork, but it has been applied to their evidence in retrospect. The ideas of Malthus have left us less able to deal with food insecurity and precarity in our own times, so we must forge new ways of thinking about land use and resources. At least one thing is certain: when returning to the questions raised by Malthus, we are more likely to arrive at clear approaches to the production of food by using a wider gauge for humanity.

Acknowledgments

I would like to thank Shannon Stimson for giving me the opportunity to return to the subject of Malthus more than a decade ago, when she invited me to join a group of scholars contributing essays to a new edition of *An Essay on the Principle of Population: The 1803 Edition* in the Yale University Press series "Rethinking the Western Tradition." Shannon gave me encouragement long after that assignment was complete, and though I should add the required disclaimer—the remaining faults are my own—her interest in my work on Malthus enabled me to resume work some years later. Thanks also go to Steve Pincus, who introduced me to Shannon at one of his many stimulating gatherings at Yale. Tim Alborn helped me launch an early piece of this project when he invited me to deliver a plenary address at the Mid-Atlantic Conference on British Studies in 2013. Even though the subject matter, Malthus in Lapland, seemed eccentric at the time, that lecture generated the seeds of this book.

Some projects emerge fitfully and this was one of them. It took a long time for me to understand that what I was trying to say belonged between two covers. I'm grateful to Harriet Ritvo for helpful conversations over long lunches for over a decade, when I came to realize that the study of agriculture needed to be tied to environmental studies. One of my last conversations with the late Eric Hobsbawm, an anchor for my career over many years, included a lively discussion of Malthus, a fact that has fueled my determination to see this project through to its completion. Serious thanks go to Jim Scott, who responded to my proposal with crucially timed affirmation and then offered comments on a section of the manuscript that reoriented me yet again. A moment of serendipity followed, when he directed me to his editor at Yale, who happened to be the same editor who helped me with *Milk: A Local and Global History*, Jean Thomson Black. I'm deeply grateful for her wise guidance, steadfast skill, and friendship, making me the luckiest of authors twice in one lifetime.

Tim Alborn, Steve Hindle, Penny Ismay, and Tom Laqueur read the manuscript in its entirety and gave me invaluable advice, in some cases, right up to the final moments. Important intellectual debts were incurred in quotidian time: Penny Ismay has been a true intellectual companion, responding to every stage of my thinking, sometimes even while running. Tom Laqueur issued numerous warnings against an unhealthy fixation with Malthus, while offering his incomparable friendship and intellectual insight over the years. Seth Koven made wonderful suggestions early on, Tim Alborn helped with creating a title, and Prasnannan Parthasawathi became my regular pandemic correspondent on the topic of the margins. Donna and Richard Vinter listened to the progression of my thoughts for years and provided an anchor for me every step of the way. John Walsh exercised his continuing guidance in helping me place Malthus within religious history at an early stage of my thinking. Fredrik Albritton Jonsson, Anya Zilberstein, and Thomas Wickman shared their expertise in environmental studies. Many others contributed in one way or another, including Virginia Berridge,

Ann Blair, John Bohstedt, Arianne Chernock, Brian Cooper, Steve Hindle, Marianne Kowaleski, Lindsay O'Neill, Guy Ortolano, Dotti Osterholt, Tawny Paul, Susan Pedersen, George Robb, Nick Rogers, Ellen Ross, Henry Schapiro, Pamela Smith, Selina Todd, Susan Tomes, Maya Feile Tomes, Judy Walkowitz, Merry White, and Ben Wurgaft. An animated and helpful gathering at the Early Modern History Seminar series at the Huntington Library made a difference in the final revisions. I am also grateful to the dynamic participants at annual meetings of the North American Conference on British Studies, where a great number of colleagues in British history not mentioned here challenged my thinking and sustained my commitment over the years.

The academic environment of Barnard College and Columbia University has nourished my intellectual life for many years. Without the example of my students, demonstrators of radical vision and intellectual courage, I wouldn't have been able to mount the arguments in this book. Provost Linda Bell and President Sian L. Beilock of Barnard College have given me generous institutional support. Among my brilliant colleagues, special thanks go to Lisa Tiersten, Timea Szell, Herb Sloan, Martha Howell, Dorothy Ko, Andrew Lipman, Nara Milanich, Anupama Rao, Nancy Woloch, Carl Wennerlind, and, most recently, James Stafford. Joel Hopkins, Sam Coggeshall, Barnaby Raine, and Mahir Riaz contributed impetus for the project in ways they may not recall. Madison McManus provided research assistance, and Sully Rios gave me endless administrative help.

I owe deepest thanks to my daughters, Emma and Rosa Gilmore. I hope they know that I couldn't have written this book without their remarkable love and presence in my life. My late husband, Michael Timo Gilmore, discussed the earliest phase of this project with me and would have celebrated its completion. The late Phyllis Emsig and the late Kitty Griffith were important throughout subsequent years of helpful conversation and support. The pandemic underscored just how crucial friendships were to any attempt at thinking. I remain grateful to dear friends who kept me (and this book) going: Michelle Anders, Tanya Braganti, Irene Briggin, Cy Britt, Laurie Burt, Nancy and Charlie Carney, Jomo Fray, Kim Hays, Kaia Huseby and Andrew Mathews, Amulya Iyer, Dorothea Nelhybel, Janna Malamud Smith and David Smith, Ruth Smith, Rudy Williams, and Lewis Wurgaft and Carole Cosell. My musical friends sustained my life beyond books, especially during the summers: thanks go to Stephanie Engel, Laura Goldberg, Nadja Gould, Makiko Hirata, Lynn Nowels, Anna Williams and Misha Veselov, along with Ari Isaacman-Beck, Anthony Marwood, Anita and John Ranelli, Viki Roth, Lynn and Bruce Waxman, Margaret Everett, John Burt, and Catherine Stephan and Seth Knopp.

The earliest years of this project were supported by fellowships from the Guggenheim Foundation and the American Council of Learned Societies. The following libraries and collections deserve thanks: the British Library Rare Books Room and Manuscripts Collection; Jesus College Library of Cambridge University; the Malthus Library, Jesus College, Cambridge; the Wellcome Library; the Bodleian Library of Oxford University; Butler Library of Columbia University, including the Rare Books and Manuscripts Division; and Widener Library of Harvard University. Because a good deal of this book was written during the pandemic, I am grateful for the many digital collections available through Columbia University. For their kind responses to requests for images, I owe special thanks to Åsa Henningsson, Uppsala University Library; Alexia Boyd, Greenville County Art Museum; and Brianna Gormly at Butler Library, Columbia University.

At Yale University Press, in addition to Jean Thomson Black, I would like to thank Elizabeth Sylvia for her tireless expertise and support, along with technical assistance with images, and Elizabeth Casey for her superb copyediting. I am also grateful to Joyce Ippolito for expert management of the final stages.

My final debt is to Ruth Smith, professor emeritus of philosophy and religion at Worcester Polytechnic Institute. Her intellectual courage and creativity led us to collaborate on the topic of marginality many years ago, when we wrote an article together for *Signs.* It finally occurred to me that almost every one of our conversations has continued the thread of argument begun back then. The dedication of this book is a small gesture of thanks for her unwavering friendship and for helping me see, among other things, that Malthus negated the margins.

1
Immortal Malthus

Food is essential to human survival. Without sufficient nourishment, people are unable to perform ordinary tasks and they eventually weaken, sicken, and die. Given the wealth and plenitude of modern nations today, starvation is an unconscionable form of suffering, which governments over the past several centuries have aimed to eliminate. These statements stand as commonly held assumptions, yet they exist alongside defiant misunderstandings that act as barriers to achieving basic goals. For example, the general public doubts that enough food currently exists to feed everyone on our planet. Typical views often echo the erroneous bestseller of 1971, Paul Ehrlich's *The Population Bomb,* which presented human beings as hapless creatures on an inevitable path to numerical self-destruction. Starvation appears as inherently related to scarcity and a surplus population. According to this line of reasoning, the fault lies in reproduction, particularly when it occurs among poor populations and in economically vulnerable nations. Aiding people in such circumstances, so the reasoning goes, will only result in their passive dependence and heedless numerical growth.

At a more strategic level, serious problems of food distribution stymy efforts at eradicating hunger. The production and supply of cheap food in modern western countries overwhelms local economies elsewhere and enforces particular market practices. Farmers in wealthy nations are often paid to take land out of production or destroy crops that are deemed overabundant. At the same time, people who live on the land—in rich countries as well as poor nations—can lack the resources to eat, just as urban residents find themselves in food deserts that obstruct the way to affordable nutrition. In the realm of global politics, food exists within a complex web of transactional assumptions: powerful players demand certain conditions in exchange for basic necessities, including food. Vulnerable nations are forced to accept terms dictated to them, while lacking resources for alternative agricultural strategies. Universal in nature, food is relentlessly entangled in circumstances that limit its production and distribution.[1]

This complicated picture presents a strong case for revisiting the world of the eighteenth-century population theorist Thomas Robert Malthus. In a brief polemic, *An Essay on the Principle of Population* (1798), Malthus presented "two fixed laws of our nature," the necessity of food for existence and "the passion between the sexes," as unavoidable and constant. He then made an incendiary move: he linked the two laws to each other, arguing that while food increased at an arithmetical rate (1, 2, 3, 4, 5, 6, and so on), population would proceed at a more rapid rate, doubling with each interval (1, 2, 4, 8, 16, 32, 64, 128, . . .). In a perfect world, Malthus reasoned, a man (his use of the gendered pronoun here is worth noting) might "ask him[self] whether he may not bring beings into the world for whom he cannot provide the means of subsistence." "Restraint" from marriage could mitigate the necessary effects of upward pressure on resources. In reality, he argued, "constant effort towards an increase in population" (simply translated as sexual activity) rolled forward, meaning that ordinary people, especially when well fed, nevertheless coupled and reproduced without inhibition. "Misery or vice" generated a downward spiral, particularly among the lower classes, who could not afford to support their numerous offspring yet seemed incapable of limiting their own numbers. The ultimate outcome was inevitable depletion of the earth's food supply. According to Malthus, without proper restraint among those who could not afford their own maintenance, humankind was likely to remain locked within a perpetual cycle of biological peril and necessary famine.[2]

Malthus's essay instantly ignited debate and passionate rebuttal; in his own decorous phrase, the work "excited publick attention."[3] Contemporary readers could discern glaring contradictions between the lines of his Newtonian reasoning: the rich were not in danger of starving, nor did they give much concern to limiting their own numbers, while the poor were threatened by the rising price of food, unemployment, and political repression in the wake of the French Revolution. Since the time of Elizabeth I, propertied English people had assumed responsibility for rescuing the needy poor, whose resources were sometimes limited to the brink of starvation. The path to civility was not easy: a long and complex history of grain marketing in times of dearth reveals the self-interest of merchants and landowners alongside tumultuous popular conflict over distributing food and resources to the masses. By the late 1790s, stopgap arrangements showed signs of strain, as poor rates climbed and prices soared. Just as market forces and customary benevolence collided, Malthus's formula linking food production and human reproduction entered the maelstrom. From 1798 onward, the age-old debate over the entitlements of the poor and the responsibilities of the wealthy classes was forever colored by his polemical utterances.[4]

The methodical thinking of Malthus, perceived as scientific by the standard of the time, appealed to his fellow Britons: even when the logic of his argument came under attack, his intellectual toolbox would preoccupy economic theorists for a century. Events of the 1790s generated a special receptivity to the kind of polemic embedded within Malthus's pages: political turbulence lent force to the fear of the famished and distressed poor that was felt by propertied elites, who recoiled from news from France following the revolution. The conservative establishment in Britain embraced Malthus as a valuable truth-teller and, remarkably enough, his essay helped to bring about a complete overhaul of the Elizabethan Poor Laws, accomplished in 1834. More crucially, his principle of population lived on as the foundation of scarcity in formal economic terms, applied with shocking disregard across the colonial world and enshrined in later nineteenth-century neoclassical economics.[5]

Like his near contemporary Adam Smith, Malthus still stands as shorthand for an entire system of thought, despite the need to interrogate multiple issues at stake, all of them rooted in eighteenth-century contexts. Tracing the genealogy of basic assumptions about food and its production and consumption provides a surprisingly illuminating exercise: through re-reading Malthus, we can see how food became conceptualized as a transactional variable, subject to particular logics that trapped many people in precarious circumstances. Some observers understood this at the time, at least with regard to European settings. As Marx wryly commented, Ireland was the "Promised Land of the principle of population," proof that a potato-consuming population multiplied to the limits of subsistence, while a market-driven supply of Irish wheat and meat bypassed powerless inhabitants. During the halcyon years of the Corn Laws, Irish grain and beef fed the populations of London and the Caribbean, crowning the trade strategy that enriched landowners while starving the lower ranks of Irish society. The link between the food supply and Irish reproduction rates appears grossly irrelevant when placed in the context of these larger connections having to do with the British state and trade policies. In fact, Malthus's tract can be seen as minor punctuation in the attenuated emergence of free trade, a development that did more to determine the history of food than public debate over assistance to the poor could ever hope to accomplish.[6]

By training our gaze upon eighteenth-century food production and its environments, this treatment of Malthusian ideas focuses instead on the structural inequality at the heart of Malthusian thinking. Political scientists and anthropologists have been particularly attuned to this fact when tracing basic Malthusian arguments as they circulated swiftly throughout modern economies. Malthus's principles easily migrated to remote settings, serving to legitimate theories of eugenics, colonialism, and the Cold War. Eric B. Ross's *The Malthus Factor: Poverty, Politics, and Population in Capitalist Development* tracked the lethal effects of the "demographic determinism" embedded within the nimble formula. As Ross argued, formulations provided by Malthus served to support unequal distribution of resources, including control over land use, within British colonial expansion, leaving a lasting imprint on developing nations.[7]

Voices from postcolonial settings have attacked "the Malthusian scarecrow" to expose the truth about food supplies behind the condition of hunger. As Amartya Sen forcefully theorized, famines only occur when populations have no way of exchanging labor for food. His "entitlement theory" of famine, delineated roughly 180 years after Malthus released his genie from the bottle, demystified the theory of population as it operated within contemporary economics. Sen argued that the only way people have been able to exercise entitlement to food is through market practices, either by earning wages or by selling their own goods. These terms have left many poor landless laborers and urban workers dangerously vulnerable to arrangements that exclude them and economic downturns that render them unemployed. Nevertheless, such obvious limitations seldom have discredited conventions of governance and trade. Sen spoke from the experience of witnessing deficiencies of distribution leading to the Bengal famine of 1943. "Starvation is the characteristic of some people not *having* enough food to eat. It is not the characteristic of there *being* not enough food to eat."[8]

And yet, "Malthus's Zombie" continues to stalk our efforts to think about food and justice. Alex de Waal, executive director of the World Peace Foundation, coined this term to help disentangle the simplistic ideas of Malthus from lived realities. A zombie concept, borrowed from Ulrich Beck's writings, is "an idea that cannot be killed by normal means, and with limitless endurance keeps coming back to torment and infect the living." The "canonical concept" of Famine (capitalized) is one of these.[9] Actual causes of famines, de Waal argues, lie in political conflict and the "weaponization" of food. He shows that famines almost disappeared from world history before making a more recent resurgence as a highly specific feature of warfare. Yet contemporaries often default to crude reasoning that relies on incorrect suppositions. According to Malthusian thinking, population and starvation remain locked in a fatal embrace: if people are starving, it must be because they are too numerous. Even while sufficient food exists to feed hungry populations of the world, the simplification provided by Malthus enables appalling atrocities to take place in the shadows of conflict. De Waal worries that environmentalists may be conjuring up a refurbished version of Malthus's zombie in the form of arguments about famine resulting from climate change and the natural environment. "Greedy and short-sighted mismanagement of our planetary resources may bring about catastrophe, but it won't bring gigantic and inevitable Famine," de Waal contends. Human beings have always been problem-solvers, finding ways out of such dilemmas through inventiveness, science, and dogged persistence. The issue then becomes one of reasoning. Either management or thinly disguised greed needs to come under scrutiny.[10]

Of course, this perspective presumes a certain shared set of objectives, as well as a wish to expose fallacies overlooked because of the shorthand of Malthusian thinking. Historians and literary critics certainly have applied energy to the issues raised by Malthus, sometimes critically, though not necessarily with an eye toward escaping the gravitational pull of his fabricated universe. Scholars have scrutinized his theological views,[11] his contribution to the field of political economy,[12] Victorian culture,[13] and modern economics,[14] along with his place in Enlightenment debates about sexuality and gender.[15] The 250th anniversary of his birth in 2016 witnessed a flurry of reassessments, including a recent issue of a scholarly journal devoted to the ideas of Malthus reconsidered in an array of global settings.[16]

Yet so much energy has exerted its own force of gravity: scholarly labors have led to harmonizing Malthusian ideas with a canonical view of the past, melding his values into the normative ideological perspectives of the nineteenth century. His later status as a clergyman, deceptive to those unfamiliar with how appointments in the Church of England were made, encouraged incorrect notions of why he authored such a work. (Malthus's interest in religious life was minimal when he wrote the *Essay.*) An argument that originated as a way of punishing precarity now appears as prescient wisdom to scholars of the environment, even though Malthus knew very little about alternative ways of interacting with the land, the sea, animals, and the natural world and was generally dismissive of their providing solutions to his problem of population. Despite the tools available to historians and writers, obstacles have stood in the way of seeing how his formulation had its own peculiar power to erase alternative ways of thinking that may be of value to us. Most crucially, the methodological apparatus that accompanied his argument, like malware smuggled in by some unknowing agency, may be preventing us from seeing the true factors at work in each new set of circumstances having to do with the production of food and its producers.

To refute Enlightenment views that envisioned a constantly improving world—what one historian has aptly called "cornucopianism"—Malthus needed to characterize essential resources as limited.[17] He chose grain as the basis for his calculations, given its historical role in supplying the staple food of bread. The choice seemed natural enough at the time: bread or corn (wheat) signified literal and abstract commodities, representative as well as symbolic, so that no one felt any need to question it. But much more was at stake. Setting aside the issue of money and wages that laborers needed in order to purchase bread, we need to recognize the limitations of this picture of the food landscape of Malthus's day. Historians can ask, at the very least, what kind of food it was that wage earners, lacking access, might starve without. What arrangements brought that food to the market? What about those few who had access to land? Were they capable of producing food? What was the justification for the allocation and management of land resources in Britain? In other words, we need to describe both the game and the players with regard to food production and market practices undergirding the law of population and sustenance.

For all these reasons, I have laid out several paths for a fresh examination of the life and work of Thomas Robert Malthus. In advance, I should point out that this is not a history of political economy in any traditional sense but rather a social history of ideas about economy, society, and nature. In fashioning an interdisciplinary approach, I have avoided customary ways of accounting for theories of political economy; such scholarship, though venerable and illuminating, has had other objectives. Many such histories describe the contributions of leading philosophers as though they were isolated intellectual Goliaths, handing on their ideas like so many batons in an enduring relay race across time. Some of the most basic assumptions of capitalist economies thus go unexamined. My interest lies more in the set of ideas about food production and the "rules of the game" as they were established for the rural world and the urban populations fed by agricultural producers. Malthus carried forward the agenda of a new regime, one that effectively marginalized those without a claim to property and the labor-intensive alternatives that made up an informal economy of the countryside. My questions have to do with how these particular exclusions, absorbed into important economic discussions, acted as vectors of attitudes and social categories that became deeply imbricated in western capitalism and British economic history across the globe.[18]

If we begin by investigating Malthus's limited diet for humanity—namely, bread— important historical issues come to light. Staple foods in the eighteenth century, like ours today, were dependent on both culture and environment; over time, they had become inextricably bound up with property, capital, and technology, as well as geographical location. Malthus's emphasis on grain showed perspicacity: his privileging of the dominant monoculture of Britain helped to construct and reinforce a modernizing vision of the countryside. But he had in fact simplified a more complex picture of the British landscape, which at the time was straining to retain its dynamism and adaptability. The long-term consequences of the monoculture of wheat, environmental as well as social, reveal the costs of Malthusian simplification over centuries and across continents. We need to ask how much Malthus and his contemporaries missed and how their exclusions might have had an impact on thinking about food production, then and later, in a global context.

Malthus's essay presented a bifurcated society riven by stark social difference, a stipulation of his argument that struck many contemporaries as peculiar. Though Malthus assumed the voice of propertied interests within what seemed to be customary paternalistic society, he effectively jettisoned eighteenth-century notions of community. Ties between classes became conditional; laborers (rendered as male) were entitled to belong to Malthus's nation only according to conditions spelled out in transactional terms. Propertied people had inherited responsibility for a recalcitrant population and now found themselves, according to the catastrophic thinking of Malthus, on the edge of an abyss. Custom indicated that the poor and vulnerable should receive "bread," but given food, laborers would only reproduce more freely, forcing society back to the edge of the abyss. Herein lay the basis for another "zombie" concept: Malthus's lower orders were repeatedly presented as people who lacked intellect and human agency; their only power was that of reproduction, a relentless drive capable of reversing the achievements of Albion. Henceforth, food became entrusted to more intelligent rulers, who would employ its necessity as a way of controlling the masses.

The laboring population thus became imbued with the characteristics of inexorable difference, deficient in the wish or will to work unless made to experience hunger. Though this argument might resonate with biblical command and indeed enjoyed future life as a cherished Victorian maxim, for Malthus and his contemporaries (who were not yet Victorian), hunger provoked judgments dissociated from the realm of sympathy. Malthus's arguments, illustrated by what contemporaries understood as primitive peoples of the New World, helped to cement an association between the condition of hunger and a dehumanized state proximate to the animal world. Like copulation, hunger linked humans to their status as creatures condemned to precarity in the state of nature. Not even Darwin would go so far as to make the human race a function of brute instincts, but Malthus had every intention of presenting a view that he argued was based on natural philosophy, the science of his day. The timing of his configuration mattered, given its context within the era of the French Revolution: by rendering people without property—that is, the majority of the population—as either primitive and brutish or a simple numerical, Malthus erased any distinct sense of human potentiality embedded in the mass of ordinary Britons.

Historians of political economy may object to the dark version of Malthusian thinking that I have sketched here. Victorian economic thought recovered a somewhat broader vision implanted in the liberal ideas fostered by Adam Smith and subsequent thinkers precisely because Malthus had provoked consideration of the role of workers as consumers and generators of national wealth. As Robert Mayhew generously stated the case, "Malthus wrote at just the moment when the socioeconomic dynamics he analyzed were being superseded." Malthus himself revised and softened his thinking over time, while cultivating a reputation as "a kind and benevolent man in his personal relationships," as J. M. Poynter put it in his definitive treatment of the history of poor relief during this formative era. "But the same cannot be said of all early Malthusians," Poynter added, "the men who welcomed the principle of population as social conservatism pure and simple." Contemporaries responded to the "definite ambivalence" in the writings of Malthus and mined his arguments for positions that would have been socially unacceptable a mere decade earlier. Powerful men in favor of abolishing relief for the poor developed a remarkably resilient body of arguments that became grafted onto industrial capitalism and made their way into later theories concerning the distribution of aid, particularly notable in policies applied to the British colonies. This linkage ought to direct our thinking into a deeper channel of inquiry. What else do we lose when we dispense with a full potential of human subjects in these settings?[19]

Answers to this question arise from an investigation of eighteenth-century ideas about the use of land and other resources. By placing Malthus's text in conversation with the production of food, we may be able to see him as providing closure to the long debate over proprietorship over land, what historians often abbreviate as the enclosure movement. Implicit throughout Malthus's *Essay* is the erasure of subsistence agriculture taking place in the margins of society. Though he was not alone in embracing cultivation as the highest form of agriculture, he may have been unique in effectively erasing all its competitors. Dairying, fishing, trapping, and gardening figure nowhere in his thinking. This erasure also allowed him to eradicate what were, at the time, traditional channels of rural self-help. When asked if Arthur Young's suggestion of giving a cow to rural families might aid in their survival, his answer was curt and dismissive. Such weak measures, he argued, would only prolong their untenable grasp on the edges of rural society. With an eye on the "ghost acres" of the colonies, later in his career, he sought answers from his own questionnaire about farming practices in India. "Is there much internal commerce of grain, or is the greatest part of it consumed on the spot where it is grown?" he asked. "Are there any impediments to the free commerce of grain from government?" His trademark point of view became more transparent in his final question: "Are there many small properties in land on which men just support their families and do little else? This is the class of people that I should expect would be most subject to scarcity."[20] Malthus was a modernizer without vision, less interested in learning from regional and ecological variation than in deploying a universal principle that gave him his reputation.

Classical economists of the Enlightenment may have known about the economic diversity of the countryside, but they failed to take adequate account of it. For Malthus, a conventional propertied view of a paternalistic rural world imposed its own form of selectivity. Stadial history, shored up by the classical past, provided a classificatory system that he and his elite contemporaries applied to their own localities as well as to the New World. Prehistory was essential to comprehending one's environment and the use of resources. In telling the story of overpopulation, Malthus deployed a common form of judgment provided by his education, identifying a typology of human activity and behavior operating along the lines of a bifurcated sense of society. Using the upward trajectory of the sequence of modes of subsistence, writers like Malthus could move easily from earlier forms of food-getting to a dismissal of marginal activities that compared inadequately to grain cultivation. A maximum of sophistication—another way of anointing a British vision of concentrated landownership and capital investment as the destiny of progressive agriculture—could be found in intensified farming. Additional benefit lay in the paternal oversight and economic subordination imposed upon those who labored in the fields. Only then could population be contained and a narrowly defined and limited amount of food find its proper levels of distribution.

This modern set of goals for food production, with particular social arrangements and objectives, overrode competing visions in Britain from 1750 and gradually influenced much of western Europe before spreading across much of the globe. The march of intensive agriculture has also been the underlying template of most histories of rural economies in Britain and Europe. "Roundabout routes to economic growth are not readily recognised by economists," Joan Thirsk pointed out years ago, "who build their theories on much more straightforward examples" drawn from a model of large-scale grain cultivation. In order to present an alternative vision of what was taking place during Malthus's lifetime, we need to look at the full picture of the countryside, including the participation of those who were gradually diminishing in number and power. These minor figures, for example, included "peasant polyculturalists," who produced a variety of food and other agricultural commodities alongside larger-scale neighboring operations, which concentrated on a perpetually enhanced output of grain. For small establishments, "involvement in the market would have been restricted to garden, farmyard, and dairy products in the main." Yet these households provide evidence that at certain times in British history, the countryside thrived on diverse activities and so did consumers of their produce.[21]

Marginal activities emerged from the shadows during times of economic contraction and depression; this is why, for example, the distressful years of the seventeenth century revealed a spectrum of lucrative alternative strategies for working on the land, participating in the market, and feeding a growing population. The same dynamic was at work at a much later phase of agricultural history, the Great Depression of the late nineteenth century, but by this time expectations regarding food production had embraced modern standards of technology and capital outlay. As the entry requirements for participation in modern agriculture grew out of reach for most rural inhabitants, the picture of who inhabited the countryside changed. The full potential of rural society was set aside, along with a multiplicity of inhabitants, in favor of a model dictated by the global market for foodstuffs.[22]

The project of recovering a comprehensive understanding of rural productivity also reveals differing attitudes toward the environment in history. Characteristics of the land, local animals, and plant life shape any chosen vision of the rural world. Population history requires unpacking "very different spatial visions that might lie behind our apparently objective territorial label[s]."[23] Classification can begin by examining the environment as it presented itself to humans and animals. By asking "what kind of agrarian life profited from this environment as it existed?" rather than "how can this environment be made to support cultivation?" we can reclaim alternative pathways obscured by the pressure of conformity to a more general model of rural progress. Such a reclamation will enable us to identify what we might call the axes of alterity created by the Malthusian perspective, sources of exclusion reinforced by modernization that still operate today.

The concepts of spatiality and social alterity are essential to the following reassessment of Malthus. My use of the word "marginal" in the following pages depends on both geographical and abstract understandings of spatiality involved in generating sustenance. Production of food in history necessarily involved land, which operated according to laws of private property limiting its use, the application of capital, and mobilization of resources. Malthus's depiction of production obscured this primary fact, making scarcity appear as part of abstract nature rather than the product of human determination and social organization. It was this mystification that repeatedly prompted Marx and Engels to respond to the arguments of Malthus and David Ricardo. As David Harvey points out, "Scarcity presupposes certain social ends, and it is these that define scarcity just as much as the lack of natural means to accomplish these ends."[24]

A particular social structure underwrote this rural landscape, and it clearly served as a backdrop for Malthus's theory of population. By rewriting the agricultural revolution, I aim to propose ways of plotting out this world in a symbolic way in order to reimagine the rural past as a realm of multiple alternatives. Concentration of landownership in fewer hands grew in the seventeenth century, as England outpaced its European counterparts by orienting its economy of foodstuffs toward the market. The eighteenth century was the final age of transition, when a diminishing number of smaller-scale tenant arrangements could still be seen across the map of Britain, summarized by Eric Hobsbawm as "an undergrowth of economically marginal cottage-labourers, or other small independents and semi-independents," a situation that obscured the structure of capitalist farming that had been increasing in importance over several centuries. "By 1790 landlords owned perhaps three quarters of the cultivated land, occupying free-holders perhaps fifteen to twenty per cent, and a 'peasantry' in the usual sense of the word no longer existed." The "margins," in this sense, refer to the status of certain labor and activities in relation to the hierarchy enforced by capitalist agriculture present in large-scale grain production, notably in the south of England.[25]

Marginality constituted both a spatial and social "otherness," an important aspect of the contextualization of economic life in this particular historical continuum. It will become clear in the following pages that Malthus understood the margins in this larger sense, as he interpreted the lessons of stadial history embodied in Scottish Enlightenment writings that relied on descriptions of the New World. Into these vast territories of different geographies, Malthus would project ideas about British advancement as representative of a developed civilization, thus rendering subsistence activities like hunting and fishing as belonging to earlier eras of human history. At the same time, New World inhabitants stood in for the English poor in his account, demonstrating their proximity to bestial conditions through their behavior, which threatened to arrest the progress of the British nation. Indigenous claims to territory were beside the point: the desideratum of mastery over nature supplanted all prior considerations in this formula of life-or-death necessity.

Enlightenment writers recognized the unresolved implications of geography as contributing factors in the history of human society; as David Harvey put it, "'all geography is historical geography,' no matter where it is to be found." Geographical characteristics, such as boundaries and nomenclature, depended on evolving knowledge of geological time, features of the land, its history of human use, and social organization. Malthus was writing at the end of a long age of improvement in agriculture, when the renowned figure of Arthur Young had championed the best practices of scientific methods of cultivation and informed breeding of animals. Such state-of-the-art knowledge bolstered a sense that farming was more than a gentleman's pursuit: it rested on a technical body of knowledge unmatched in most other parts of the world. Thus the lands far from the centers of power and knowledge provided the substrate for speculation. Malthus, however, was no agrarian expert: his intimate reactions to travel in the northern parts of Scandinavia revealed the distance between his own modern mentality and what he categorized as alterity. His determined rigidity in observing alien forms of subsistence gathering among the Sami people may not be surprising, yet it serves to indicate a stark lack of respect for Indigenous knowledge and resourcefulness, an indicator that formulaic thinking would cancel out alternatives, even in environments remote from British soil.[26]

To some readers, this may seem as though I am making a sentimental case for a lost world of small and rural activities, a position hardly tenable when considering the tremendous demand for food accompanying an increase in urban and global populations since the time of Malthus. This is not my intention. Instead, I am asking the reader to consider the powerful way in which Malthusian categories of labor and production, with their exclusions and appropriations, altered expectations in the realm of food production. The narrow formula of early nineteenth-century Britain, once championed as an essential component of modern industrial society, placed powerful limitations on how western colonial powers approached other cultures and their environments. It is worth our while to go back to the history of the elisions enforced by Malthusian thinking in order to reframe the problem of population as one of vision, power, and scope. Who eats what and how and where it is grown constitute fundamental assumptions within agricultural studies, environmental history, and interlocking disciplines. Ultimately, the intersection of multiple fields of study enables us to locate important common ground in which to think hard about food production. Only then can we redefine the problem of survival as a question of critical perception and historically informed imagination.

2

Nature's Mighty Feast

How Scarcity Became Established Fact

Readers of Malthus have mistaken him for a pious clergyman, intent on a moral mission, or a full-fledged political economist, authorized by the theorists of the era; he was neither when he wrote the *Essay,* though he became both at different times in subsequent years. It helps to see Malthus the author as a mortal being, whose career was shaped by tendencies of his own human nature against the background of the late eighteenth century. For personal and physical reasons, Malthus struggled to find his place in the world. Biographical details of his first thirty years illuminate details behind the writing of his little book and force us to see the arrival of the *Essay* as a highly fortuitous event. Formative experiences drove Malthus to rebel against the optimism that characterized the Enlightenment, a mutiny he was well equipped to carry out. Timing was everything: his publishing debut came at the height of a turbulent decade of radical expression and political repression following the French Revolution. Economic theory matured over the next two decades, so when

Ricardo published his *Principles of Political Economy* in 1817, the field had achieved a stable footing in the public sphere.[1]

Rather than subscribing to the belief that the satisfaction of every individual coincided with the needs of all, Malthus identified a wayward, destructive impulse in all human nature. No element of his bad news was original, yet the *Essay* ultimately gained an appreciative audience and even brought about "a new turn of thought" in economic and social theory. Despite considerable outcry, the arguments of his *Essay* would find a haven within an influential circle of conservative opinion, insuring acceptance into a gradually cohering discipline of political economy and its supportive Evangelical wing within the Church of England. As Boyd Hilton aptly phrased this shift, "Natural theologians had argued from the design of the universe for the existence of a beneficent and omnipotently purposeful Creator, but the dismal science's picture of the world seemed to suggest that, on the contrary, God was mad, bad, and dangerous." Henceforth, Malthus's theory of natural scarcity became crucial to modern economic theory, where it worked as a bulwark against questioning the basic terms of the distribution of resources across society.[2]

The goal of collectivity lay at the heart of social theory of the Enlightenment. Political and moral philosophy concentrated on analyzing the characteristics common to all humanity, particularly those that resulted in binding humanity together. Economic theorists enjoyed the best vantage point in this regard, given that they focused on how society organized the project of sustaining human beings by distributing the fruits of labor. For Adam Smith, one of the most influential British voices of the century, the problem was solved via ethics: through sympathy, humanity shared a common goal (the sustenance of society) and mutual dedication to that task. This was coupled with individual drives and interests, explained through the workings of labor and wealth within his *Wealth of Nations.* Subsequent generations, aided by the turn of thought reacting against the French Revolution, would mount objections to the imposition of universality implanted in Enlightenment ideas.[3]

Though not immediately apparent to modern eyes, the Malthusian problem of population engaged with crucial ethical issues animated by the radical ideas of eighteenth-century revolutions. Was society based on an awareness of mutuality and interdependency, or was it simply a collection of atomistic actors, who fortuitously reinforced each other's efforts toward survival? And seen in a historical context, what role did institutions play in this? Was the state a necessary agent in insuring that social and economic connections remain strong and mutually reinforcing? Historically, had humankind advanced beyond the stage of existence in which life had to be nasty, brutish, and short? Or were the bodies and labor of those without a propertied stake in society assigned a precarious existence, which they necessarily navigated by their own efforts alone? To what extent were ordinary individuals, those lacking particular characteristics and privileges, excluded from a concept of a flourishing society?

In fact, Malthus's theory of population and food production adhered to a historical model of society only implicitly elaborated within the pages of the first *Essay.* His understanding of these issues becomes more legible within biographical details, which reveal a fascinating, if chilling, reversal of the outlook of the Age of Enlightenment. Malthus's model of society jettisoned liberality in the eighteenth-century sense of the word in favor of a pared-down notion of what would become liberalism under nineteenth-century capitalism. Individualism, the preeminence of property, a historically naïve disregard for paternalistic commitments, and an inordinate trust in select empirical evidence of "truth" (often mistakenly called "scientific"): these were the features of a broadly utilitarian middle-class politics. At its height, this position championed the individualism, self-help, and abstract freedoms based in the legal framework of the liberal state. Although those in power never wholeheartedly acknowledged the perilous aspects of this arrangement, they profited from an edifice of humanitarianism and charity that allied with their efforts. The consequences of structural inequality stemming from economic arrangements would grow over time, becoming visible in "the social question" of the nineteenth century. What contemporaries could not predict was the powerful durability of the myth that grew out of the Malthusian diorama of society. Even as notable liberal thinkers such as John Stuart Mill departed from hard and fast positions, social assumptions underlying economic principles developed along an independent pathway. While hope resided in the belief that free trade would benefit all members of industrial society, the imperatives governing the transformation of rural life remained unquestioned. The immortal Malthus would prove more powerful and toxic than the energetic debaters of an island nation could ever imagine.

Malthus lived within a cultural milieu stirred by fascination with nature. At every level of society, countless English people took an interest in the permutations of the natural world, whether for practical purposes (soils, weather, and crops), as part of a shared dedication to cataloguing scientific fields of knowledge, or simply as a readily available form of aesthetic experience. A broad public followed the lead of John Locke and Robert Boyle, familiar within the orbit of a powerful print culture, in taking up the practice of recording meteorological events. Ordinary almanack readers were joined by diligent clergymen, ever aware of weather as active demonstration of divine presence. Botany similarly captivated scores of enthusiasts, reflected in numerous editions of guidebooks as well as public displays of collections. Led by George III, a king noted for bringing with him "a trio of enthusiastic botanists," the 1760s witnessed the foundation of the Royal Botanic Gardens, the recent enlargement of the University Botanic Garden at Cambridge, and the further diffusion of English editions of Linnaeus's work that had appeared in the 1750s. England's own John Ray had supplied an encyclopedic guide to the natural world in the late seventeenth century, which was translated from Latin into English in 1744. The fact that Rousseau, an avid botanist, used Ray's guide during his explorations in Britain in 1766 went down in English lore as a celebrated event, proof that such interests were, paradoxically, imbued with national character even as they were widely shared across Europe.[4]

These enthusiasms directly infused the world of the Malthus family. Daniel Malthus II, father of Thomas Robert ("Bob" to family members), claimed his own place in the historical record, oddly enough, through his limited but markedly persistent relationship to Rousseau. As a man of solid fortune, Daniel pursued his passions with few restraints. As a descendant of Royal Apothecaries, he and his wife (a cousin with her own esteemed pedigree) enjoyed connections to well-positioned professionals. Daniel, however, chose to style himself a peripatetic man of letters; he amassed a fine library of Enlightenment volumes, which he adopted as true guides to the good life. He developed a pronounced (one might venture to say consuming) admiration of Rousseau, which suggests that the French philosopher somehow embodied a stance that made sense to this eccentric English gentleman. Always attuned to his surroundings, Daniel studied nature, took up botanizing with alacrity, and faithfully recorded the weather, urging his son to obtain a thermometer while at university so that their exchanges might be more precise. For Daniel Malthus, Rousseau's importance lay primarily in his Romantic, rather than his republican, tendencies: this meant a

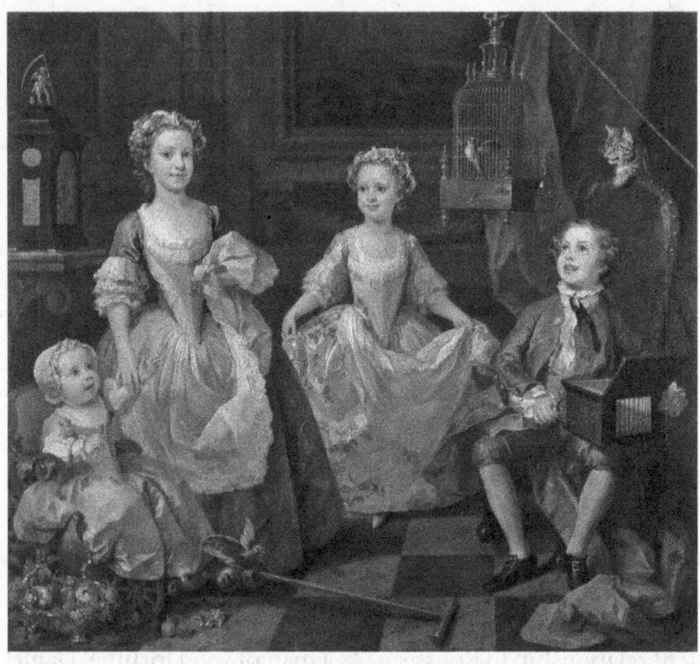

William Hogarth, *The Graham Children*, 1742. A celebrated family portrait embodying the values of the Age of Enlightenment, this depiction of Henrietta Graham Malthus, the mother of Thomas Robert, displays many features of the prosperity and status of her childhood household. Pictured on the left, Henrietta assumes the knowing expression of the eldest child, holding fast the arm of her youngest sibling, Thomas, who had died by the time the portrait was completed. Henrietta would give her own younger son the same name in 1766. (The National Gallery, London)

rejection of convention and excess, the spirit rather than the letter of the law. In missive after missive, Daniel attempted to woo the philosopher with what he believed were kindred sentiments of the outcast, confessing at one point "that loneliness is a beautiful thing."[5]

Henrietta, Malthus's mother, embodied the enlightened era in a different way: as one of the Graham children painted by Hogarth, she represented the eighteenth century's new attitudes toward childhood innocence and well-mannered indulgence. The scene is littered with objects of amusement and play. As a record of family progeny, Henrietta holds the hand of an already deceased baby brother, Thomas, the namesake of her own son, Thomas Robert. Her other brother, Richard Robert, is pictured seated at a children's organ. Her later life in the Malthus household would not be easy, given the rejection of convention dictated by her husband. She "would not have been supposed happy by those who knew her," her granddaughter tactfully recorded. Though Henrietta was an educated woman, her voice is inaudible in much of the remaining records, with only these words and a description of her as "most affectionate and indulgent." For unclear reasons, Daniel forbade her from wearing a wedding ring and insisted on an unusually nomadic existence. Even after all seven children were born, the family moved about repeatedly. Daniel allegedly ruled the rather large household in a heavy-handed manner; he was "a person whose will was imperative and to whom everything gave way."[6]

Daniel pursued almost constant independent travels, and on one excursion in Switzerland he spent six hours with Rousseau. He was at pains to tell the philosopher that his visit to the town of Môtiers was not simply to seek him out (it was a haven for British travelers at that time), yet this was clearly a relationship he wished to develop. On the eve of Rousseau's visit to Britain, Daniel urgently confessed, "I have long loved you through your writings—if you will allow me to love you differently, what I started to do in the few times that I saw you, come see me in your turn, in a small country house that looks a bit like the one you imagine in your Emile." ("The Rookery" was a pleasingly rustic homestead, one of the few that anchored the

Malthus family for a handful of years, situated in a particularly picturesque site in Mereden, Surrey. Daniel had the place remodeled according to his stipulations in 1761.) In later correspondence, he took the trouble to inform Rousseau that he had nothing to do with the quarrels between landlords and poachers; he was more familiar with cottages than castles. Desperate to convince Rousseau to stay at the Malthus home during his visit to England, Daniel insisted that the philosopher would not be put off by pretensions but rather would be hosted "merely in the house of a farmer, a rude hunter, and without ceremony."[7]

While Malthus the elder disavowed the customary role of a man of his stature, Rousseau, for his part, made use of the bookish man's admiration, asking him to procure texts on botany and specimens of plants for him. When Rousseau finally conferred a visit upon the Malthus home in March of 1766, a sixth child, Thomas Robert, had been born just three weeks earlier. The convergence of the philosopher's visit and the arrival of this particular child invites speculation and even a certain justifiable pause in our consideration of how the infant and later young Malthus faced the challenges of his life. Thomas Robert was born with a serious physical disability, a harelip and, most likely, a cleft palate. His biographer Patricia James, the only person to delve into the problem with interest, noted that his ancestor the Reverend Robert Malthus "was evicted from his vicarage of Northolt in Middlesex in 1662; his parishioners had a number of grievances, including the fact that he had 'not only a low voice, but a very great impediment in his utterance.'" She speculates that this may have been due to this man's harelip and a cleft palate, and she adds (in the insensitive language of her own time), "Malthus had this defect and it should be appreciated at the outset that he was a badly handicapped child."[8]

The Rookery, Surrey. The birthplace of Thomas Robert Malthus, this agreeably situated farm was purchased around 1761 by Daniel Malthus, a choice possibly influenced by his intense fascination with Rousseau. He made many changes to the site, creating a residence described some years later as "unparalleled in rusticity and picturesque effect." The family lived there for seven years. (John Timbs, *A Picturesque Promenade Round Dorking*, 2nd ed., 1823, 202. Album / Alamy Stock Photo)

Eighteenth-century medical discussions of harelips speak in similarly dire tones, especially because infants would be unable to suck nourishment and would require special care in feeding. Sometimes medical men were able to perform a procedure to correct the palate, but they could do so only in the first year of life and at great risk to the infant. It seems safe to assume that the Malthus family decided not to proceed with such a solution and thus Robert's speech would be quite labored and difficult to understand. No family members offered an account of what must have been difficult early months of his life. Frustrating to any biographer, all that remains are references to Daniel Malthus's urgent and even obsessive efforts to track the movements of Rousseau across England. This seriously disabled second son, a child of nature in a cruelly ironic way, began his life in a household thoroughly distracted by erratic movements of the French philosopher famously enamored of nature's charms.[9]

The fate of Thomas Robert, who stood to inherit none of the property of his large, migratory family, sat in stark contrast to the two other men, father and son, of the Malthus family. Daniel's nomadic bent, somewhat strange for the father of seven children, reappeared in the behavior of his older son, Sydenham II. Sydenham was twelve when Robert was born; his early life and education remain obscure, apart from the fact that his father was said to favor his eldest daughter and youngest son. An outline of Sydenham shines through the demographic data with its own touch of irony: living the life of a peripatetic gentleman, he fathered one "natural daughter" and four children, in addition to the six stepchildren he acquired through his marriage to a widow, his cousin, at the relatively late age of 45.[10]

It is clear that Daniel Malthus adopted a protective and controlling attitude toward his disabled son. During Robert's childhood, Daniel bore down hard on a plan for his education, presumably because this son would require a means of earning a living but perhaps, too, because the child's intellect contradicted the misfortune of his physical disability. The Malthus family would later discuss the possibility of Robert acquiring an appointment in the Church of England, like several relatives before him, but his speech defect must have made them apprehensive about such a plan. Soon young Bob came under the tutelage of the Reverend Richard Graves, who proved an eccentric choice but a convenient one: the family rented accommodations from him at Claverton beginning in 1773, when Robert would have been seven. Robert remained there, even after the family had left, until he was sixteen. Depending on the source, assessments of this arrangement varied. One estimation concluded that Malthus "was taught little but Latin and good behaviour." Yet correspondence between Graves and Daniel Malthus indicated that the young boy had successfully read Horace and showed a precocious appreciation of the satires of Juvenal. Despite the narrowness of his schooling thus far, the young Malthus was gathering the skills to advance within the elite educational institutions of his time.[11]

Graves clearly left an impression on his student, if only as one more mentor against whom Malthus would rebel. He was described as "short and slender, . . . eccentric in both dress and gait[;] . . . his features were expressive and his conversation was marked by a sportive gaiety." Graves seemed to be something of a cut-up (not unlike the boy Malthus, who was said to enjoy antics) and he enjoyed rustic versifying, even composing a poem about members of the Malthus family. Graves's true claim to posterity resides in a satirical novel about a Methodist minister, *The Spiritual Quixote* (1773), thought to be a veiled portrayal of the infamous Joseph Townsend, later author of *Dissertation on the Poor Laws* (1786). Malthus would borrow heavily from Townsend in his *Essay*, absorbing the author's own principle of population and repeating his criticisms of the Old Poor Law, rather than embracing the rebel reformist outlook of Graves. As an ordained minister, Graves had associated with the Holy Club at Oxford, the seedbed of Wesley's Methodist movement, though he shunned the excesses of religious enthusiasm. His personal behavior was not exactly proper: as a young man, he eloped with his landlord's sixteen-year-old daughter, marrying at the Fleet, and then, in a gesture of enlightenment, arranged for her education. Income from his school at Claverton enabled him to cobble together a comfortable living and to cultivate friends among the Bath intelligentsia, including the famous Bluestocking set.[12]

Robert moved next to the home of Gilbert Wakefield, dissenting minister and an outspoken critic of the established church, who was later imprisoned by the British government for provocative statements during the reactionary years of the late 1790s. For a time the sole pupil at Wakefield's home near Warrington, Malthus benefited from his tutor's avowedly liberal approach to education. Wakefield believed the student resembled "a delicate and tender plant, which must be protected with equal solicitude from the chilliness of neglect, and the inclemency of rebuke." Here again was the spirit, if not the letter of the text, of Rousseau. Wakefield's decidedly radical position on religion had already been laid out in the public eye. When Robert first met him, Wakefield had recently given up his appointment as curate, rejecting not just the 39 Articles but also the doctrines of the trinity and incarnation. A deeply moral and often passionate character, Wakefield lavished a great deal of time on his pupils. He furthered Robert's study of mathematics and classical languages and also helped him in a material way: recognizing the young man's abilities in his own field of mathematics, Wakefield intervened to gain Robert admission to Jesus College, Cambridge, where Wakefield himself had been ranked Second Wrangler. The plan was not the immediate wish of his parents, but Robert was resolute in his insistence and, thanks to Wakefield's support, he eventually got his way.[13]

The most curious thing about the educational sojourn of Robert Malthus is how he later struck poses that were perfectly contrary to his father's romantic attachment to Rousseau and the outlook of his two tutors. Graves spotted contradictory tendencies in Robert at the age of fourteen. In a letter to Daniel Malthus, Graves reported (in a somewhat bantering tone) that Robert sometimes revealed a bellicose streak: "Don Roberto, who tho' most peaceably inclin'd & who seems rather to give up even his just rights, than to dispute with any man, yet (paradox as it may Seem) loves fighting for fighting's sake—& delights in brusing [*sic*]." Perhaps thanks to permissive and even doting parents, this English Émile was learning how to be a stubborn contrarian. While living with Wakefield, Robert wrote home repeatedly about his shooting excursions, despite the fact that his tutor was known to avoid even fishing because of the pain it inflicted.[14] The pugnacious tendency of the adolescent boy metamorphosed into an intellectually reactive posture at Cambridge. Malthus's earliest known attempt at publishing would spring from his difference with the definition of "happiness" offered by William Paley, the most celebrated (and optimistic) theologian of the age, whose work was required reading at Cambridge. Paley the Eudemonist could imagine nothing made by a benevolent deity that would lead to human torment. Malthus, on the other hand, saw humans as the inevitable spoilers of their own capacities.[15] This position likely would have offended his old tutor, Wakefield, who championed the poor and oppressed (including animals) throughout his life. As a dedicated empiricist, Malthus never lacked a way of finding fault with the assertions of others; or, as a friend put it in a posthumous review of his work, "Mr. Malthus was not fond of storms, . . . [but] he usually turned out in one."[16]

Robert's correspondence with his father reveals a determined son who was respectful but resolutely independent. This strain, once apparent in print, betrayed a rather perversely contentious dimension of the otherwise polite young man. "The chief study is mathematics," Malthus reported to his father from Cambridge in the autumn of 1784, "for all honour in taking a degree depends upon that science & the great aim of most of the men is to take an honorable [*sic*] degree." Their exchanges show how the issue of the breadth or narrowness of Robert's education was a concern, as Daniel (who had never finished his studies at Oxford a generation earlier) strained to understand what his son was doing at university. The father extended a palm to his son, after they had differed over Robert's program of study, by elaborating his views on mathematics. "There is scarcely any part of learning which I esteem more, & all I have ever said to you which cou'd possibly be misunderstood . . . is that I cou'd always wish to see it applied, & that I desir'd to see you a surveyor, a mechanic, a navigator, a financier [this last, inserted], a natural philosopher, an astronomer, & [not] a meer speculative *algebraist.*" Malthus answered by assuring his father that "[I] am rather remark'd in College for talking of what actually exists in nature, or may be put to real practical use." More than once, he pointed out that his course of mathematics was not confined to abstractions: "The greatest stress is laid on a thorough knowledge of the branches of natural philosophy," he explained. He asked for permission "to proceed in my own plan of reading for the next two years. . . . I promise you at the expiration of that time to be a decent natural philosopher, & not only to know a few principles, but to be able to apply those principles in a variety of useful problems."[17]

The older Malthus seemed ill positioned to criticize "meer speculative" fields of study, so perhaps his principal worry was the need for an income for the younger son. The prospect of entering the clergy remained in the air, but at least one of Robert's advisors at Cambridge indicated that owing to Robert's speech impediment, he doubted that he would be able to perform the expected oral duties assigned to a man of the cloth. But Malthus soon obtained a second opinion and reassured his father that an appointment would be possible; he had, after all, declaimed in chapel and been understood by his peers. At this point in the century, the typical curriculum at Cambridge sufficed as background for a career in the clergy. As William Paley had proven just a generation before Malthus, excellence in mathematics merely paved the way for prowess in moral and theological disputation. Because appointments in the Church of England were obtained through favor and influence, Malthus's parents should have had little reason to worry. Their family's sphere of influence extended in several directions among a prolific number of propertied relatives, who would ultimately supply him with financially lucrative livings. Yet this did not remove the personal and inner conflicts most likely generated by such a disability, which may in fact explain the protective posture of Daniel Malthus and the negative view of Bob's mother when he indicated his wish to go to university. In a more abstract sense, too, the experience was fairly certain to leave some mark on the thinking of this young "natural philosopher." We might speculate that Malthus experienced nature as remorseless in a very personal sense.[18]

Reactions of contemporaries to Malthus's speech and appearance make clear the salience of his disability. James's thorough researches turned up several remarks confirming this fact, most of them from Malthus's female acquaintances. Mary Berry commented on having had "interesting" conversation with him, "when one gets over his painful manner of speaking from wanting a palate to his mouth, and having a hair-lip [*sic*]." She added a point evident from the portrait of him by Linnell, which politely obscured the affected area of his mouth: "not, however, at all unpleasant in appearance." Harriet Martineau, notoriously hard of hearing and dependent on an ear trumpet, recorded his "inability to pronounce half the consonants in the alphabet," but she was pleased to find his speech "slow and gentle, with the vowels sonorous, whatever might become of the consonants," enabling her to understand him. Maria Edgeworth confessed to her mother that when Malthus was in the company of more fluent speakers, his "snuffly" way of speech became "intolerable." She admitted, like "all who know him declare," that he was "a most amiable man," not the "ogre" described by

Cobbett. Then she added, "For if I were a child and had heard of his being an Ogre I should run away if he were to come near me and begin to speak." While on a tour of the Lake District when he was twenty-nine, Robert recorded an incident in which "a remarkably pretty girl about sixteen" had this exact reaction to a question he posed, though he believed that "she mistook me for a fine gentleman at first" until a close view of his countenance revealed him to be one of "the swinish multitude." His journals include several other instances of his admiration of female beauty, suggesting that he suffered from his condition in more ways than just in speech.[19]

One fact seems certain: Malthus's disability accompanied him throughout the course of his search for a place in society. He did not have an easy time of it and the ten-year endeavor laid the groundwork for his contentious arrival with his *Essay on Population.* After he was made a fellow at Jesus College following his degree, he returned home to live with his parents and remained there even after he accepted his first clerical appointment as a curate at Okewood in Surrey. For an unmarried man, this arrangement made sense in more than simply a financial way, but the situation would have some bearing on the intellectual path that the maturing Malthus would take. Surviving copies of Malthus's sermons constitute unremarkable performances; it is also likely that he struggled with them, given the marks in his manuscripts, which indicate places where he probably paused to catch his breath.[20] The young curate methodically applied "natural reason" to principles of the Bible and arrived at injunctions to obey conscience and seek goodness through correct behavior. Historians of the Church of England have long pointed out that until the spiritual revival and reforms of the nineteenth century, most posts were held by undistinguished members of the landed classes not noted for their religious sensibility or their intellectual acuity. (Even a posthumous memoir of Malthus damned the profession with faint praise: "We never knew one of this description so entirely free from the vices of his caste.") Parishioners in rural Surrey most likely did not hold the bar high. In any case, this was not where Robert Malthus devoted his real energies.[21]

Of these critical ten years at home, much remains a mystery to those who have written about the life of Malthus on the eve of his appearance as the author of the *Essay.* Patricia James refers to this time as "the unknown decade."[22] Two memoirs written by close associates suggest that Malthus was attempting to enter the public sphere as a writer and likely met with frustration. Fragmentary evidence of a rejected manuscript in 1796 appeared in a memoir by William Otter, Malthus's friend from Cambridge years, and also the posthumous memoir by William Empson, Malthus's colleague at the East India College. They agree that this effort, entitled "The Crisis," was probably best left unpublished, as it represented a youthful, somewhat naïve set of thoughts on dealing with the problem of the poor. Otter indicated that Malthus's father discouraged him from publishing it, and a rejection from a publisher underscored the failure of it. Interestingly, excerpts disclose a more charitable view of the poor than the one Malthus revealed in the *Essay* in 1798. He showed sympathy for the poor widow with children and articulated his support for Pitt's Reform Bill, which was not critical with regard to the number of offspring of poor families. Yet if Malthus's objective was to gain the attention of a patron who would offer him a more lucrative clerical living, as one historian has argued, then this somewhat lifeless attempt did not offer the correct approach. His father consoled him with what turned out to be shrewd advice. "The truth is that the market overflows, and if there is not some particular abuse or known name, the booksellers are not willing to risk their money." Daniel also expressed a wish that Malthus had sought the help of his former tutor Gilbert Wakefield, who was certainly much in the public eye at the time and might assist with his connections to booksellers.[23]

This was no ordinary age of print: the 1790s witnessed momentous ruptures in the political debates of the British nation. Harvest failures and wartime inflation created widespread hunger across the British Isles, with sentiments posted across the social spectrum. "We will do some Mischief if you don't lower the Brade [*sic*] for we cannot live," began one incendiary broadside. Alongside the cost of bread was the rising tide of poor rates, which attempted to address problems of unemployment together with pervasive hunger. Popular excitement about the French Revolution soon became the target of reactionary fear. By 1792, the wave of opinion turned against British reformers and agitators for liberty and freedoms of speech and the press. Several of Malthus's acquaintances and mentors were among those who were pursued and ultimately crushed because they had expressed views that were on behalf of liberty and against the repression that came from higher quarters. Gilbert Wakefield's career as a defender of English liberty spanned these years and ultimately became the test case at the end of the decade. As a historian of the Wakefield trial argued, "the overriding political character of the state trials in the 1790s" reflected the position that "defendants should be condemned, not because their opinions were untrue, but because they were untimely."[24]

By 1800, "many of the leading radicals were either dead, exiled, or imprisoned." Wakefield was convicted of seditious libel in 1798 and imprisoned early the next year. The impassioned schoolmaster and minister died of typhoid shortly after being released in 1803, but there is no record of Malthus communicating with or visiting him.[25] Scholars have lamented "a lost generation" of literary and philosophical writers. Important figures have been "pushed to the margins of our literary histories of the period: Joseph Priestley, James Montgomery, William Frend, Thomas Beddoes Sr., Helen Maria Williams, William Drennan, Robert Bage, Gilbert Wakefield, James Mackintosh, and others." Along with Wakefield, Malthus could claim close personal history with William Frend, who had been his tutor at Cambridge.[26]

In the midst of a conservative backlash in every aspect of British life, the overwhelming power of the British state found its spokesman in Edmund Burke, who, in addition to his *Reflections on the Revolution in France* (1790), also laid down the law on the issue of bread. His *Thoughts on Scarcity* in 1795 abandoned all pretense of charitable attitudes toward the poor. Several aspects of this publication proved important for the future of Malthus. His stance on labor, "a commodity, like anything else," drew from Adam Smith, yet Burke located the principle in a socially bifurcated society of high and low, propertied and the poor, and he insisted that tampering with the market constituted the worst policy in times of scarcity. Here was a flag signaling that the triumph of agrarian capitalism was finalizing its victory. Burke, like Townsend before him, felt that the problems of the poor could be explained by the simple fact that there were too many of them. In a striking gesture, he presented their claim on the wealth of society as equal to what they ate:

> The laboring people are only poor, because they are numerous. Numbers in their nature imply poverty. In a fair distribution among a vast multitude, none can have much. That class of dependant pensioners called the rich, is so extremely small, that if all their throats were cut, and a distribution made of all they consume in a year, it would not give a bit of bread and cheese for one night's supper to those who labour, and who in reality feed both the pensioners and themselves.

Burke's contemporaries recognized the precise sources of his fire-and-brimstone rhetorical strategies (the Bible and Milton) and saw how he called upon his earlier concept of the sublime by employing it as a weapon. Hazlitt fittingly described Burke's method as the equivalent of "forked lightning" and "loud thunder," which shocked the reader into fear so effectively that his argument met approval in the face of stunned silence. Here was a formula that Malthus would not ignore: praise be to the bulwarks of power and tradition as safeguards against the marauding demands of the people, portrayed as unnatural rights of the ignorant.[27]

Malthus's struggle to express himself in print, rendered more acute by a disability that challenged his "fitness" in other senses, brings to light another facet of the first *Essay*, namely, its viciousness. Even without historical knowledge of how the publication influenced the course of British social policy, any reading of the original *Essay* must come to terms with its deliberate punitive attitude toward the poor. Even a sympathetic biographer like Patricia James was forced to speculate that had Malthus inherited the comfortable living of his cousin, the rector of Walesby, Lincolnshire, five years earlier, the work might never have been written, or at least not written the way it was, "by an impassioned and frustrated man." Malthus was, as yet, without independent means, owing to the inadequate income from his curacy in Okewood. As a second son, he fell into the category of what Joan Thirsk classified as the stock figure of "angry young man," comparable to "stepmother" or "mother-in-law," in early modern England, though she adds that "people without social pretensions saw little merit" in primogeniture. He most likely chafed under the tutelage of his father, who was clearly involved and invested in all of his son's doings, even while encouraging him to keep looking for a willing publisher.[28]

Even more convincingly, Gail Bederman has argued that the key trigger for the *Essay on Population* came with the publication of Godwin's memoir of Mary Wollstonecraft, which touched off a public firestorm of antipathy toward the reformer and his late wife. As Bederman shows, the precise timing of the *Essay* points to Malthus having read the memoir alongside *The Enquirer* of 1797, the work by Godwin that he publicly refers to as the inspiration for a "conversation with a friend." Bederman's careful dating of these publications in conjunction with events in Malthus's life suggests that his reaction to Godwin and Wollstonecraft's sexual freedom may well have fueled the bold and somewhat cavalier argumentation in the first edition. Add to this his own sexual frustration and one finds the "almost sadistic gusto" of the first *Essay* coming into clearer focus.[29]

The unmarried author of the first *Essay*, impeded in speech yet well trained in rational disputation, had not seen much of the world in either its human or geographical variety. By his own account, Malthus claims to have penned the essay with few books to hand, though this was neither true nor relevant. The statement was obviously meant to excuse awkward mistakes and lack of sufficient knowledge evident in the first *Essay*. Without census data, Malthus had gotten the population of Great Britain wrong by 56 percent in the first *Essay*. New figures available to him, along with an altered perspective, influenced later revisions.[30]

Regarding the fixed laws of nature in the realm of sexuality, Malthus most likely had little direct experience, though it would be fair (and characteristically clinical in a Malthusian way) to say that he knew of sexual longing. Whether he had heard of *coitus interruptus* and its frequent application by rich and poor, we do not know; other forms of contraception were well known to his peer group at Cambridge, including his own tutee, Samuel Taylor Coleridge, who had to be rescued from a sortie with prostitutes at one point during his years at Jesus College.[31] Malthus could not have been aware, as we are, of periods of early modern history when population increases were obviously slowed by deliberate means. What he did know, or believe, was that sexual urges in young men generated ungentlemanly, disorderly behavior and were often procreative in their effect. Malthus's older brother, Sydenham, offered a case in point: his complicated personal affairs and those of the cousin he finally married "would have been worrying the family throughout the 1780s and '90s," according to Patricia James. Sydenham had fathered a daughter out of wedlock and then gained six stepchildren as a result of his marriage; he and his cousin subsequently had four more children together. Malthus's several grievances had begun with Paley's depiction of happiness connected with large numbers; he would end his case by attacking Godwin's (and Wollstonecraft's) demonstration of the related version of heedless sexuality and incongruous optimism.[32]

Marginalia in family copies of the works of Wollstonecraft and Godwin indicate agitated objections to Godwin's account of sexual freedom and his argument that sexual activity would eventually wither away in a more perfect society. Malthus family readers, whoever they were, harbored intense dislike for Wollstonecraft. (Malthus's cousin, Jane Dalton, the owner of Wollstonecraft's *Travels in Sweden,* most likely left her own marks in that volume.) If one reads the *Essay* as a polemic against Godwin and Wollstonecraft, the issue of human sexual behavior is hard to miss. Godwin's memoir of his late wife made public the nature of her former liaison with Gilbert Imlay, an American journalist, with whom she conceived a daughter, Fanny. Wollstonecraft was pregnant when she and Godwin married in 1797; dying ten days after the birth of a daughter, she became the subject of Godwin's grief-stricken efforts to immortalize her. His memoir of her life, published in January of 1798, echoed Rousseau's candid revelatory style in his *Confessions.* Yet given the temper of the times, Godwin's book brought mainly condemnation, and it would help seal the fate of his publishing career. It is more than likely that Godwin's faith in nature and love in the face of his personal experience also contributed to Malthus's contrary motion, his "almost sadistic gusto" in writing "of small-pox and famine, babies exposed and children starving." Coated in hellfire, the venom of Malthus's attack is unmistakable.[33]

His insistence on "what actually exists in nature" captures the spirit of Malthus's endeavor when he set upon Godwin's publications as the fertile texts from which he would generate his famous principle. In the first edition and more systematically in the second, he mocked what he believed to be Godwin's chimerical construction of human nature, which, he objected, had no basis in observed behavior. His most trenchant statements about nature often appeared in conjunction with his descriptions of the twin forces of population and the passion between the sexes, as they combined with natural and social forces acting upon human offspring. In truth, Godwin had laid the groundwork for his own ambush by including a passage of speculation about human behavior in the future that was at best utopian and at worst excessively optimistic. The infamous chapter attracted Malthus and other critics like bees to honey:

> The men therefore who exist, when the earth shall refuse itself to a more extended population, will cease to propagate, for they will no longer have any motive, either of error or reason, to induce them. In addition to this, they will perhaps be immortal. The whole will be a people of men, and not of children. ... There will be no war, no crimes, no administration of justice as it is called, and no government.... Besides this, there will be no disease, no anguish, no melancholy and no resentment. Every man will seek with ineffable ardour the good of all.[34]

Ironically, the passage preceding this conjecture argued for a check to wanton sexual activity. There Godwin rather diplomatically stated that sexual gratification initially disguised its rewards via "a false road of danger and deception," failed to deliver much in the way of "sympathy and intercourse of minds," and, moreover, became less viable in an aging male body. This was his version of the centuries-long debate over pleasures of the senses against those of the mind. He concluded his tome of more than five hundred pages by indicating that the chapter was "given only as a matter of probable conjecture" meant to be "altogether" separate from the "leading argument" of the volume.[35]

In the eyes of the Cambridge Ninth Wrangler, this line of reasoning must have lured like bait. Godwin had achieved considerable acclaim as the author of *Political Justice,* but he was a writer without the privileged tutoring in disputation and logic that Malthus had received at the hands of Wakefield and at university. The ironies can be savored in hindsight. Godwin's strict and somewhat humble education, the product of a family of three generations of devoutly Calvinistic dissenting ministers, led to an unsettled ministerial career for four years. By 1782, he had moved to London in an effort to support himself as a writer. *An Enquiry Concerning Political Justice,* published in 1793, was his most ambitious and successful publication and it went into three editions by 1798. Its central argument was on behalf of the power of individual judgment in the pursuit of knowledge, not one with which Malthus should have quarreled. Yet even without the melodrama of his personal life, Godwin's lack of credentials made him the perfect straw man. Malthus had excelled in an examination system that rewarded syllogistic logic and binary oppositions. Godwin's formal training was one of theological orthodoxy; the rest of his knowledge had come from hours of independent study and participation in discussion groups afforded by life in London in the heady years of the 1780s and 1790s. Godwin's work offered Malthus the opportunity to marginalize the renowned author of radical and liberal opinion who presumed to rewrite the terms of reality.[36]

What the Enlightenment had rendered sunny, Malthus repainted as overcast: the previous century had held that a large population made possible a greater degree of productivity and a stronger defense against enemies, yet Malthus turned the increase of humans into a detriment and a burden. Feed the poor and they will reproduce; support them in any way and they will indulge in idleness. The commandments of the body governed the lower orders, a principle Malthus claimed to have observed as a scientist in the laboratory of British society. An honest observation of nature would recognize that it operated "like a kind though sometimes severe instructor, with the intention of teaching us to make all parts strong, and to chace vice and misery from the earth."[37]

By putting nature in charge, Malthus was able to enlist the teleology of natural theology in a wholly new task, a dreadful scenario that shook off the platitudes of an earlier age. The contrast between his version of nature and that offered by William Paley's *Natural Theology* could not have been more pronounced. We justifiably might wonder if the young Malthus had felt condescension when he read that text as a twenty-year-old Cambridge student. It is highly likely that his oral examinations had demanded that he systematically critique it. Nevertheless, it was Paley who had captured the conventional outlook of the eighteenth century:

> It is a happy world after all. The air, the earth, the water, teem with delighted existence. In a spring noon, or a summer evening, on whichever side I turn my eyes, myriads of happy beings crowd upon my view. "The insect youth are on the wing."

> Swarms of new-born flies are trying their pinions in the air. Their sportive motions, their wanton mazes, their gratuitous activity, their continual change of place without use or purpose, testify their joy, and the exultation which they felt in their lately discovered faculties. . . . If we look to what the waters produce, shoals of the fry of fish frequent the margins of rivers, of lakes, and of the sea itself. These are so happy, that they know not what to do with themselves.[38]

Not so for the Malthusian universe, where swarms of any creature suggested imminent decline. Malthus singled out the basic fact of instinct—primarily, sexual desire—and made it the motor of ultimate destruction. The other bodily need, food, drove humans to engage in arduous labor. Problems arose from the drive for basic satisfaction without thought of consequences. Malthus believed he was introducing a necessary historical perspective on this scenario, one he had gleaned not only from the sophisticated pages of Gibbon and Hume but also from the invisible template provided by the middlebrow Townsend.[39]

Malthus did not argue that all humanity would suffer from excessive reproduction; he was quite clear in pointing out that only those who were too poor to support themselves would suffer or perish. He was careful to aim the harsh lessons of nature at the wanton disregard and ignorance of those who married without the means to feed numerous offspring. Malthus went as far as to label subsequent misery as the will of God. It was this unkindness, disguised as moralism, that attracted the criticism of theologians as well as British radicals. Learned clergymen found it needful to point out to Malthus that divine will did not punish humankind for its existence alone.[40] The direction of his thought, willfully dismissive of Christian charity toward the poor, erred on many fronts. As Daniel LeMahieu put it, "Parson Malthus thus espoused a Christianity which equivocated on original Sin, neglected Jesus, and denied Hell." Moreover, "sluggishness [was] not depravity." This "new way of thinking about poverty and inequality" proved "quite as momentous as the proposals of Condorcet, Paine and Godwin, which provoked it, and with far more immediate effect." Nowhere in his description of the effects of populousness did Malthus reconcile his picture of calamities with the biblical assertion that "the poor shall inherit the earth." The Christian duty of charity was remade as conditional, redefined according to elite interests.[41]

Malthus twisted his presentation in such a way as to make nature the accomplice of divine will (and vice versa), but his astute and theologically educated readers were not fooled. A paragraph about food stood as one of the starkest examples of Malthus's account of history according to the will of nature:

> Famine seems to be the last, the most dreadful resource of nature. The power of population is so superior to the power of the earth to produce subsistence for man, that premature death must in some shape or other visit the human race. The vices of mankind are active and able ministers of depopulation. They are the precursors in the great army of destruction; and often finish the dreadful work themselves. But should they fail in this war of extermination, sickly seasons, epidemics, pestilence, and plague advance in terrific array, and sweep off their thousands and ten thousands. Should success be still incomplete, gigantic inevitable famine stalks in the rear, and with one mighty blow levels the population with the food of the world.[42]

Arguing against the extension of poor relief to those who were hungry, he pointed out in his revised edition of the *Essay* that the needy laborer "should be taught to know that the laws of nature, which are the laws of God, had doomed him and his family to starve for disobeying their repeated admonitions." The chimerical abstractions of Godwin and others only interfered with a clear comprehension of the proper lesson about true nature and its punishments.[43]

Departure from Scripture and theology was no matter: Malthus was not writing as a theologian, nor had he been educated as one. Except for his few years under Graves, he lacked the most basic exposure to conventional practices of the Church of England owing to the fact that the Malthus family did not attend services. In fact, his appointment to a clerical post, as it happened, was threatened by the fact that he had never been confirmed, causing him to lean on family connections to accomplish the rite during a holiday in the Lake District in 1795. All of this inattention to convention alongside an extraordinarily liberal education came to roost in the *Essay on Population.* Eschewing the role of moralist, Malthus set out in search of the truth in philosophy, and so he reached for lofty companions in the first chapter: he cited Hume, the notorious skeptic, "Dr. Adam Smith," and Robert Wallace as sources of his principle. Only Wallace had serious training in divinity, which informed his defense of a morally ordered universe in *The Various Prospects of Mankind, Nature, and Providence* (1761). Here, Malthus found a critique of utopian logic with regard to burgeoning populations, and he also borrowed heavily from Wallace's exercise in arithmetic on display in his *Dissertation on the Numbers of Mankind in ancient and modern Times: in which the superior Populousness of Antiquity is maintained* (1753). (The book included a table with eight columns illustrating the "scheme" of population increases.) In complete contradiction of Wallace's argument—that the current state of the world was comparatively less populated than in ancient times—Malthus the contrarian turned the dial of Wallace's calculus to different ends. While Wallace criticized the upper rungs of society for luxury that interfered with procreation, Malthus trained his gaze on the lower, excoriating their fecundity.[44]

Many elements of the first *Essay* have the quality of utterance that no one of a polite or educated temperament would have deigned to say in public. Malthus repeatedly cited popular parlance or common knowledge as a way of permitting such statements. "The sons and daughters of peasants will not be found such rosy cherubs in real life, as they are described to be in romances," he asserted in an obvious reference to the Rousseauean taste of the era. "It cannot fail to be remarked by those who live much in the country, that the sons of labourers are very apt to be stunted in their growth, and are a long while arriving at maturity." Bad-mannered prejudices of the propertied classes paraded through the essay, inserted within descriptions offered as scientific observation. "The laboring poor, to use a vulgar expression, seem always to live from hand to mouth," he argued. "Their present wants employ their whole attention, and they seldom think of the future. Even when they have an opportunity of saving they seldom exercise it, but all that is beyond their present necessities goes, generally speaking, to the alehouse." To this opinion he added his all-important commentary on policy: "The poor laws of England can be said to diminish both the power and the will to save among the common people, and thus to weaken one of the strongest incentives to sobriety and industry, and consequently to happiness." Give the poor the means to spend and they will dissipate their cash in immediate gratification: this was more opinion than scientific observation. Even his assertion that rising poor law rates only contributed to lowering the price of provisions and the wages of labor was, in fact, hearsay and not truth. Yet the image of freeloading on the rates was a powerful trigger for reactionary views. Malthus's approach to the social question of the age fit the bill for a best-selling book at the turn of the century.[45]

It bears repeating that the first *Essay* emerged into the public arena just as the field of political economy became established as a social science. Reflecting the high stakes of such public attention and patronage, Malthus's polemic generated challenges from every quarter, including working-class radicals like William Cobbett, the Lake poets Wordsworth and Coleridge, and more conservative critics like Robert Southey, the irascible Tory. Objecting to "Malthouses rascally metaphysics," Southey wrote to his friend John Rickman, the compiler of census data for the British Parliament: "I shall be very glad to lend a hand in some regular attack upon this mischievous booby, and if you will put your shoulder to the work we may in a few evenings effectually demolish him." In print, Southey was scarcely more polite: "Mr. Malthus is said to be a man of mild and unoffending manners, patient research, and exemplary conduct. This character he may still maintain; but as a political philosopher, the farthing candle of his fame must stink and go out."[46]

Soon Malthus would find no need to bother with a response, as his high position in influential circles guaranteed him respect and a kind of immortality that even his famous critics would not enjoy. Given how often Malthus was cited as the inspiration for the New Poor Law, which embodied his proposals, both the calumny and the esteem are not surprising. In a memorial memoir, one of his colleagues sought to rescue him, though not without revealing the extent of public dislike. "Political economy—the science of civilization—is sought to be discredited by the help of private slander and the name of one of the best men is made an ignominious by-word for inflaming the passions of the poor," William Empson complained.[47]

After the *Essay* had created considerable stir and made a name for its no longer anonymous author, William Godwin attempted to engage the new celebrity in a productive dialogue about the implications of his argument. He visited Malthus on August 15, 1798, after Malthus had moved from his parents' home in Surrey to rented rooms in London. Clearly, he saw himself embarking on an independent path as the author of the *Essay*. Their conversation seems to have been fairly amicable, yet Godwin wrote Malthus immediately upon his return home to say that he had "omitted the most material part of the subject" of population, "the most striking view in which it may be placed," when they had spoken. Reminding Malthus that he himself had admitted that Britain at present had fewer people than it could support, Godwin added, "if human beings are of any value, it is certainly desirable, *ceteris paribus*, that every country should contain its greatest practicable number of inhabitants. Shall I not then be the irreconcilable foe of the present system of society, which practices so melancholy a consequence, it seems to cut us off from hope which must be inexpressibly dear to every lover of his kind?" The emotional tenor of the plea was pure Godwinian disposition. The response it received was pure Malthusian reason: "I do not see how the present form of system can be radically or essentially changed," Malthus wrote, "without a danger of relapsing again into barbarism."[48]

Singular in his focus and method, Malthus thereafter adopted the posture of a "hedgehog," knowing one important thing, for the rest of his career.[49] As his friend William Otter observed in a memoir after Malthus's death, "From the moment the principle of population had been struck out from his mind, and had taken hold of the public attention, it became to him the dominant and absorbing subject of his thoughts, constraining him to grave reflection, and causing every other tendency to yield to it." A former student put it less charitably: preoccupied by "the terrible increase of our population," Malthus "was so constantly harping upon this theme that we always called him 'old Pop.'" All of his arguments bent toward his principle and the persistent physical needs of the lower orders confronting a finite set of earthly resources. Persuaded by friends and critics alike, Malthus softened his position on "positive checks" to population, admitting in the second (1803) edition that laborers might well voluntarily postpone marriage or check their rate of reproduction without resorting to "vice," or mechanical methods of birth control. The *Edinburgh Review* conceded that Malthus had "weeded out, from time to time, a few obnoxious metaphorical expressions which had given offence to certain readers," while leaving the substance of his argument fundamentally unchanged.[50]

Once his pamphlet had reached the public and created a stir, Malthus clearly felt some belated humility and set to work to enlarge his knowledge of the surrounding matrix of his argument. Buoyed by the public response to the first *Essay*, Malthus inflated the matrix of the second edition to an entirely new proportion, enabling him to relegate Godwin's role to the margins. He changed the subtitle of the book, eliminating Godwin's name, along with that of Condorcet. (To be precise, Godwin appears in Book III, chapter 2, on page 366 of 604 pages of text.) In a tone of condescension, he dismissed Godwin's reply to the first *Essay* as a misguided response to his own argumentation. Malthus's "disingenuous" behavior—that is, his erasure of the debates that spawned his theory—is worth noting, for it sheds light on the careful path he constructed for himself in the years following 1798. In the shifting context of public opinion, Malthus could now claim that his abundant evidence, not a simple disagreement with optimism, made the case for his principle.[51]

In the 1803 edition, now considered the standard text of the *Essay*, Malthus added a more pointed assertion about the lack of rights of the poor. In a passage that has become notorious for its mean-spiritedness, he intoned:

> What [the real rights of man] are, it is not my business at present to explain; but there is one right, which man has generally been thought to possess, which I am confident he neither does, nor can, possess, a right to subsistence when his labour will not fairly purchase it. *Our laws indeed say, that he has this right and bind the society to furnish employment and food to those who cannot get them in the regular market;* but in so doing, they attempt to reverse the laws of nature.

He continued with a clarification of how society should be reordered according to the "laws of nature":

> A man who is born into a world already possessed, if he cannot get subsistence from his parents on whom he has a just demand, and if the society do not want his labour, *has no claim of right to the smallest portion of food,* and, in fact, has no business to be where he is. At nature's mighty feast there is no vacant cover for him. She tells him to be gone, and will quickly execute her own orders, if he do not work upon the compassion of some of her guests. If these guests get up and make room for him, other intruders immediately appear demanding the same favour. The report of a provision for all that come, fills the hall with numerous claimants. The order and harmony of the feast is disturbed, the plenty that before reigned is changed into scarcity; and the happiness of the guests is destroyed by the spectacle of misery and dependence in every part of the hall.[52]

By his own admission, Malthus was arguing against the laws of the land, which were narrowly defined as the Poor Laws; but according to any reasonably educated person, the laws themselves would be justly construed as representing centuries of customary law and humanity. The *Essay* was a "paradigm changing move," which, in the first instance, aided the critics of the Poor Laws in advocating for their removal.[53]

More important to posterity was its implications for a broader picture of social justice. In this scene of "nature's mighty feast," where we might picture a groaning board of animal, vegetable, and plant products, the hungry poor had no claim "to the smallest portion of food." Hence, scarcity is assumed to be a natural condition of life for those without property or sufficient employment. In effect, Malthus was spelling out what Amartya Sen has called "exchange entitlements," the means that ordinary people have to either labor or trade what they own for food. If the opportunity to work vanishes and they own nothing, they are simply subject to starvation. The rules of the game had been set by the administrators of property, and the poor had little choice but to accept them or, in the words of Malthus, "be gone."[54]

With the publication of Malthus's second edition in 1803, his usefulness became readily apparent. Malthus was offered an appointment as "Professor of Political Economy" at Haileybury College, which became the training school for the East India Company, at a generous salary of £500 a year with housing. This same year, Malthus would also take a rectorship at Walesby, Lancashire, an appointment controlled by his cousin, Richard Dalton, worth a comfortable £300 a year. (He would never officiate or reside there; he appointed a curate at £70 a year.)[55] As an instructor of young men destined for India, many of them seventeen years old, he had secured his place in an institution that would encourage the application of his assiduous reasoning. The College took its mission seriously, as the Company had come to understand that its ministers faced serious responsibilities. The College at Haileybury was to replace a school on site at Fort William in India, and with this shift came a decided change in curriculum, from one of liberal studies, including India's customs and history, to more technical training in law, finance, politics, and commerce. A fulsome appreciation of the ancient civilization of India was no longer deemed necessary for administration of the colony.[56]

These crucial years make clear that Malthus participated in the construction of a nineteenth-century definition of political economy, even as he never actually published another definitive treatise in the following thirty years. "It should be recalled that at this time the domain of political economy was neither clearly defined nor hierarchized in the manner that was shortly to occur," Keith Tribe has pointed out. Malthus's additional material in the 1803 edition, which dealt with food supply and the danger of imports, mattered more than his arguments about demographics to the subsequent field as it unfolded. In a sense, his points about population were now subordinated in relation to more difficult matters of balancing an agrarian with a commercial economy. At Haileybury College Malthus focused much of his instruction on Smith's *Wealth of Nations* and thus aided the college in the canonization of that text as the centerpiece of political economy. Malthus's own *Essay*, which he continually revised, also became required reading.[57]

Malthus's disputes with others continued, coupled with his practice of professing friendship with those with whom he quarreled. Godwin would continue to entertain visits from Malthus and call on him in return. Their meetings clustered around times when Malthus was revising the *Essay* for republication in 1803 and 1806, but after that they became infrequent and finally ceased after December 1822. Mutual respect could not have been the foundation, given Malthus's letter to Frances Place two months after dining at Godwin's home: "Mr. Godwin, in his last work, has proceeded to the discussion of the principles of population with a degree of ignorance of his subject which is really quite inconceivable," he wrote with palpable condescension. The contrarian, it seems, harbored an ill opinion of his host and was eager to score at the expense of his old rival, even at his relatively advanced age.[58]

Malthus's manners in public served him well at a handful of the famous dinners hosted by his publisher, Joseph Johnson, among such unlikely compatriots as Henry Fuseli and Godwin, along with noted mathematicians and medical men. At the time, he was known for his independence of mind, which, from the perspective of those who were silenced by the age of repression, was a considerable charity indeed. Subsequent biographers of Malthus, viewing the early influences of Wakefield, Graves, and Frend with undisguised distaste, would remark that young Bob had emerged unscathed. "Nothing of the wayward father or the eccentric novelist, of the scrupulous non-conformist or the presumptuous polemic" appeared in his character, but all of those influences brought about "the early habit of having to think and decide for himself" and "a steadiness [in him] beyond his years." The pattern of "differing from those" close to him was clearly apparent in retrospect. All too clear from these posthumous memoirs written by Otter and Empson, hyperbolic with praise for Malthus's disposition, is the need to rescue their friend's character from widespread calumny. By the time of his death in 1834, coinciding with the inauguration of the New Poor Law, the fact that Malthus had differed from the sympathy of the Age of Enlightenment no longer warranted any recognition at all.[59]

3
Rewriting the Agricultural Revolution
Unnatural Selection in the Malthusian Origin Story

Modern-day investigators need not look far in their search for reactions to Malthus following the publication of his first *Essay* in 1798 and its revised edition in 1803. One is tempted to say that all subsequent writers on social problems defined themselves in relation to Malthus, whether for or against, though as one astute literary scholar has noted, "but not against the same Malthus." In one corner, political economists jousted over questions of labor, wealth, and resources; in another, moral commentators reacted to the suggestion that people reproduced like animals and had no regard for fellow humans. At the head of a legion of critics stood the Romantics, who saw Malthus's malice-infused picture of nature as a vicious distortion of reality. Wordsworth, Shelley, and Coleridge joined the ranks of Godwin's supporters, along with Robert Southey, who fully recognized the self-perpetuating qualities of public hysteria generated by Malthus's polemics. Figures unknown today, such as John Rickman, largely responsible for the first census of Great Britain in 1801, commented on Malthus's ignorance of numbers—"not likely to dogmatize less because he knows less"—with undisguised distaste. But lines drawn between camps were not always visible to the public eye: once the census was launched, the people of Britain were more likely to see it "as a tool of Malthusian logic, being used . . . to identify and enumerate groups as 'problematic' or 'surplus populations,'" than as a corrective to the groundless speculations of Malthus. In short, the Malthusian zombie had burst forth, replicating itself across important sectors of society.[1]

The paths of these many public disputes exerted power in political and social realms for well over a century. As Robert Mayhew has amply documented, Malthus's legacy was "at the core of debates in political economy" and Victorian cultural arguments even when his principles were deliberately contradicted. John Stuart Mill wrestled with the twin problems of producers and consumers in relation to the creation of wealth and eventually settled on a more liberal and beneficent distribution of resources than imagined in Malthus. Stanley Jevons contributed an "extended exercise in Malthusian projection" in his book *The Coal Question* (1865), replacing Malthus's concern about wheat with a fearful mathematical prediction about fossil fuel energy. Alfred Marshall, whose *Principles of Economics* (1890) set the terms of the modern field of study known today, pointed to "Malthus as 'the starting point of all modern speculations' on population growth and its economic implications." The considerable impact of Malthus on John Maynard Keynes, the architect of liberal spending in the public sector, deserves much more space than is possible here. That influence, Mayhew shrewdly pointed out, was best telegraphed by Keynes's undergraduate students, who called their instructor "Jeremiah Malthus."[2]

Our purpose here is somewhat different. As an initial task, we need to achieve analytical distance from the Malthus zombie by setting aside the reflexive tendency of all discussions about population linked to resources as they follow the limited circuitry of his arguments. We need to disentangle ourselves from his primary assumption that scarcity of food is a planetary inevitability. Only then can we interrogate the way in which Malthus constructed a sense of closure around his argument, not least, through the "empirical allure of narrative" within his population tale, which effectively coincided with the origin stories of western society. By uncovering epistemological strategies assisting his compact formula, we should be able to make room for more creative thinking about resources that made food production possible in the late eighteenth century. We can also redirect attention to the larger issues at stake at that time, concerns vanquished by historical forces and thus rendered invisible to us now, which nevertheless suggest possibilities within our own world of food production. Although those circumstances of subsistence were specific to time and place, the dynamics of property and power have reproduced strikingly familiar circumstances in the twenty-first century.[3]

In order to redirect our thinking, we need to render the spatial idioms of the world of Malthus more legible. In his *Essay*, the aspiring political economist mobilized powerful cultural conventions of eighteenth-century Enlightenment thought, particularly with regard to property and land use. As a mediating force, these conventions acted as both a lens and a frame through which he and his contemporaries perceived the problem of population. The problem remains one of perception for us, too. As a lens, culture enables us to see, fathom, and encode the features of our environment. As a frame, culture delimits and directs our attention. Culture is transactional in the way it prompts associations with historical forces and institutional structures. For example, when we look at a picture of a hoe, we immediately conjure up images of the application of the tool to soil by a particular human for particular purposes; yet significant and variable details will be determined by our own cultural lens and frame. Each tool, in fact, inhabits an ideological universe; "no rigid boundary can . . . be drawn between technology and ideology." By contextualizing the *Essay on Population* within strategies of the time, we might see its arguments as part of an intellectual universe of limited options; yet this is not to suggest in a rather teleological way that the era was simply less competent than a later age in its capacity to create a food supply. In order to think outside historically specific constraints, we need to imagine alternatives within these same late eighteenth-century settings. This vantage point should help us verify the fact that Malthus painted an overdetermined universe, one that was deceptively conjoined to selective conditions.[4]

The Malthusian universe depended on culturally circumscribed assumptions that operated as theories of social hierarchies and human history in the eighteenth century. Central to the argument of the *Essay on Population* was a stark opposition between civilization and a barbaric struggle for existence. This particular tension, built upon fundaments as old as ancient myth, represented a form of ideological commitment: it implied a narrative pointing in a particular direction, looking forward to modern achievements like the city, technology, and a scientific knowledge base. On the face of things, this strategy might appear as common sense at that time and even now: why not trace the behavior and values that promised a form of order, along with greater efficiency and abundance? Accepting this narrative would simply "connect the dots" between particular conditions of the past and the world we know today.

But as historians, we must be more mindful of the terms in which such accounts are conveyed; in a sense, we must do the work of translation that uncovers how words like "nomadic" close off certain pathways, forbidding complex thinking about possible modes of existence, while narrowing expectations along predictable paths, in this case, a particular form of agriculture. To borrow from François Hartog's study of "representation of the other in the writing of history," the *Essay* can help us see that "what counts" is "the way the text elicits belief," "not so much the quantity of new information it presents as how it is treated by the narrator (who not only says what is said but says it in a particular fashion and says what is most 'notable')." Malthus was not alone in founding his claims on the narrative of civilization and its obverse, so a brief examination of this familiar strategy should give us useful insight into the dynamics at work within his argument.[5]

Recent scholars studying the Global Middle Ages have exposed a pervasive "origin story for the development of civilization" that depicts the struggle between settled agriculture and the nomadic other. No less a source than the Book of Genesis shows "how humans moved from a hunter-gatherer mode of subsistence—foraging at will in the garden of Eden—to one based on agriculture and the sweat of the brow." The "Mesopotamian model" of the rise of cities depended on this same dichotomy. Implicit in the standard account was a relationship of power: the civilizational epicenter, the city, overshadowed the hinterlands, where unruly outsiders roamed and resisted law, taxes, and improvement. There is no mystery about who wins this struggle. Its lineaments are visible in another ancient narrative, that of the *Epic of Gilgamesh,* written more than a millennium before the earliest books of the Bible, which "ends . . . with the death of the pastoralist." Enkidu, the shaggy pastoralist, must cut his hair and change his diet according to the stipulations of his urban captors. As the adopted sidekick of Gilgamesh, he must wage war upon his own people; he is not without a memory or conscience, so consequently he feels overcome by despondency. The gods ultimately extinguish him, making room for Gilgamesh's reflections on civilization and the price it must exact. For Europeans, this narrative carries the aura of a "just so" story: no other cast of players or sequence of events seems imaginable. For Enkidu, it is the story of subverted existence and stymied evolution.[6]

The same dichotomy pitting civilized cities and barbaric hinterlands in conflict informed political relationships between the center and the periphery in ancient and medieval times. In twelfth-century Rome, pastoralists were "classified not simply as poor and peripheral but also backward, in the literal evolutionist sense of the word."[7] Voices from the time endorsed the superiority of regions where grain-growing agriculture supplied urban centers of power and wealth. As Gerald of Wales, a well-traveled twelfth-century clerical scholar explained, progress already meant that "human beings [had] advanced from the woods to the fields and from the fields to villages and urban groups." What he saw of the Irish caused him to lament their resistance to settlement. "This race despised agricultural labour and continued the life of woodland and pasture to which it was accustomed," he recorded. His characterization remained influential for four centuries, when consolidation of Tudor political authority needed its foil of the hinterlands as a mirror for its own military achievements.[8]

Over time, the dyad of civilization and pastoral nomad provided the template for a powerful model of human relations across space; its essence charged the urban-rural axis with a concentrated sense of hierarchical difference between people. Lauro Martines located one wellspring of this powerful relationship in northern Italian cities, where "the image of the 'hick' had appeared" in courtly advice books and poetry as early as the thirteenth century. Regions in Germany and the Netherlands witnessed the same growing chasm between urban sophisticates and "the hulking, bent figure of the countryman . . . rendered commonly in caricature or with amused condescension." Peasants were "sub-human," according to the humanist Felix Hemmerlin of Zurich. In *The Courtier* (1528), Baldassare Castiglione depicted the peasant as a gullible fool, the butt of jokes played on him by the sardonic city slicker. Sebastian Franck described rural workers as "wild, treacherous, and untamed," reminding his contemporaries of the threats posed by venturing outside the policed space of the seventeenth-century city.[9]

Common assumptions about agricultural history rested on related beliefs and worked to support the expansion of political authority. Using the term "barbarian" to denote people who remained outside the reach of early states, James Scott points out the "ironic, tongue-in-cheek sense" of the word. " 'Savage,' 'wild,' 'raw,' 'forest people,' 'hill people'—are terms invented in state centers to describe and stigmatize those who have not yet become state subjects," he explains. At the same time, "the superiority of farming was underwritten by an elaborate mythology recounting how a powerful god or goddess entrusted the sacred grain to a chosen people." No mystery shrouded the identity of such beneficiaries: mandatory systems of fiscal and military organization, which commandeered food supplies, usually followed on such pronouncements.[10]

Most often, grain underwrote the European staple food, bread, and it also presented the ideal unit of taxation exacted from estate holders and citizens. As early as the ninth century, European peasants had no choice but to adapt to this system, driven by the demands of an increasingly powerful market circuitry. Many households eked out a precarious existence by combining wage-earning with raising crops for subsistence alongside those they sold or used as tax payments in kind. Farmers with claims to small holdings felt pressure from rising fees and taxes in a multitude of forms. By the eighteenth century, the inequities of the system were clear to contemporaries. "The grain which feeds man has also been his executioner," Sebastien Mercier wryly observed in 1770. The vice-like grip of the market "held producers, middlemen, transporters and consumers" in a kind of "slavery," yet the structural support for providing the people with their daily bread rendered the arrangement unassailable.[11]

From the perspective of centers of political power in Europe, existence outside this intricate fiscal and market apparatus appeared increasingly subversive, and sometimes it was. Transitional periods like the seventeenth century offered abundant proof. A growing chasm between rich and poor fueled daily conflicts and sporadic rebellions from the late sixteenth century through the seventeenth century. In Fernand Braudel's memorable account of the Mediterranean, "disturbances broke out regularly, annually, daily even, like mere traffic accidents which no one any longer thought worth attention." Vagrancy and banditry became the rule rather than the exception. David Hackett Fischer's study of the crisis of the seventeenth century combined disparate data on rebellions categorized as both political and broadly socioeconomic, showing that economic downturn exposed breaches in social trust that had been maintained with concerted effort under more sanguine conditions.[12]

With the spread of Enlightenment ideas in the eighteenth century, the spirit of perfectibility promised to solve the problem of the rural margins peacefully: the diffusion of knowledge and simple technology would eventually carry the barbaric "other" forward into the future. Everyone benefited, according to Scottish writers, including women, who were spared the brutish labor of toiling on behalf of mere sustenance. Even without formal knowledge of the gold standard of civilizational narratives, the rise of Mesopotamia, eighteenth-century historians offered the lineaments of agricultural modernization. When nineteenth-century British archeologists finally uncovered physical evidence of the Fertile Crescent, they constructed a story that harmonized in striking ways with developments already internalized from their study of ancient history. Human exceptionalism thus became locked in an embrace with a particular trajectory of urban-rural relations and food production.[13]

The task of feeding expanding urban populations is a problem familiar to historians of long trends in history. Fernand Braudel insightfully commented, "If there was a Neolithic revolution, it is still going on."[14] Cast in terms of "deep history," the path of agricultural revolution, often depicted in standard history texts as a northern European and British achievement, instead takes on a universal character. "The great revolutions, as they are commonly characterized, of the nineteenth and twentieth centuries—in industrialization, energy production and distribution, agriculture, and the genetic modification of food sources—were in a sense extension or further stages of the process launched at the beginnings of farming, by which humans became producers of their own food: a sort of 'unnatural selection,' which replaced the impersonal role of evolution in changing and launching species with the power of the human hand." This grand narrative, we should note, has the ironic effect of producing a panorama with remarkably little trace of identifiable agencies.[15]

In reality, the makers of agricultural progress were particular people with access to land and power over labor; in the European context, many were inhabitants of the Low Countries and England, who possessed sufficient capital and land to make a go of modernizing their farming techniques. Under the banner of improvement in this grand scheme of history, they interfered with the forces of nature to prevent humanity from suffering from the exigencies of hunting and gathering and natural catastrophes. Students of the past were (and still are) encouraged to identify with those who vanquished nature without giving too much attention to the terms of their own alliance with the improvers. The benefits of progress came along with a contract presented as rational; pleasing stories about nature and animals needed to be set aside as puerile. In a sense, this is how Malthus encouraged his readers to think.

The continuing force of this learned pathway of history is so strong that we can hardly see our way out of the ramparts that enclose us on all sides. That metaphor can help us reimagine a different route through the map of agricultural history. By examining a wider array of elements in historical context, we can begin to imagine competing lines of reasoning that were fighting for survival during the second half of the eighteenth century. A visual map of value in the British eighteenth century will help us to see vectors of power established between dietary practices and the forces of nature; a simple binary between nomad and settler does not do justice to the complexity of relationships involved in extracting food from the earth's resources. In this initial attempt, the British model remains central to this schematized map. Ultimately, we must try to theorize a wide variety of settings in order to accommodate the spaces and methods of producers of food outside Britain and Europe.

The "semiotic square," a symbolic system first proposed by A. J. Greimas and François Rastier, provides an effective tool for imagining oppositional concepts as ever-present and conjoined in constant movement within an enclosed matrix of possibilities (see diagram). We should note the similarity between this model and Lévi-Strauss's culinary triangle, a venerated tool of food studies, which posits interlaced cultural meanings of raw, cooked, and rotten foods. Food production can be as instructive as food consumption in seeing how our

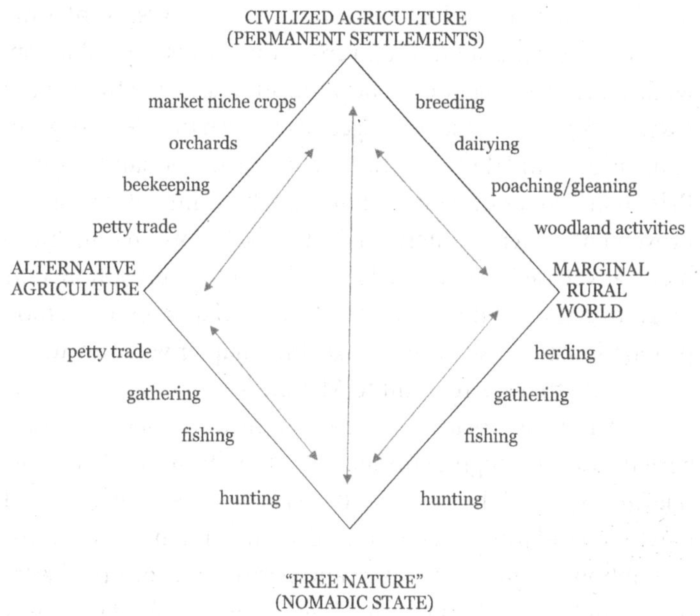

Spatial trajectory of the agricultural revolution

concept of society has arranged itself around what we consider conventional (and universal) dietary needs. But while Lévi-Strauss suggested a basic model in which nature and culture, aided by the human hand, worked upon food in a universal manner, and our model will employ more historically specific agencies. As James Clifford explained when using such a vehicle in evaluating art, one must "stress the historicity" of movement within such a system, which remains in perpetual flux.[16]

Our diagram of Malthusian reasoning ultimately points to a model of connected social and political formations within civilizational development. This emphasis will show that within modernizing European culture, the passage of time conferred benefits upon certain crops and means of production, while marginalizing or even negating others. At the time of the *Essay on Population*, the privileged place given to sedentary grain cultivation validated changes occurring in the landscape of Britain and areas of western Europe. The print culture of improvement, which proliferated during the European Enlightenment, advertised the material rewards of grain cultivation. Our diagram can simulate many different connections between food production and historical change; this chapter will only touch upon a few that are relevant to Malthus's *Essay on Population.*

At the top corner of the diagram lies sedentary grain agriculture, the high achievement of civilization. The most relevant aspect of this activity, the permanent settlement, could as easily stand for contemporary Britain as for ancient society. As Gibbon pointed out, "fixed and permanent societies" were designated as "modern nations," which he compared favorably to the unsettled way of life of the Germans in the ancient past. In fact, in Gibbon's time, this was an accurate representation of where British and European agricultural developments had been heading for several centuries. Robert Bartlett's account of the making of the European continent underscored this "highly particular form of land use" involving "a more densely populated monoculture." Europeans recognized wheat as "the aristocrat of cereal grains." Barley and rye, suited to different climatic conditions and diets, were designated as lesser relatives of wheat, and these also expanded across low-lying plains and arable regions in Europe and Britain.[17]

The evolution of concentrated grain cultivation, often imprecisely translated into the term "enclosure movements," is familiar to students of western European history. Large estate holders aimed to maximize returns from their holdings, precociously thinking along the lines of economies of scale. Draining and ditching became bywords of husbandry: landowners converted marginal scrub and marsh areas into arable fields, which they sowed with grain for the market. As leases of tenants came due, landlords increased rents to the point of breaking the smallholder's grip on land use, thus incorporating adjoining allotments of land into their burgeoning estates. Political influence of landowners led to a raft of legal restrictions that buttressed exclusive rights to property. Such laws prevented hunting and foraging in forests and marginal areas, and violators were prosecuted for poaching. In Britain, even charitable customary laws permitting gleaning ceased to take precedence over private mandates, the law of Leviticus eventually succumbing to the laws of private property.[18]

Significantly, Malthus was witnessing the final phase of enclosure in England. Over time, the number of small farmers and peasants diminished in breadbasket regions of England. In strikingly candid terms, political economists had already designated Ireland as the breadbasket for urban Britain. As Europe and Britain urbanized, the market for grain in cities grew, we might say in Malthusian terms, exponentially; the cultivation of grain for the urban market became tacitly understood as the foremost goal of agriculture. Malthus's disregard for the sufferings of the landless laborers who could not find employment was at the heart of the criticisms aimed at him in 1798. But few people even among his critics imagined that the tide of history would ever turn in favor of the doomed smallholder or, unimaginably, the landless laborers who were driven from the countryside by the inexorable consolidation of landholdings.[19]

Opposite this dominant system of settled agriculture, at the bottom corner of our diamond, lies the realm of "free nature." A play on words helps us locate our thinking along a line of historical progression: in the beginning, access to nature and its fruits was allegedly free and, according to the Edenic state suggested by the Book of Genesis, obtained without payment of the sweat of the brow. But exactly what constituted "nature" or the true beginning of natural or agricultural history was largely conjectural in the late eighteenth century. This corner of our diamond, then, can operate as a site of imaginative thinking. During the Enlightenment, the state of nature came into its maturity as a hypothetical ideal, rescued from the destructiveness and chaos of the century of Hobbes. According to Rousseau, we might imagine a vast reservoir of human and natural resources, unspoiled by the luxurious tastes of civilization. If barbarians inhabited this corner, ideally, they were depicted as noble savages, uncorrupted by worldly materialism and vanity. In more realistic terms, accounts of the superabundance of fish in the New World, for example, constituted the empirical evidence for what Europeans labeled as "free," though conflicts with Indigenous Americans over territories and resources provide us with the means of redefining the raw materials of subsistence in settings outside of Europe.[20]

Yet the eighteenth-century realm of the imaginary entertained contradictory notions. The pastoral nomad, often substituting for the barbarian in narratives of ancient history, provided a perfect foil for the negative forces at work on this end of a historical continuum. He might convey the fallen state of man, through the original sin of Adam, attempting to survive by dint of virile efforts, notorious or otherwise. As the opposite of civilized man, he functioned as "the dark twin," who wandered the earth, lawless and idle in the sense of being untethered to systematic production.[21] He and his animals subsisted outside the bounds of domestication. Sedentarists were Aristotelian creators, while nomads were opportunistic parasites. Sedentarists decoded the secrets of nature and released its bounty for the benefit of human flourishing; nomads simply merged with nature and siphoned off its by-products.

The significance of this bifurcation of society cannot be overemphasized. It is here that the claimants of civilization based their entitlement to land and power over the Other, cast as a bestial scrounger dependent on nature's whim. The arguments of Aristotle, transferred and translated through the ages, became the arguments of later-day cultivators. In this way, the spatial organization of the earth's resources extended its power into political and social organization, dividing up humanity into a distinctive hierarchy. Sedentarists used the justification of cultivation in order to overpower, displace, and sometimes enslave those who had a different relationship to their environment. Justifying their claims through the guarantee of abundance, cultivators marshalled resources and assumed their management. Based ostensibly on the fear of having too little to survive, their claims translated subsequently into the power to extend that fear to their subjects, whom they viewed as too inattentive, ignorant, or lazy to labor unless goaded by hunger.

No matter what characteristics we attribute to "free nature," we can say that it represents the realm of "prehistory," a time prefiguring the impact of historical forces like political and social organization, greater knowledge, technology, and marketing arrangements. The dominant pressures of change are indicated by central vertical arrows: these represent the dynamic impact of states, social forces, and economic arrangements. The inevitable upward trajectory of historical development sustains population growth, and this is where the arrangements of food production enter into the picture.

Grain cultivation as "mainstream agriculture"[22] claims a very long historiography stretching back to archeological excavation of the early societies of the Middle East. Here is where we find the paradigm generated by archeologists and historians of the mid-twentieth century. Gordon Childe's *What Happened in History,* first published in 1942 as a work for the British "bookstall public," explained the achievements involved in the "Neolithic Revolution." As the foremost prehistorian of his time and a committed socialist, Childe aimed to inform his readers of their heritage at the onset of World War II. Settled agriculture presented the origin of society by validating the ingenuity and forethought involved in cultivating crops, particularly grain. Childe's "distinction between food-gathering and food-production" identified the move to settled agriculture as "an economic and scientific *revolution* that made participants active partners with nature instead of parasites on nature." His conceptual apparatus became part of the intellectual framework for subsequent discussion of "the agricultural revolution" and a later extension of this same progressive thrust, which included industrialization. "The ox was the first step to the steam engine and petrol motor," Childe asserted with unabashed Whiggism.[23]

What were the winning features of settled agriculture? Sedentarism was inextricably linked to "brain work" of a particular kind; what followed from this was the special human march to higher forms of organization. Domesticated grain offered systematic bounty with predictable outcome that allowed for other, more sophisticated activity to go on. Cultivation seemed to promise a savings in time and effort. And because its returns were predicated on design and delay, those who carried on such activity demonstrated superiority of intellect on account of their foresight; in moral terms, they gained credit for their ability to forgo immediate gratification. Given all these benefits, Enlightenment texts on the "four stages" theory of history understood this social formation to embody moral value, too. Gibbon offered his own example by inserting a brief telling of Zendavista's story within *Decline and Fall of the Roman Empire*, including the maxim "He who sows the ground with care and diligence, acquired a greater stock of religious merit than he could gain by the repetition of ten thousand prayers."

Gibbon reached for the ancient Persian prophet Zoroaster as a worthy decorative flourish for his archaic story of western empire.[24]

Technology wedded to a moral outlook appears incontestable as advancement, especially when linked to a powerful concept like revolution. Yet, in context, these same elements present a certain amount of difficulty when defined as universally advantageous. The mortarboard plow, heralded by historians as crucial in transforming the medieval European landscape, looks a lot like its precursor and never fully convinces a classroom of students scrutinizing PowerPoint images. One begins to suspect that the really crucial issue within this narrative is the "who" behind the brainwork in the turn to monocultures of grain. If the most powerful landowner in the region decided to organize grain production in a certain way, employing a plow in the process, his passage to future success was highly likely even without the plow. Put in more abstract terms, diffuse activities of history, like natural forces, don't actually know or see the way to such logical progression. Efforts to grow food are interactive, as elements of the environment respond to human involvement. The efforts of cultivators must adapt to subsequent challenges as they experience successes or confront resistances that inevitably shape their pathways along irregular rather than straight lines. Our search for a complex, diverse agricultural past should make us suspicious, then, of the straight vertical arrow upward.

Our diagram can reconstitute multiple paths to the present by releasing nature from what is actually a highly constrained—some would say vanquished—historical path. Let's instead imagine nature as a set of multiple forces emanating in all directions from the distant free nature corner of the diamond. Along with representing untouched resources such as remote land and forests, nature also generated weather in the form of wind (both helpful as a source of power and destructive in terms of crop yields) and precipitation. In some epochs, such forces worked alongside those elements contributing to the central upward arrow. Nature drove rivers and streams along their courses and governed the complex ecologies of oceans and their coastal areas. On a microbial level, nature generated plant and insect life, while promoting a constant cycle of growth and decay. Involved in constant chemical transformations, microbes replenished the soil in the form of manure and plant life and interacted with foods like bread, milk, and cheese to transform them into enriched, longer-lasting foods. In each instance, we might imagine multiple alternatives to the formulas involved in the classic eighteenth-century agricultural revolution.

For Malthus, a different drama unfolded: natural forces worked upon humans as vectors of correction, checking mistaken actions caused by human ignorance, while rewarding actions taken along the vertical line of historical change. Malthus did acknowledge that some natural events—spectacular storms and epidemic disease—could check intelligent actions, too. But like the retributions issued after the Lisbon earthquake in 1755, his equivocations left room to speculate about divine punishment for imprudent behavior. Such occasions, he would offer, only reinforced an argument in favor of a carefully marshalled grain supply, overseen by paternalistic stewards laying down disciplinary provisos. In fact, Malthus's aim had to do with restricting the extent of demand on this high order of sustenance. Certain people were more likely to indulge repeatedly in sexual desire without thought for the future, bringing forth offspring whom they could not afford to feed. They were, in a sense, undomesticated human beings. For Malthus, the organization of plants, animals, and landownership under one system was very much a process masterminded by an intelligent deity. According to natural theological teachings, those who were wedded to a world of unrestrained behavior would face consequences in the form of biological hardship impeding their survival. On a more practical level, such conditions called for wise stewardship by the landed classes. The paternalism underlying Malthusian arguments pointed to real-life equivalents in the form of a class of trustworthy, improving landlords in eighteenth-century Britain.

Our contrasting concept of domestication can help us evaluate this important issue in Malthus's argument. In the revised 1803 edition of the *Essay,* Malthus notoriously presented nature as a "great mistress" of a "mighty feast," who was strict, exclusive, and merciless in managing limited room at a metaphorical table. His choice of imagery signaled a domestic space and, indeed, he was positioning food production behind domestication in a metaphorical as well as a social sense. This particular passage (expunged from later editions because of the outcry it provoked) perfectly illustrated the argument that it was the "who" involved in marshalling resources within the grand household of nature that ultimately mattered to his story. At the banquet, participants derived their place at the table by either the possession of property or the claim to employment. Woe to him who arrived with neither of these assets:

> A man who is born into a world already possessed, if he cannot get subsistence from his parents on whom he has a just demand, and if the society do not want his labour, has no claim of *right* to the smallest portion of food, and, in fact, has no business to be where he is. At nature's mighty feast there is no vacant cover for him. She tells him to be gone, and will quickly execute her own orders, if he does not work upon the compassion of some of her guests.

Under these conditions, Malthus presented human compassion as lacking necessary foresight. Given the generative power of human nature—that is, wanton sexual behavior—the supply of "intruders" was limitless:

> If these guests get up and make room for him, other intruders immediately appear demanding the same favour. The report of a provision for all that come, fills the hall with numerous claimants. The order and harmony of the feast is disturbed, *the plenty that reigned is changed into scarcity*; and the happiness of the guests is destroyed by the spectacle of misery and dependence in every part of the hall, and by the clamorous importunity of those, who are justly enraged at not finding the provision which they had been taught to expect. The guests learn too late their error, in counteracting those strict orders to all intruders, issued by the great mistress of the feast, who, wishing that all her guests should have plenty, and knowing that she could not provide for unlimited numbers, humanely refused to admit fresh comers when her table was already full.

Like a parent allowing a child to make a mistake for the sake of a harsh lesson, Malthus lured his readers into a domesticated space and then challenged them to see the outcome. This vision of nature, anthropomorphized as an ultimate authority, punished, destroyed, and vanquished human actors in a zero-sum battle for survival.[25]

We need to step out of Malthus's constrained great hall and imagine other pathways of domestication, including other forms of social organization. Now we can fully situate the reasoning behind the limited discussion of diet found in the pages of Malthus's *Essay.* Alternative ways of thinking about food production and social organization can be found along the adjacent sides of our diamond. By dispensing with the Aristotelian notion of human mastery of nature, we can be better positioned to see human relationships embedded within a variety of environments of the past, replete with animals and plants supplying multiple sources of food. These might be fishing villages, forested areas, mountainous terrain, or tidal bays. Rather than aiding a progression toward a particular agricultural destiny, historical actors of many kinds appear within a spectrum of ways of working alongside nature, ranging from borrowing and syphoning to negotiating and collaborating. Not all actors are human: through multispecies ethnography, we can bring to the fore a variety of entangled relationships with animals, fish, plants, and marine life, which a modernizing model regards as separate or marginal to mainstream economic life.

The result is a wholesale rearrangement of the questions we ask about sustenance. How, for example, does "a multitude of organisms' livelihoods shape and [in turn become] shaped by political, economic, and cultural forces[?]" In order to succeed in this new manner of inquiry, we would need to undo the process of inversion that has "othered" rural inhabitants, as well as animals and plants—revising the "nature and I are two" position—and imagine a different array of simultaneous activities. What if the narrative of agricultural revolution had been interrupted by myriad alternative story lines? This is the act of "resuscitation" that the semiotic diamond is supposed to make possible.[26]

It turns out that our historical accounts have been too sparsely populated to provide a full understanding of "what happened in history," to borrow Gordon Childe's memorable title. Our diagram should help us turn our attention away from the dominant upward arrow representing the classic account of agricultural progress in the center of the diamond so that we can envision multiple paths to the present. Formulas of domestication have been useful in tracing the evolution of particular animals and plants, but they have undoubtedly constrained our thinking. "The paradigm of an 'agricultural revolution' that most of us learned in our introductory anthropology classes can now be seen to be at odds with much of what archeology has revealed," Dorian Q. Fuller asserted a decade ago. Domestication of sheep, goats, and cattle (not to mention humans) took centuries to occur and was "highly contingent on particular cultural practices that need not have unfolded in a similar way for each domestication" across the globe. To fully comprehend selected pathways, we need "to instead consider in more detail the interplay of particular human practices as strategic choices in subsistence and how these were entangled" with specific changes in plant and animal life and the environment.[27]

A more comprehensive geographical framework immediately forces us to see the transition to modern food production differently. Just as important as human actors, specific natural settings played a part in determining food resources. "Landscapes are historically accretional and cultures like cultivars fit into and contribute to this accretionary process. For this reason, some authors promote thinking about agricultural origins as evolutionary 'niche construction.'" The British agricultural revolution was just one configuration located in one type of place. The human effort required to shape this particular space, along with the ecological costs over time, shows how manipulated this setting actually was. As we trace activities on either side of our diamond, we can see that niches do in fact inform historical change and often supply alternative methods and outcomes that could sustain populations and coexist alongside mainstream agriculture. Certain niches offered resources to those not taking part in the larger economic structures supporting large-scale cultivation. As a result, such activities became available as a means of rescue when mainstream activities experienced hard times.[28]

On the right side of our diamond, pathways to the historically marginal rural world hosted their own, distinct claims to land, plants, and animals. This segment reveals activities not formally excluded from civilized neighbors and yet not included in the same frameworks of organization. Immediate use determined much activity on the lower side of the diamond. Hunting and herding might represent many different approaches to obtaining meat as a dietary feature; some methods were derived from custom, depending on community practices that included shared use arrangements. Moreover, herding cultures were capable of depending on wild animal populations, which they followed within bounds set by generations of ancestors. In the case of deer, as Tim Ingold has shown, animals might even remain rooted to their wild habitats and retain morphologically wild features. His arguments based on an example of Scandinavian Sami herding shattered the conventional definition of domestication and framed new questions about animal populations as forms of capital and subjugated workers.[29]

Fishing deserves an important place on both lower sides of the diamond: the ocean's borders, along with the edges of lakes, rivers, and streams, provided plentiful sustenance throughout history. Mediterranean and Baltic cuisines depended on fish, both fresh and cured, as a staple of a varied and nutritious diet for millennia. First Nations in North America depended heavily on "the shoreline's robust estuarine ecology." As Andrew Lipman illustrated for the colonial Northeast, "the abundant tiny plants and animals held in the region's bays were attractive food sources for both shellfish and finfish." Not surprisingly, Algonquian diets included "fishy porridge" blended with corn and "large servings of seafood." Such protein sources were not to be scoffed at, though it took several hard winters for colonists to learn how to reorient their thinking away from English expectations.[30]

English foodways were not the only methods of survival, of course: fishing combined well with nonagricultural pursuits like merchant enterprise. The Dutch considered coastline activities as the preferable way to sustain their populations; their perpetual view of the world facing the sea shaped their approach to colonization. Their foothold in New Amsterdam depended on trade more than land acquisition; the English, wedded to wider territorial expansion, challenged them and easily bargained for the island of Manhattan. The Dutch moved on to distant islands in the Pacific. Such a strategy, John Gillis explained, "may puzzle us but made perfect sense to them." The fact that Malthus, on the other hand, failed to recognize such approaches to land and food should be underscored. His comprehension drew from his personal aspirations with respect to the propertied hierarchies in which he lived as well as his relationship to historical time, space, and national identity.[31]

Movement upward along the sides of the diamond, toward the middle points, brings greater engagement with rules, methods, and laws governing how sustenance is gathered or produced. Poaching occurs when private property prevents claims to wild animals like deer and rabbits. Gleaning similarly belongs to a marginal world of contested rights. On the right-hand side, inhabitants generally see their lives as taking place outside the systems of legal and marketing rules of the center, but they are not primitive simply because of that. On the upper-right segment, approaching civilized agriculture, forms of gathering may include knowledgeable adaptation to seasonal changes and plant use. This may include practical understanding of what, under civilized agriculture, might be considered scientific approaches.

If herding is highly developed, dairying becomes possible; this includes dairying with goats, sheep, and even deer and the marketing of cheese, even fancy kinds. Proximity to civilized agriculture presumes a more restricted, exclusive approach to land use; thus, breeding becomes desirable, as the market would reward the rearing of animals with a greater ratio of meat to weight and size.

On the left side of the diamond, the operations of alternative agriculture suggest a more entangled relationship with civilized cultivation and its markets. Both property rights and legal restrictions come into specific play here, and participants may be landowners and fully participatory members of rural social networks. On the upper side of the diamond, involvement with capitalist markets shapes the perspectives of participants; their alternative aspects have to do with the crops and environments they oversee. Hunting and foraging also take place on the lower left-hand side, but with a difference: alternative agriculturalists are aware of a full spectrum of possibilities for sustenance and their engagement may be systematic and fully alert to prospects in the marketplace. Petty trade sometimes takes the place of autarkic activity and contrasts with a systematic, venture-bound relationship to the center. Variability in output makes this necessary: climatic and seasonal impact on products raised mostly without highly capitalized equipment renders their viability uncertain. However, such livestock and cultivated crops can be highly desirable to inhabitants of the center of society. At times, alternative products appear more attractive than those produced at the center, which may be more abundant and, depending on the cycles of market and seasonal conditions, more or less expensive.

Alternative agriculturalists owned less capital in terms of land and equipment than did concentrated grain cultivators, but their operations were successful because they exploited the one factor they controlled in abundance: their own labor. Most of their practices were, in fact, labor-intensive, which is why their endeavors were often seen as less viable from the point of view of large estate managers. For example, eighteenth-century smallholders sowed lucrative crops of canary seed with the use of teapots. One can hardly imagine the Earl of Suffolk investing time in such a byway of the rural economy; even if pegged at subsistence-wage level, the long-term costs of labor and more eccentric marketing channels compared poorly to the assurance of income through cereal production.[32]

The paradigm of alternative agriculture may seem counterfactual when viewing the world inhabited by Malthus and his contemporaries, yet in fact the concept fits very well within the historical view of the changing landscape of England from the mid-seventeenth century onward. Joan Thirsk devoted a great deal of attention to keeping track of experiments with crops and methods, a tendency visible in the rural record when an abundant supply of grain (and a drop in price) drove a search for alternative ways of making a profit from the land. The pattern began as early as the fifteenth century, when "expanding cow-dairies" offered greater income than sheep. Dairying exemplified the characteristics of all types of alternative activities: the basic unit was the small farmer, who used family labor and viewed such enterprises as extensions of households, right down to the methods used to work with soil.[33]

These families were, in effect, gardening their land, with all the labor-intensity that implied. Flexibility and adaptability marked their approach to horticulture and poultry-keeping, along with crops like cabbages, potatoes, and artichokes; industrial crops like rapeseed, hemp, and teasels, "essential to the cloth industry"; and fashionable items like saffron and canary seed. Orchards of plums and apples also promised serious profit margins, so it is not surprising that the people who grew such crops might mount resistance to tithe collectors. (Thirsk cites William and Elizabeth Payne of Thanet, Kent, who went down on record throwing "a plum, an apple, a turnip, and a rosemary sprig" at the collectors who came in search of payment.) An increasing number of tithe disputes after 1650 indicates that income from such crops caught the eye of authorities, whose sagging revenue from grain led them to investigate the subsidiary ways in which the rural population was managing to support itself.[34]

Assessing the value of these activities presents a conundrum for the historian: what is the appropriate metric with which to measure alternative agriculture? The activities sometimes don't appear on record at all, or, if they do, their significance is hard to tally. "The penetration of alternatives into the economy is only perceived in briefly documented episodes, as a flashlight momentarily illuminates dark corners," Thirsk admitted. Comparison by means of measures imposed by grain-growing, such as acreage used or workers employed, diminished their importance in the annals of history. Voices sometimes leapt out of correspondence of the time: in 1734, a farmer near Edinburgh noted that "you may have a better return from kitchen garden than from corn" and, a year later, raspberries "will yield you more than wheat" and "they'll require less husbandry than a crop of wheat." There is little doubt that rural inhabitants understood the distinction between mainstream agriculture and pursuits that were sometimes referred to as "small things," regarded as the marginal work of women. This form of dismissal most likely used gender as a gesture of disdain rather than an accurate description of who was involved. Yet such labors brought their own reward in terms of financial survival and even prosperity, what Thirsk described as "life-saving value in whole villages." These niche areas supplied the "wiggle room" financially necessary for many forms of supplementary activities undertaken by independent households, but such pursuits were factored out of the economic model of modern agriculture.[35]

We have traveled a long way from the world of Malthus and his calculus. Without resorting to sentimental statements about lost village life, we might consider the oppositions presented through this examination of the limits of agriculture as grain cultivation impelled forward by the dictates of the capitalist market for wheat. A clearer definition of the margins comes into view when we restore inhabitants to the land and consider a greater range of activities pursued according to the dictates of the environment. Consider, for example, the critique of Malthus by the Scottish political economist James Anderson, who, as a farmer, lamented the loss of London's human and animal excrement. With that mother lode of nutrients, Anderson pointed out, the soil of the countryside might be regenerated ad infinitum in order to feed hungry humans. Anderson's arguments provoked Malthus, though the empiricist population theorist never quite comprehended what Anderson was advocating. It was Anderson who sent him back to his books, causing him to focus on rent as a problem in need of explanation.[36]

Karl Marx, in turn, seized upon Anderson's insights to conceptualize the "metabolic rift" occurring between the cities and the countryside, emblematic of human disavowal of its oneness with nature. As John Bellamy Foster has shown, Marx was particularly attuned to the "main ecological crisis of his day—the problem of soil fertility within capitalist agriculture," and he used the issue as a lever to pry open the larger problem of the relationship between humans and nature. He believed that large-scale agriculture ran counter to the interests of the earth and its resources and pounced on the irony that "rational agriculture . . . needs either small farmers working for themselves or the control of the associated producers." Scrutinizing the work of Liebig, Marx foresaw the implications of soil enhancement for theories of rent and labor value, not to mention the structural basis of property ownership that would ultimately determine how land was inhabited and used.[37]

Malthus's rural laborer, with his thin legs and undernourished appearance, stood in for a much more actively engaged population of previous years: even among those who were precariously employed, marginal people operated as agencies of adaptation and change, the very definition of resilience. Small farmers and cottagers were positioned to devise ways of surviving outside the crushing dictates of market agriculture, which would turn many of them into rural proletariats without property or resources. Recent scholarship forging new definitions of human interaction with the environment have turned to the concept of moral ecology, which takes into account resistances to dispossession and vernacular practices that were sustainable and viable until challenged by predatory economic interests, bureaucratic states, or elite conservation strategies. Through an alliance of economic history, cultural history, and anthropology, moral ecology creatively animates marginal or hidden rural actors and resources in a complex space of historical change. What was once seen as a polarized conflict of oppression and resistance in the countryside is now a more demotic field of interactions, which highlight environmental factors of critical importance to specific localities. The right to dwell or, as Tim Ingold has described it, "an alternative mode of understanding based on the premise of our engagement with the world, rather than our detachment from it," brings to light much of what was missing from earlier historical narratives. We need a more useful paradigm of protraction and entanglement: we are still in the midst of change and the findings of population studies make us acutely aware of how much we need a flexible form of agrarian vision.[38]

4
The Ignoble Savage
Categories of Human Difference and Population History

Malthus forecast the future based on the human past; in this sense, the *Essay on the Principle of Population* was a work of history as well as social science. He offered a clear lesson to his readers: civilization rested on a fragile and hard-won foundation secured through bestial struggle, a version of history marked by simple, unmistakable polarities of good and evil. In the first *Essay,* he set the stage for his theory by supplying the barbaric prehistory of western Europe. Hallmarks of this era included "constant war," the mistreatment of women ("unremitting drudgery" for the sake of "their tyrannic lords"), a failure to honor the elderly ("thus violating the first feelings of nature"), constant misery and hunger, and a restless search for food ("like so many famished wolves in search of prey"). His liberal use of animal metaphors signaled an important strategy that depended on what he understood as historical constructs of barbarian and savage and "the struggle for existence" across time and space.[1]

That potent phrase, "struggle for existence," echoes from the pages of the first *Essay.* Many scholars see this as an invitation to highlight Malthus's anticipation of Darwin's insights a half-century later. Though the obvious parallel interest in struggle links their arguments and language, Darwin theorized and celebrated the idea of variety in nature. Nothing could be further from Malthus's findings, which collapsed differences into simple categories of behavior. The mistake lies in thinking forward rather than back: Malthus had borrowed the phrase from Edward Gibbon's *Decline and Fall of the Roman Empire* (1st volume, 1776), the multivolume work that acted as one of the mother lodes of the *Essay on Population.* It was there that Malthus absorbed several key assumptions about hunger and human behavior. The dynamics of barbaric life and the pressing necessity of migration in Gibbon's history provided an important model for Malthus's generic natural cycle of human history. "[T]he westward movement of barbarians into the Atlantic provinces of the Mediterranean empire of Rome . . . becomes the history of Europe, and very nearly of mankind," J. G. A. Pocock pointed out in his analysis of Gibbon's *Decline and Fall.*[2] Whether speaking of "tribes" or "bands," the story repeated itself in "the perpetual struggle for room and food" within the pages of Malthus's *Essay.*[3]

Gibbon was by no means the sole exponent of this brand of history, or even an especially influential one. Yet he serves as a useful entryway into the style of thinking that permeated elite British society during the formative years of Malthus's life. Both Gibbon and Malthus employed the model of historical development known as four stages theory, or stadial history, which informed Enlightenment thought during the middle decades of the eighteenth century. Voices on both sides of the Channel based their discussions of human history on the same assumptions, which explained social arrangements according to the prevailing form of subsistence production. It is easy to forget that Quesnay, Turgot, Rousseau, Smith, and Millar, to name a few, located the structural support for their ideas about progress in the logic of how food was procured.

This narrative exerted definitive explanatory power over the final decades of the century, as travelers, naturalists, and merchants encountered peoples in other parts of the globe. Earlier modes of economic life came into clear focus as they were drawn from living examples, at first in nearby Scotland and northern Scandinavia but more importantly in the Americas. It was there that four stages history generated typologies of human behavior corresponding not just to phases of human subsistence labor but to regional and even racial categories of human difference as they were understood in the eighteenth century.

The concept of human difference moved to center stage during the last quarter of that century, as Europeans gathered a plethora of information from remote encounters. Categories generated at this time might be seen as part of a larger problem of handling knowledge overload through a historical watershed, much like the way a cascade of information during the Renaissance called for the creation of organizational techniques in the sixteenth and seventeenth centuries.[4] Yet differences perceived as "human" also intersected with existing social categories, which were firmly planted in a nation with a long history of administering to an ever-shifting body of poor laborers. The English state had not shied away from creating administrative categories that objectified ethnic and regional types. William Petty's seventeenth-century political arithmetic is a useful reminder of how early preoccupations with populations outside of England generated an impulse toward objectification.[5] As a way of eradicating problems related to the Irish population, for example, Petty added transplantation and forcible marriage to established strategies like impressment and the workhouse; he even imagined "obliterate[ing] [Irish] Names of Persons and Land" as a way of literally erasing ethnic difference.[6] Britain's continuing entanglements around the globe accentuated the move toward some form of reckoning with peoples generally typified as Other. As Roxann Wheeler has pointed out, even when skin color is not invoked, racial categories can operate in important and powerful ways. Commercial ambitions joined with a civilizing mission, as "*Christian* and *savage* participate[d] in a visible economy of race outside of a color paradigm."[7]

Such differences modulated according to increasingly fervent claims of national and racial superiority. Kathleen Wilson's exploration of elements of London's cultural scene illuminated the ways in which Cook's voyages played through "drama, science, and religion," which combined forces "to classify the English and British as a superior and distinctive people" characterized by particular manners and customs. Historical narratives employing racialized notions of Anglo-Saxon identity found receptive audiences in theaters and print culture during the 1770s and 1780s, fueling a sense of special British endowments. "The central myths of Anglo-Saxonism" were recast as building blocks in the historical foundation of a rejuvenated nation.[8]

Stadial history participated in these developments and merged with political sentiments, as warfare on three continents and historic challenges to colonial supremacy forced Britons to find an explanatory model for patriotic ambitions as well as commercial success. Historians have regarded Malthus's handling of stadial history as a means to an end, namely, reinforcement for his principle of population, but there is more to be said about its implications in his work. His predecessors in political economy, notably, Adam Smith and James Millar, were far more optimistic and nuanced in dealing with human differences, and they imagined a coherent moral polity constituted by an alliance of social ranks moving through the history of time. Malthus purposefully mined their data with a more partisan set of objectives. Targeting subsistence activities of Indigenous populations, he cast them as unintelligent food-gatherers, doomed to disappear, and, more than this, their degraded condition stood in as a proxy for the lower classes in Britain. Malthus made the equation explicit in his cursory examination of information about primitive populations around the globe. Comparative ethnology became a means to an end that had consequences for those who stood outside the social contract imagined by a theorist who saw nothing noble in the contemporary savage.

Malthus first read Gibbon's *Decline and Fall* as a student at Cambridge, and he recorded feeling stirred by its dramatic narrative, which began in Rome with the earthquake of July 21, 365 CE. Gibbon supplied generous detail about catastrophic environmental events and their imperial surroundings. As an avid recorder of the weather and a fervent admirer of classical history, Malthus obviously found the volume to be exciting reading material. He offered his father a decorous report of his appreciation of the first volume: "He gives one some useful information concerning the origin & progress of those nations of barbarians which now form the polished states of Europe," Malthus wrote to Daniel Malthus in 1786, "[and he] throws some light upon the beginning of that dark period which so long overwhelmed the world, & which cannot I think but excite one's curiosity."[9]

It was undoubtedly true: Gibbon painted an action-packed portrait of the Huns, Tartars, and Germanic tribes, whose pastoral nomadism, cast as "undoubtedly a life of idleness," provided enough leisure time to pursue "the violent and sanguinary exercise of the chase" across the plains of western Asia and Eastern Europe.[10] Malthus would adopt a style strikingly similar to that of Gibbon, but with added purpose: he devised a historical account of late ancient migrations combined with elements of natural history in order to stage a dire human predicament underscored by environmental destruction. Both writers took advantage of considerable authorial license in crafting their stories. As Karen O'Brien argued in a survey of Enlightenment narratives, "few historians registered the generic proximity of history to fiction as a threat to the epistemological validity of their work." Authors and readers assumed that "political, emotional, and aesthetic choices" could be made to "create, not an imagined, but an interpretive community engaged in a rhetorical arbitration of their own history." Malthus, like Gibbon, was clearly aiming to appeal to a particular "interpretive community," one with a solid classical education and an unquestioned belief that particular historical tropes conferred veracity upon evidence and argument.[11]

By the 1780s, as Gibbon published the last of the six volumes of *Decline and Fall*, a stadial account of history was "beginning to appear as something very like orthodoxy."[12] Ronald Meek defined the theory this way: "In its most specific form, the theory was that society 'naturally' or 'normally' progressed over time through four more or less distinct and consecutive stages, each corresponding to a different mode of subsistence, these stages being defined as hunting, pasturage, agriculture, and commerce. To each of these modes of subsistence . . . there corresponded different sets of ideas and institutions relating to law, property, and government, and also different sets of customs, manners, and morals." For our purposes, we should note how information about the natural world and methods of subsistence production regularly came up for re-evaluation. Despite its clear structure, four stages theory was never a static set of principles. Given the flux of Enlightenment knowledge, it is worth emphasizing that the construct functioned as a constantly evolving set of structures through which data new and old were subjected.[13]

Ancient antecedents of four stages theory set the pattern for its later forms, but the Enlightenment injected new life into the model through heightened attention to encounters with the land and peoples of the Americas. "As the European vision of the world moved westwards, so it moved also inexorably backwards." Readers of Enlightenment literature regarded the western continent as a kind of living diorama of the past, replete with peoples engaged in primitive modes of subsistence that preceded the zenith of agriculture designed by contemporary Europeans. Most famously, Locke inscribed words discussed and debated since their publication in his *Two Treatises on Government* (1689): "in the beginning all the World was *America.*" While "cleverly echo[ing] the scriptural tradition of creation," Locke pointed the way to a justification for the settlement of the North American continent through staking out private property for the sake of cultivation. "In Locke's labor theory of value, human beings used their bodies to convert natural resources into property," Alison Bashford and Joyce Chaplin have argued, providing the rationale for "population and what it was good for." This particular image of the historical origins of property served as an anchor for subsequent discussion of agriculture in the evolving discipline of political economy.[14]

The genealogy of social science in the Enlightenment moved forward in relation to these same central preoccupations: the creation of wealth through the establishment of private property and agriculture. Four stages theory assisted this act by showing how advancing stages of subsistence labor demanded increasing levels of organization, embodied in codes of law and governance. Montesquieu's *The Spirit of Laws,* first published in 1748, might be seen as "providing a kind of green light, an *ex cathedra* 'go ahead,' for the new social science. . . . [T]his is what the pioneers of the four stages theory saw fit to read into it," Meek observed in his study. *The Spirit of Laws* went into 124 English editions between 1750 and 1793, dispensing its classificatory system to a reading public. From the 1750s, Scottish and French writers on natural history, language, travel, and, most important, economic life readily absorbed the methods of four stages history. What people did, how they produced subsistence, was understood as the guiding principle for the social organization, customs, and behavior of different peoples around the globe.[15]

Intertwined with this approach and equally important as an analytic framework was the fact of human classification. This aspect of four stages theory provided the actual "social" within the Enlightenment's science. Yet historians have placed much greater emphasis on the economic activity under discussion, so much so that the act of human classification appears as an ancillary activity.[16] Something like stagecraft diverts our attention: out of the ashes of the struggle against migrating and marauding barbarians, "that dark period which so long overwhelmed the world," according to Malthus, came the light of law and reason. Here was the ground-clearing that opened the way for the rational and scientific breakthroughs of the Baconian age. The establishment of laws, government, and, ultimately, agriculture and commerce: this particular arc of evolution made possible a form of European exceptionalism, which then metamorphosed into human exceptionalism in the narrative of what became known as the history of civilization.[17]

If we shift our focus from the agents of Enlightenment (the European narrators) to the savages who served as a foil for European intelligence, we immediately see how much power was wielded through the act of categorization. Europeans were emphasizing human difference as a means of insisting on their own intelligence. But did this imply that those classified as primitive were simply on their way to a similar human destiny? Insuperable difference was bound to persist, and writers generally viewed Indigenous North Americans as "incapable of any cultural change, unlikely to progress through the transformations that would lead from a hunting stage of subsistence toward pastoralism and agriculture."[18] Blocking the way to their rehabilitation were elements of geography and climate, which clearly played a determinative role in the subsistence activities of many peoples under investigation. Climate theory persisted as "the common sense of the day and a magnet for contradictory beliefs" at this time, despite the fact that its close correlate, humoral theory, lost credibility by the 1700s.[19] As Montesquieu had pointed out, the "empire of climate is the first of all empires," and Georges-Louis Leclerc, comte de Buffon's influential *Histoire naturelle* contributed a theory of racial differences linked to geographical regions. Adding their own twist to these theories, Scottish philosophers overlaid moral and behavioral differences as products of stages of subsistence labor. (Millar astutely linked romantic love with the condition of claiming private property, aligning patriarchal ownership with gender roles.) Knowledge and economic culture became inextricably bound together, making the path to contemporary achievements belong solely to industriously complex Europeans.[20]

Popular culture eagerly absorbed these assumptions and embedded them in wider discussions of nature and geography. By the 1780s, when Malthus was at Cambridge formulating his assumptions of natural philosophy, London theaters were eagerly mining informative accounts of distant places. Functioning as purveyors of constructed natural history, they offered audiences dazzling visual projections in "naturalistic and spectacular stage designs." The malleable figure of the Indigenous American fit into this busy theatrical context with perfect ease. Lessons of antiquity might merge with human representatives and artifacts from other parts of the globe, so that those designated as "primitive" acquired "Spartan courage, fortitude and austerity" or, alternatively, "Elysian innocence, luxury and sensuality." In one instance, the noble savage, presumably enlightened by his superiors, even appeared as an "ambassador for England."[21]

It did not matter that Indigenous visitors to London voiced their own thoughts on issues like the intellectual and moral capacities of the savage. Their demonstrated achievements made little impression on the popular view that they were "inherently lacking." Fictional narratives and voyeuristic opportunism only heightened the impact of contemporary manipulations of indigeneity. As Brian Cooper has shown for this period, "Categories not only help produce and organize facts as descriptions of the social state, they serve as prescriptions for governance." The lessons of political economy would serve to "make people like the types in their theories." These uses indicated a shift in perspective taking place in the larger arena of public awareness, preparing the ground for a more imperial and masterful approach to arguments about cultural difference.[22]

Rousseau's noble savage, with his oversized posthumous life, thus requires some recalibration when we consider its important role in eighteenth-century economic thought. The savage of *Omai, Or a Trip Around the World* might edify the public in search of expanding its mental horizons, but in matters of political economy, the Indigenous producer of subsistence hardly got a hearing in the court of elite opinion. Writers and ministers wielding power regarded him as marginal at best; in Turgot's succinct summation, "to express a preference for the savages is ridiculous bombast." Rousseau's seminal text, the "Discourse on Inequality," received low marks from Adam Smith, who dismissed it as "a work which consists almost entirely of rhetoric and description." Repeatedly, theorists depicted Indigenous subsistence activity as ineffectual and primitive.[23]

Gibbon's stark binary opposition between roaming hordes of primitive peoples and civilized society perpetuated yet more confusion: he notably failed to "distinguish between 'barbarian' and 'savage.'" As J. G. A. Pocock has pointed out, he used "the terms interchangeably . . . as denoting a stage of vagrancy preceding stationary cultivation, social space, and the exchange of goods, words, and ideas."[24] Civilized space harbored numerous fine distinctions, among them, many behavioral traits that indicated heroic virtue derived from the *polis.* But the *barbaroi* lacked access to noble characteristics because they had no powers of language, no laws, and thus, no sense of happiness or justice. Christianity adopted these principles but held out the requirement of conversion. At the same time, medieval philosophers like Albert Magnus kept alive ancient definitions. "Physical handicap and deprivation, or . . . disease causing deprivation" made men "bestial . . . with no spark of humanity," he explained in book 7 of the *Ethics.* Quoting Cicero, he reminded his readers that barbarians were "wild men leading the life of animals with the wild beasts. . . . [Such] bestial men eat raw flesh and drink blood, and are delighted to drink and eat from human skulls." The slippage between barbarian and savage invited a post-Enlightenment free-for-all that was ably demonstrated by Malthus's dramatic and polemical prose.[25]

In his analysis of this classificatory preoccupation in ancient literature, Brent Shaw argued that the binary opposition between cultivation and its nomadic precursors operated as a fully fledged ideology within the foundations of European thought. Members of the two groups were seen to be at war with one another, each hoping to extinguish the other in order to survive. The opposition had far-reaching consequences. By pitting systems of food-getting against one another, contemporaries effectively deprived them of temporal coexistence: "[F]irst, a complete separation of nomads and sedentarists into two polarized and isolated taxonomic compartments wherein the two economies or 'human types' never merge or are perceived to have any dynamic interaction. And secondly, the nomad is seen as the ultimate barbaric human type who is directly opposed to the 'civilised' sedentary agriculturalist." Barbarians had nothing to offer sedentary agriculturalists, who regarded them as aliens lacking any redeeming traits whatsoever. Shaw noted the existence of "prejudices commonly associated with mobile people even in our own society," but he insisted that the "written accounts" of antiquity "contain more than mere prejudices," because "the views in them about nomads are a more organized and structurally consistent set of ideas" worthy of the term "ideology."[26]

As a way of accomplishing such a division, ancient writers presented barbarians replete with characteristics that were disgusting to the civilized person. Herodotus's description of the ancient Scythians, the quintessential "eaters of flesh" and "drinkers of milk" (which was believed to be transformed blood), demanded the "categorical imperative" of physical revulsion. Their mode of subsistence displayed a proximity to bestial behavior that the civilized person should learn to abhor. In the eyes of Enlightenment writers, the Scythians' form of flesh-eating ("on the hoof" rather than from the butcher) approximated the bloodthirstiness of cannibalism. And their habit of drinking the fresh fluids of their animals, given this relatively early date in the civilized history of milk, called up associations with coarse diets and uncouth bodily constitutions. Eighteenth-century accounts were not above recycling old images of alien identity to signify what was unfamiliar and unacceptable to Europeans. Savages displayed physical "deformity" and were presented as lacking intelligible language—hence the use of the word "barbarian," rooted in the syllables ("the people who mutter ba-ba-ba") first employed by the Greeks to designate the Other. Use of the word "race" to denote their kind did not signify skin color, but rather a larger notion of differences eventually absorbed under the heading of "culture." As an indicator of just how far these alien types were on a vertical hierarchy of difference, their proximity to animals located them as far from contemporary (civilized) Europe as conceivable.[27]

This nearness to animal existence had important intellectual and moral implications. Aristotle underscored the notion that nomads were undeveloped in their relationship to production by highlighting the absence of purposeful activity among their type: in fact, they followed their animals (hardly a masterful approach) and were idle and lazy in comparison with their settled contemporaries; they never appeared to be in the act of doing anything. Their dependence on unpredictable forces of nature, he argued, demonstrated a passive, unthinking approach to obtaining subsistence when compared to sedentary agriculturalists. In contrast, those who tilled the soil not only labored in their fields but also set their minds to accumulating knowledge and technique that enabled them to further exploit the land and its flora and to flourish as a result. The herder remained in an endless, repeating cycle of nature, never evincing a sign of development. If he occupied a grade above his animals, he hardly differed from them in his imprisonment in nature.[28]

As long as such people were classified as nomadic, they could be cast as structurally deprived and, at times, driven to desperation. Thus, sustenance became mere subsistence, which rendered food acquisition similar to the foraging of animals. Gibbon introduced the arithmetic of natural history into his account, foreshadowing Malthus in this way, suggesting that food shortages restricted the numbers of migrating peoples:

> The measure of population is regulated by the means of subsistence; and the inhabitants of this vast peninsula [of Arabia] might be out-numbered by the subjects of a fertile and industrious province. Along the shores of the Persian Gulf, of the ocean, and even of the Red Sea, the *Icthyophagi,* or fish-eaters, continue to wander in quest of their precarious food. In this primitive and abject state, which ill deserves the name of society, the human brute, without arts and laws, almost without sense or language, is poorly distinguished from the rest of the animal creation.

Compared to cultivation, fishing, as shown in the previous chapter, was categorized as part of the savage life. Its signal characteristics were indolence and precarity. According to Gibbon, the descent into a never-ending pursuit of food disqualified these types of humans from legitimate forms of society by their divorce from activities of the mind.[29]

For Gibbon, as well as Malthus, settled agriculture served as the foundation of modern historical time; until that condition was established, human collectivities exhibited all sorts of failures, whether technological or moral. As Gibbon had expressed it, "Modern nations are fixed and permanent societies . . . bound to their native soil by arts and agriculture." Cultivation of the land was the means of civilizing the roaming hunter, depicted as a "lazy warrior" or "indolent" savage who was driven by bodily urges and thus "addicted to deep gaming and excessive drinking."[30] As Gibbon explained,

> If we contemplate a savage nation in any part of the globe, a supine indolence and a carelessness of futurity will be found to constitute their general character. In a civilized state, every faculty of man is expanded and exercised; and the great chain of mutual dependence connects and embraces the several members of society. . . . The same extent of ground, which at present maintains, in ease and plenty, a million of husbandmen and artificers, was unable to supply an hundred thousand lazy warriors with the simple necessaries of life.[31]

Malthus repeated this same image of the lazy warrior in his "history of the early migrations" in the second edition of the *Essay,* published in 1803. Only the "strong goad of necessity" could move such peoples to action. "The natural state of man" was far from noble; it could be characterized as a universal tendency toward "a state of sloth."[32]

The first *Essay on Population,* with its dramatic argument boosted by rhetorical strategies, made a deep impression on the minds of late eighteenth-century British readers. Reviewers begged for more evidence of Malthus's principle in action, preferably from examples in the real world. Now Malthus seized the opportunity to tell a fuller story of humanity as an unceasing struggle against scarcity. As part of a move to prove that "theories of human happiness should rely on observations of humans as they were and had been," he turned to North America and other "new worlds" for evidence of population history.

Alison Bashford and Joyce Chaplin paid meticulous attention to this effort in their lengthy study of the second edition, which they recognized as "a significant anthropology of Indigenous people and history of colonial encounters." In their view, Malthus showed originality in the way he "showcased settler information about new world population dynamics as a distinctive form of modern knowledge." At the same time, they point out that Malthus joined a number of writers who never actually visited the North American continent themselves—the armchair travelers discussed earlier in this study—and relied on sources written on average around 1755. By ignoring a number of major texts that had appeared since then, along with additional evidence from Spanish sources and settlers, Malthus presented a highly selective and distorted view of Indigenous culture, showing Native Americans as weaker than they actually were. He argued that their numbers were doomed, not simply because they were being exterminated by settlers but because of their bodily predispositions and their mode of subsistence. Thus, Bashford and Chaplin contend, Malthus "naturalized native population decline," revealing his "underlying racist assumptions."[33]

Malthus's handling of sources demands a brief examination here in light of his underlying wish to gain favor as a newly fledged theorist of political economy. It seems odd that someone wishing to adhere to the standards of truth belonging to natural philosophy would fail to consult major scholarly sources in favor of bestsellers in a more popular vein. Malthus's footnotes bulge with references to histrionic travel accounts in New South Wales (including a scene of rape perpetrated as tribal competition), Cook's exotic voyages, and Reynal's popular (and exaggerated) account of the Indies. What the public had enjoyed largely as sensational, if illuminating, literature Malthus repurposed as sound historical data. Even as eighteenth-century "savages" in contemporary environments provided living demonstrations of subsistence work in the distant past, Malthus would pluck evidence from these settings in order to illustrate the ceiling placed on human progress by the perpetual multiplication of hungry mouths. His search for support for his principle shaped what became a highly selective gathering of evidence.[34]

Malthus's strategy of omission becomes clearer when we examine his reliance upon another bestseller, Scottish Enlightenment historian William Robertson's *History of America*, first published in 1777, which provided him with copious data for the second edition of the *Essay*. Bashford and Chaplin showed that the author of the *Essay* "leaned hard on Robertson's work in the fourth chapter of his 1803 edition," proven by his thirty-six footnotes to the work (compared to the average of 7.3 references to any other single source). In addition to what he learned by reading Benjamin Franklin, Malthus would absorb the lengthy explication of stadial history in *The History of America*. And just as Malthus leaned heavily on Robertson, Robertson's account of the Americas leaned heavily on Aristotle, alongside Spanish accounts of the sixteenth century. Aristotle's framework of five "pure types" of modes of subsistence originally placed the nomadic pastoralist at the bottom of the evolutionary ladder and cited the Scythians as a prototype. In their place, New World hunter-gatherers would qualify as the least evolved of any human type in future representations such as Robertson's. In Brent Shaw's words, "it was their turn to shoulder all the nihilistic-anarchic characteristics once attributed to the nomad."[35]

Deeply educated in philosophy, theology, and the classics, Robertson (born 1721) brought formidable intellectual breadth to the market for enlightened historical works. His first major success, *A History of Scotland during the Reigns of Queen Mary and James VI* (1759), saw four editions in two years, and his later *History of the Reign of Charles V* (1769) would "[seal] its author's reputation as the leading historian in Europe." As a consummate clerical intellectual, he combined active participation in urgent public issues of contemporary Edinburgh with continual scholarly activities. In the 1750s, he and other local luminaries joined together in a debating club called the Select Society, a group that included David Hume, Adam Smith, and Lord Kames. His election to the post of principal of Edinburgh University in 1762 may have been "the most important single step in institutionalizing Enlightenment values in Edinburgh during the eighteenth century."[36]

Robertson absorbed key arguments about stadial history and political economy from this milieu. His *History of America,* initially a two-volume work published in 1777, introduced what was meant to be a series that began with sixteenth-century Spanish colonization, punctuated by chapters on Indigenous Americans, and continued through the present-day former colonies. (Robertson fell ill and died before completing the project.) Appreciative audiences extended beyond Britain to Europe, where a French translation of *History of America* went through nine editions. His treatment demonstrated considerable breadth and a relative lack of dogmatism, thanks to what Jorge Cañizares-Esguerra has called his "angelic detachment." (Robertson aimed to "deliver his evidence as if upon oath," he confided to Edward Gibbon.) Seen today as "a significant landmark in the development of cultural anthropology," the *History of America* offered evidence of Indigenous life that was inclusive of variety and even nuance, though it also delivered judgments of the kind that Malthus would find useful.[37]

Malthus trained his diligent gaze upon these volumes and aimed to emulate Robertson's method while retaining his own purposeful search for Indigenous failure to achieve subsistence. It is impossible not to recognize the method, phrases, and tone of the earlier Scottish work in the second edition of Malthus's *Essay.* "In every inquiry concerning the operations of men when united together in society," Robertson explained, "the first object of attention should be their mode of subsistence."[38] Malthus followed this direction in examining each remote setting of human life and, like Robertson, he assumed that enlightened existence placed basic bodily needs far below newer and higher desires brought on by civilization. Lower wants provoked animalistic tendencies; higher wants were thought to inspire ingenuity and industry. As Robertson argued,

> If we examine into the motives which rouze men to activity in civilized life, we shall find that they arise chiefly from acquired wants and appetites. These are numerous and importunate, they keep the mind in perpetual agitation, and, in order to gratify them, invention must be always on the stretch, and industry must be incessantly employed. But the desires of simple nature are few, and where a favourable climate yields almost spontaneously what suffices them, they scarcely stir the soul, or excite any violent emotion. Hence the people of several tribes in America waste their life in a listless indolence.

This last sentence was of crucial significance in giving Malthus further evidence for the connection he was making between Indigenous people and the laboring classes of Britain.[39]

In an earlier century, Spanish missionaries generalized about human nature from climatic and environmental conditions: by their estimate, the tropical regions in the Americas proved harmful to physical and cerebral activity. The theologian and jurist Francisco de Vitoria concluded that the natives were "unfit to found or administer a lawful State"; "they have no careful agriculture and no artisans" and might be compared to "people of defective intelligence." Their pathetic diets, "scarcely better than that of wild beasts," underscored these points. Robertson absorbed the Spanish accounts without skepticism, but he did add more information regarding food procurement. Abject indolence "applies only to some tribes," he continued. "[A]mong most of the American nations, especially those seated in rigorous climates, some efforts are employed, and some previous precautions are taken, for securing subsistence." Robertson recognized their three sources of food: fishing, hunting, and agriculture, with the latter "devolved entirely upon the women." Yet he returned to evidence of a suspected problem of attitude: "labour [was] deemed ignominious and degrading" and in some instances (but not all) foresight was lacking. In the end, he handed a picture of inferior thinking and occasional sloth to his English acolyte.[40]

All of this is worthy of pause for reflection. It is quite likely that Malthus saw Robertson's account of American resources as providing a parallel to the English Poor Laws and the recent determination to give laborers cash supplements in order to augment their bare subsistence wages. The British state had created conditions of a "favourable climate" in a metaphorical sense, in his view, generating a willingness among laborers to rely on handouts in place of employment. "Indolence" was, in fact, a word that Malthus would use repeatedly in his *Essay* in a peculiarly persistent way. But more significantly, Malthus would take this example further than simply a reinstatement of the failure of savages and laborers to live by the sweat of their brow.

As his historical treatment of earlier modes of subsistence would show, savages were lesser beings, far from noble, and now subject to the greater intelligence and authority of a post-Enlightenment European age. Malthus's new hierarchy of history would render pre-cultivation methods of subsistence unworthy of serious attention. He did this by departing from Robertson's somewhat unusual account of the coexistence of hunting, gathering, and agriculture. The labor of women also disappeared from consideration. Erasure of primitive food production was a matter of human progress in this post-revolutionary era of British sovereignty. If a higher standard of living was going to serve as a reward for civilization, then these uncivilized activities needed to be negated.

In light of Robertson's scrupulous attention to veracity and variety, the erasure of Indigenous cultivation in the account of Malthus seems noteworthy indeed. Robertson had noted that "throughout all America, we scarcely meet with any nation of hunters, which does not practice some species of cultivation." Even in the most fertile and abundant places in warm climates, the need for a "regular supply of food" demanded that some "industry and foresight must be exerted." Robertson identified Indigenous methods of preservation and storage, intelligently carved from natural circumstances, which fed tribes when seasonal constraints made food scarce. His clinically descriptive account, though not particularly sympathetic, nevertheless rendered the activities of Indigenous peoples as worthy of intellectual curiosity and interest, so that the reader came away with a sense of having learned about new human relations, however distantly situated on the ancestral map.[41]

Malthus set out to achieve the opposite in order to prove his point about classifications of people: for him, North America was a scene of continuous famine among Indigenous populations, whose unthinking behavior betrayed a lack of foresight and reason. Of critical importance, obviously, was cultivation, the litmus test of civilization, yet we must recall that the Scottish philosophers understood that women were responsible for maize-growing. Women's work needed to disappear and so the Malthusian translation of this approximation of civilization was to label it as degraded and marginal to subsistence. Repeatedly, we hear Malthus, like Adam Smith, deem the crucial field work of Indigenous women as onerous and morally reprobate. (Robertson, by contrast, mentioned maize-growing thirteen times.) And so the remarkable staple food of the Americas received only marginal attention in the *Essay.*

When Malthus did recognize the occasional practice of cultivation in the Americas, he was quick to insert his own dynamic, demonstrated by the Indigenous determination to roam and hunt. The urge to hunt appeared as much a matter of bad habit as necessity. For Malthus, moral judgment crept in to imply that those who cultivated might avoid the perils associated with what he often referred to as "wandering" in the revised *Essay.* Yet during periods of duress, he explained, the men continued to "disperse themselves in the woods at certain seasons" to find their animal prey and sometimes came back with nothing. These failed breadwinners thus exposed "their villages . . . to certain famine."[42] (Robertson distributed blame to both the forest and the pantry: he cited his Spanish sources in noting "scanty maintenance" and "scanty stores" that "brought on a famine.") Malthus also found occasion to remark on intermittent periods of gluttony that showed lack of prudence, not recognizing customs of feasting that even his chosen Europeans might indulge in, depending on the religious calendar. Whatever the evidence, Malthus turned its meaning toward his principle: there was never enough food for hungry mouths in America.[43]

Robertson's rather incomplete account of cultivated foods revealed the vulnerability of his text to those who wished to plunder it for their own purposes: because he devoted fewest words to those subjects that were widely known, he gave too little value to what the New World had to teach the Old World about food crops. So in his account of important foods of the Americas, he placed "the potatoe" fourth on his list of five plants (just below the plantain and above the pimento) and said no more, because "its culture and qualities are too well known to need any description."[44] Hence, one of the greatest gifts of the western hemisphere to the rest of the world, the food that nourished urbanization and industrialization, received one sentence and was otherwise ignored. Maize scarcely received more space on the page. It was "well known in Europe by the name of Turkey or Indian wheat, a grain extremely prolific, of simple culture, agreeable to the taste, and affording a strong hearty nourishment." Robertson paid attention to manioc owing to the curiosity value of its conversion into edible food: he pointed out that the juice of the shrub's roots is a "deadly poison," yet once squeezed out of the plant, it could be made into a palatable staple food called "Cassada bread." Here was a case of Robertson joining Malthus in a negative judgment: he regarded it as famine food, no indication of the "ingenuity of the Americans," but "rather [to] be considered as one of the desperate expedients for procuring subsistence, to which necessity reduces rude nations." Such was his inadequate coverage of the Columbian Exchange, still unrecognized in eighteenth-century Europe.[45]

Both authors believed that New World inhabitants were subject to a precarious existence. In the hardest circumstances, their insecurity reduced them to the level of beasts and served as a cautionary tale. By mining a footnote that began with "Their subsistence was poor and precarious," Malthus transposed a passage in Robertson's text to underscore this point. The original lurid account came from Spanish explorer Álvar Núñez Cabeza de Vaca, who reported deplorable desperation of Indigenous people in Florida, a picture that clearly inserted judgments into what were likely to have been misperceptions. Malthus could not resist the mixture of drama and revulsion in the Spanish account:

> He describes them as unacquainted with every species of agriculture, and living chiefly upon the roots

> of different plants, which they procure with great difficulty, wandering from place to place in search of them. Sometimes they kill game, sometimes they catch fish, but in such small quantities, that their hunger is so extreme, as compels them to eat spiders, the eggs of ants, worms, lizards, serpents, a kind of unctuous earth, and, I am persuaded, he says, that, if in this country there were any stones, they would swallow them. They preserve the bones of fishes and serpents, which they grind into powder and eat.

Without agriculture, savage life descended to an animal-like existence.[46]

The Enlightenment had placed a great deal of stock in the distance that humankind had traveled from the precipice of precarity. Now Malthus built on that achievement, lingering on the degree of degradation experienced by those who were dwelling on its perilous edge. He offered a sensational tale of "a poor Indian and his wife, who, on the failure of game, having eaten up all the skins which they wore as clothing, were reduced to the dreadful extremity of supporting themselves on the flesh of two of their children." Here were two truly ignoble savages. Readers, recoil, he insisted. This is what you should know about existence outside your own hard-won civilization.[47]

Writing the *Essay* gave Malthus the ideal opportunity to desecrate the iconic ideal of Rousseau. In the first edition, he seemed acutely aware that his readers might hold too positive an image of the "natural man." Early in its pages, he took the time to point out that the able-bodied warrior might suggest a tolerable form of human existence, but he was the exception, not the rule, as a prototype of barbarian existence. "He is the gentleman, the man of fortune, the chances have been in his favour," Malthus translated for his British readers, unlike the vast majority of native North Americans who comprised "the nations of hunters." He urged the British public to imagine the large numbers of "women, children, and aged [of savages]," inhabiting a rank of society more like "the lower classes of the community in civilized states," not a social group to be admired. They dwelled on the far side of the embankments of civilization.[48]

In the 1803 edition of the *Essay*, he directly addressed the question of whether anything in "savage life" was worth admiring. By this time, Malthus clearly knew he had critics he must cultivate and so he softened his language, having deployed "annihilation" with regard to native populations an uncomfortable number of times in the first edition. These remarks followed a lengthy and often ponderous description of promiscuity, infanticide, and cannibalism on the South Sea Islands, with numerous references to the famed accounts of Captain Cook. "Savage life" had little to commend it, apart from more leisure time, which the "lower classes in civilized life" might see as a "striking advantage." But these societies, he emphasized, operated under "a most tyrannical distinction of rank," in which "the lower classes of the people are in a state of comparative degradation much below what is known in civilized nations." As if to disavow any idealization possible in this situation, Malthus concluded his comparisons with criticism of "the preposterous system of Spartan discipline" that had "sometimes been so absurdly admired," as it was said to be at work among Indigenous New Zealanders. He stressed that the "incessant war" of such societies would erase any reward of virtue, discipline, and patriotism. The civilized man, by comparison, "is taught to feel for his neighbour, or even his enemy in distress." These were ironic words from the writer who was attempting to bring down centuries of English Poor Law.[49]

For Malthus, those who scavenged for food were a race apart. His treatment of savage life in earlier stages of history shed a critical light on the laboring man also driven by bodily urges. His descriptions of British laborers revealed resemblance to the savage in more than just their lowly status: they were sluggish and work-averse, sustained by whatever handouts they could get. They demonstrated the consequences of an overwhelming state of "torpor." Once bestowed with parish relief, they fell prey to "the cravings of hunger, the love of liquor, the desire of possessing a beautiful woman"—urges potentially universal to all men but resisted by those of higher reason. "The savage would slumber for ever under his tree," Malthus indicated, "unless he were roused from his torpor by the cravings of hunger, or the pinchings of cold."[50] Such behavior summed up the specter of ignoble savage and set the parameters of social theory by summoning up popular prejudices rather than revealing the more complex interactions between humans and environment.

Malthus's claim that the laws of nature were in fact the laws of human society created what Margaret Somers and Fred Block have called "social naturalism," a system in which "the line between humans and animals is blurred since people are conceived as biologically driven by the self-interested need for food and reproduction." And in that abject position, the poor were shown to have made poor choices. "Of all Malthus's accomplishments . . . none was more portentous than his radically converting the poor from a structural position to a behavioral choice."[51] In his later writings, Malthus would emphasize a more general theory of wants as a necessary motivating force of "even civilized and improved countries." The categorization of the lowest rung of laborers would remain in place, subject to lower wants of the belly and the stewardship of their masters.[52]

Interlude

The Place of Bread in the History of Scarcity

A DEEP HISTORY OF modern western bread has yet to be written, but, judging from the evidence so far, its narrative would draw from a complicated web of developments across Europe. Many types of bread developed across a broad landscape, deriving their character from different ecosystems and tastes. As a widely embraced staple food, bread often signified sustenance generally, and any reader of the *Essay on the Principle of Population* might easily gloss over references to it as unremarkable. Yet given the connection between bread and Malthus's argument about scarcity, it is worth our while to look briefly at the implications imported into the essay by the wheaten loaf.

Aside from its abstract nature, the light loaf of bread in Europe was a product of a very particular history reaching back to Roman times. An ebb and flow of historically contingent demands for food from imperial and urban centers pressed their urgency upon the countryside. Roman preference for wheaten bread, inherited in part from contact with the Greeks, supported a system of grain cultivation and milling techniques that extended across the Mediterranean and northward to Britain. Bread symbolically linked the farmer with the needs of the state: the cultivated field of wheat functioned at one end of the fundamental binary of citizen-soldier, who was expected to produce grain and carry bread as his staple food. One of the ironies of bread history is its association with food security in Roman times. The trustworthy loaf provided sustenance when other foods, including vegetables and meat, were scarce. Surviving testimony of the inescapable importance of bread to the city and the empire stands near Porta Maggiore in Rome, where a massive tomb of the baker Eurysaces, erected around 30 BCE, chronicles the production of loaves along its friezes.[1]

Regional variation re-exerted its force in the Middle Ages, as European peasants wielded a limited degree of freedom to grow their own alternatives to wheat. Such "duty-free" sustenance eluded the tax gatherer and also insured against dearth imposed by adverse weather. A diversity of crops presented a sensible alternative, the constant counterpoint to the march of wheat cerealization across the continent. The necessary

Tomb of Eurysaces, Porta Maggiore, Rome. Circa 30 BCE. Eurysaces, freed from slavery, directed a highly successful bread-baking establishment, immortalized in this enormous monument. The friezes around the top depict the production of bread from the delivery of grain to the inspection of the final product by state officials and speedy delivery to the marketplace. (Author's photo)

consequence of this was locally determined bread made from other grains, such as rye, oats, barley, spelt, and millet, which promised greater abundance and ease of cultivation in many settings. Such loaves offered density and nutrition, despite suffering from a lack of refinement, being neither voluminous nor light in texture. Alongside pulses or beans, onions, and perhaps a serving of pork, these breads completed a hearty meal suited to supporting physical labor.[2]

Not all bread was equal, however: from the vantage point of sophisticated consumers and learned opinion handed down across centuries, bread existed within a hierarchy of color and texture. Traditional medical wisdom held that different types of bread suited different "Natures and Complexions." Only "strong bodies and laborious persons" could tolerate dark, heavy grains, such as rye, while bread made from barley was out of the question for any but the toughest constitution; oaten bread, varying according to season and recipe, could go either way. Wheaten bread was deemed "best for all stomachs" and the finest variety functioned as food for the sickly and the newborn. Or so the manuals told their readers. This kind of dicta promoted the sense that bread was as efficacious as it was inevitable. As a much-reprinted English manual on health matters put it, "Bread is never out of season, disagreeing with no Sickness, Age or Complexion, and therefore truly called the Companion of Life."[3]

In fact, the British Isles entertained a lively diversity of bread according to region. Oatcake remained common in northern areas around Lancashire, while Yorkshire preferred rye varieties and the Midlands clung to barley bread. Ordinary daily bread often included a mixture of flours, including barley, despite its low marks in terms of prestige. Housewives and cooks maintained a repertoire of methods of making more palatable loaves out of heavy grains. But in the second half of the eighteenth century, the demand for bakers' bread came to dictate the destiny of varieties of grain. The South and southeastern parts of the nation, tied to the metropolis and wealthier than the North, led the way. Wheat was less perishable as well as more prestigious, and heightening awareness of digestion as a health concern meant that lighter breads gained broader public appeal.[4]

The metropolis of London preferred wheaten bread, and such urbanite taste exercised an impact on the surrounding areas. Wholesalers sought wheat flour in large quantities, so millers followed suit, demanding higher prices for small quantities sold to home bakers. With the cost of fuel rising beyond the pockets of ordinary consumers, greater numbers of ordinary people simply purchased their bread. The trend toward wheat in turn modified popular attitudes toward bread made at home: with their mixture of grains, such loaves represented "traditional" taste compared to commercial loaves. Some elites were aware of changing times: one year after Malthus published his first *Essay*, the Earl of Sheffield pointed out in a treatise on grain shortages that "[n]o bread is now made in London but the fine wheaten bread." Like their Parisian counterparts, Londoners demanded and got the institutional structures that light bread demanded.[5]

Commentators on the other side of the Channel supplied illuminating discourse on similar developments in France, where fashion and taste were known to dictate patterns of consumption. While Voltaire lamented the "dainty refinement" of the Parisian consumer of the light wheaten loaf, physicians celebrated its perfectly digestible qualities. A shrewd social critic of the 1760s, Simon Linguet, attempted to demystify what he regarded as the tyranny of bread in any form, blaming it for trapping humanity in a web of exploitation and misery. Its universality, he charged, was a myth; most of humankind flourished on other foods. (As examples, he cited the rice of Asians, the cassava of Americans, and the hunting and fishing of Africans.) Bread constituted "a tedious and costly compound" consumed in a "little corner of the planet . . . our little Europe." His screed pointed to bread and its agricultural superstructure as "the secret of perpetuating famines" at the heart of social exploitation ("the plough opens the tomb of our species"). All of this was to no avail against the supremacy of the master grain and its offspring, the fine wheaten loaf.[6]

When Malthus wrote the first *Essay,* he was living at his parents' home in Surrey, adjacent to a region characterized by large estates dedicated to the master grain. At the leading edge of capitalist development in agriculture, the Home Counties of the South and Southeast were entirely devoted to wheaten bread by 1750. Even more remarkable, in nearby Kent, bakers "had gone one stage further and stopped using unsifted flour." Bread for sale in Malthus's region of Britain therefore would have been distinctively white, a sign of affluent taste and an indicator that such preferences were spreading downward to the laboring classes.[7]

Malthus hadn't failed to notice these developments. Despite widespread acceptance of tastes changing with the times, he viewed laborers' demands for white bread as an indication of their self-defeating sense of entitlement. (Unlike Linguet, he added no criticism of the commercial system that governed the price of the chief ingredient.) More important, however, was the way in which the subject of bread brought to light his own hierarchy of dietary classification, drawn from what was essentially a customized historical and imperial map of civilization:

> The labourers of the South of England are so accustomed to eat fine wheaten bread that they will suffer themselves to be half starved, before they will submit to live like Scottish peasants. They might perhaps in time, by the constant operation

> of the hard law of necessity, be reduced to live even like the lower Chinese: and the country would then, with the same quantity of food, support a greater population. But to effect this must always be a most difficult and[,] every friend to humanity will hope, an abortive attempt.

His trademark principle repeated that once a people were well fed, they would reproduce more prolifically. A rhetorical use of the notion of humanity served to underscore the alliance Malthus attempted to forge with his readers, uniting them along an axis of elevation over an overpopulating peasantry. Notably, even when Malthus admitted the desirability of a laborer who was a consumer as well as a worker in his revised *Essay* in 1803, he did not broaden his concept of the foodscape of the lower classes. For him, the hierarchy of food represented an important difference between the British gentleman and those below him, who were required to walk a fine line between purchasing power and hunger.[8]

Scottish peasants ate oats (one-third the price of wheat in 1795) according to custom and preference, yet Malthus implied that English laborers would regard the diet of northerners as beneath them, and perhaps he was correct, as popular prejudice against the Scots was a known feature of metropolitan English life. In truth, most British people (of any class) would recoil from unfamiliar food. The Scottish medical authority William Buchan lamented the misconception that rice "prove[d] injurious to the eyes," given that it was "the most general article of diet among mankind." As most physicians of the eighteenth century admitted, Buchan pointed out that bread could create blockages in the digestive tract. He also noted that bread was more expensive because of the way it was marketed: it "pass[ed] through the hands of both the miller and the baker" before reaching the consumer. For several reasons, then, too much bread could be a bad thing.[9]

Unlike the "lower" Chinese peasants who ate rice, Malthus might have realized, Chinese elites enjoyed a cuisine of high quality and prestige, which was far in advance of the notoriously rustic cuisine of British elites. Consumption of a new and different staple food was out of the question in eighteenth-century Britain, of course, and the cursory attention to exotic foods was simply an academic exercise, as Malthus hardly intended to calculate ways of supporting a larger population. His comments aimed to address current debates over the Old Poor Law, including a proposal to provide each laboring family with a shilling supplement per week per child. Malthus predicted that this strategy would only result in the birth of more children and a less sufficient division of produce. His model suggested that the sum produce of the region, like a pie divided among family members at the table, would remain the same over time.[10]

The issue of hunger remained unresolved between the lines of the first *Essay*, and Malthus's subsequent writing on the subject remained focused on the inescapable problem of scarcity. In *An Investigation of the Cause of the Present High Price of Provisions*, which went into several editions immediately upon its appearance in 1800, he expounded on the law of supply and demand with regard to wheat and other food commodities. Malthus maintained that "butter, cheese, bacon, pickled pork, rice, potatoes, &c." might offer temporary sustenance for the poor during the current times, but not for long: their relentless demand would soon drive up prices and they would face scarcity of those commodities, too. This form of discussion most likely rang hollow for many readers, given the popularity of writers like Arthur Young, who praised the nutrition of the potato and advocated giving cows to the poor to sustain their households. Nevertheless, the fledgling political economist captured an audience and drove home the inevitability of the market as the final determinant of who would be able to eat.[11]

Tampering with diet meant putting the historical supremacy of Britain at risk. Malthus was prepared to argue against the potential of feeding more people through the cultivation of potatoes, a proposition set forth by Adam Smith. Malthus would have associated potatoes with two less civilized populations: the people of South America and the Irish. This food source gave him the opportunity to underscore the real threat of alien diets by reiterating his law of population—this time, linked to the culturally specific history of British food sources. His language here indicates generous help from Montesquieu's *Spirit of the Laws,* but in his trademark way, Malthus channeled that author's ideas to different purposes:

> Corn countries are more populous than pasture countries; and rice countries more populous than corn countries. The lands in England are not suited to rice, but they would all bear potatoes: and Dr. Adam Smith observes, that if potatoes were to become the favourite vegetable food of the common people, and if the same quantity of land was employed in their culture, as is now employed in the culture of corn, the country would be able to support a much greater population; and would consequently in a very short time have it.

Malthus's "power of population" would cancel out any efforts to alter the play of forces aiming to satisfy hunger, as the common people reflexively multiplied when supplied with more food. (A hint of rabbit behavior lingers around the "very short time" in which the multiplication would take place.) Malthus concluded this chapter with his grimmest estimation of inevitable misery, his pronouncement that "gigantic inevitable famine stalks" all of Europe, wracked at that time by war, despite the high degree of "knowledge and industry" (and methods of transport) achieved by 1798. Here was another instance of the English Émile scoring a victory for the anti-Enlightenment.[12]

A great deal was obviously at stake in this defense of grain cultivation: for Malthus, it was an emblem of historical legitimation. His vocabulary betrayed a system of classification that governed important hierarchies of knowledge and modes of production: "corn countries" and "rice countries" stood for two distinct cultures, which occupied remote geographical locations in an imaginary historical continuum of civilization. The impact of this kind of reasoning on categories of class and culture was more profound than benevolent-minded Enlightenment authors could have imagined. Theories of progress worked to the advantage of all when the end result was envisaged as universality characterized by social harmony. When the picture changed to admit deep divisions between social classes as well as between cultures, however, the categories of stadial history channeled invidious ideological ruptures into theories about society and economy. Malthus's *Essay* put forward a kind of Trojan horse for such reasoning. Even today, we mistake the surface for the content by assuming that his assertions were based on a vision of a cohesive universe identifying commonalities among humans. His critical assessment of methods of food-gathering and agricultural production proves this to be far from true.

5

A Natural History of Hunger

The Last Great Domestication

Malthusian peril rested on simple biological calculations: give people enough to eat and they inevitably reproduced at a greater rate, and, as they multiplied, more mouths devoured food supplies that failed to grow at the same pace. The net result would be hunger and suffering, leading to "the last, the most dreadful resource of nature," famine. Peppering these pronouncements with biblical ire, Malthus rendered the history of humanity as a constant struggle that pitted carnal, sensual appetites against ineffective endeavors to satisfy hunger. The punishing competition for subsistence followed upon such inevitabilities, determining the ebb and flow of human flourishing.[1]

Yet one aspect of this blunt argument remained unclear: what kind of food was Malthus talking about when he used the word "subsistence"? Resources of food constituted one-half of the argument about population, yet Malthus devoted remarkably little space to discussing the variety of ways people satisfied their biological need to eat. His assumptions about diet and food production remained mostly implicit throughout the *Essay* or limited to references to wheat. Scholars of political economy have seen this ambiguity as indication of his allegiance to grain agriculture as the fundamental source of wealth. "So taken is Malthus with the production of corn [that is, wheat] that he forgets even to include fish or fowl as sources of food," Margaret Schabas pointed out in her study of the natural origins of economics. According to his approach, dependence on trade presented a threat to the fundamental security of economic life: the nation required its own grain supply in order to survive. Viewing commerce as secondary to agriculture, Malthus promoted views very close to those of the French Physiocrats, but with less room for creative adaptation. He resolutely resisted attributing importance to the role of commerce, which Adam Smith had recognized as a crucial turn in the path to modernity. Yet his allegiance to grain actually fitted out his argument for a subsequent expansion of the nation's strength: the nation's breadbasket, wherever it might be located, would come to signify another source of British power and supremacy.[2]

Malthus fully intended to create a narrow gauge for his argument about food supplies for a specific reason: grain agriculture and the staple food of wheaten bread represented incontestable measures of the rewards of civilization. While much of the rural economy remained invisible in the pages of the *Essay*, Malthus fully recognized that the British population was divided into at least two tiers of dietary expectation. Elite demand for meat forced Malthus to confront inequalities of diet, but this did not alter his adherence to grain and bread as the staple of the laboring classes and a convenient shorthand for food in general. He simply objected to the expansion of acreage devoted to pasturing beef cattle, which he viewed as detrimental to "the maintenance of labour" because of the relatively few hands employed in bringing meat to the market. Current arrangements, he seemed to be saying, might best stand still in time. Just as the Assize, a centrally mandated price of the wheaten loaf since the thirteenth century, stood for a reliable basic entitlement for the entire population, grain stood in for the dietary intake of the English nation. As an anchor of a timeless diet, wheaten bread (or "corn") also furnished a measure of the standard of living. By way of Malthus's model of the economy, grain became both idiomatic and literal as a unit of survival.[3]

This picture may tell us more about the Malthusian genealogy of scarcity than any of the theoretical or arithmetical discussions that followed upon the polemical debut of the first *Essay.* Determined to adhere to the principle of land as "incontrovertibly the sole source of all riches," he laid down two absolute assertions seldom effectively refuted: he emphasized that the supply of arable land was fixed and that its administration in any setting rightfully resided in those who followed agriculture of the most advanced kind. The first assumption evolved into an even more incontestable principle, the law of diminishing returns, developed in the first decades of the nineteenth century. Efforts to squeeze more productivity out of the margins, fated to return less and less over time, were futile. Ricardo would take this further, deploying the argument as a useful fiction on behalf of his arguments for free trade. In Malthus's view, the diminishing margins were both a useful abstraction and an empirical fact. Britain's table must, from the start, draw from its own magisterial wealth in land, where its stewards ruled over the laboring world with omniscient discipline. Proper management of land through British cultivation remained at the heart of five subsequent editions of the *Essay.* The second point, the consecration of Britain as an exemplar for lesser nations and peoples, gathered additional force over the course of the nineteenth century through an irreversible alliance with industrial capitalism and colonialism.[4]

For Malthus, grain agriculture was destined by history, informed by natural philosophy, and rooted in a particular historical narrative of interaction with the natural environment. With deceptive simplicity, he laid out his "fixed laws of our nature" operating through the personification of a beneficent but overwhelming power. Gendered as a woman, Malthus's nature differed from that of Baconian natural philosophy, who had been an unruly, active force in need of virile mastery. Malthus's version appeared to be a moral-minded disciplinarian, a kind of didactic Ceres in British garb. Her first principle appeared to be a firm law of boundaries, which she imposed by donating a scant amount of territory to the project of feeding humans. While generative "seeds" of all kind were plentiful, property was not:

> Through the animal and vegetable kingdoms, nature has scattered the seeds of life abroad with the most profuse and liberal hand. She has been comparatively sparing in the room and the nourishment to rear them. The germs of existence contained in this spot of earth, with ample food, and ample room to expand in, would fill millions of worlds in the course of a few thousand years. Necessity, that imperious all pervading law of nature, restrains them within the prescribed bounds. The race of plants and the race of animals shrink under this great restrictive law. And the race of man cannot, by any efforts of reason, escape from it.

Narrating these facts as though telling a story to children, Malthus depicted a very local setting—"this spot of earth"—that at times stood in for a version of little England and at other times for the universe. His arithmetical orientation obscured a good deal of stage management with characteristics that any contemporary reader would easily identify. A colossal schoolmistress demanded deference to a predictable, Newtonian regularity inside a controlled, state-sponsored laboratory.[5]

Malthus inherited assumptions built upon venerated British arguments about the possession of property. Drawn from Aristotle and famously summarized by John Locke, the view of nature as a latent force waiting to be unlocked by human design known as *techne* found a receptive audience in the European Enlightenment. A tree possessed the potentiality to be a chair; a virgin meadow, with the application of human labor, could become a field productive of wheat. Through the "mingling of labour" (the phrase was Locke's), settlers might lay claim to tracts of land in the New World and elsewhere simply because they brought the intentionality and know-how of British farming to North American soil. Wedding these ideas to Christianity, Malthus linked mindful cultivation of the earth to the "Supreme Being," who reinforced the wisdom of the Greeks by "ordain[ing] that the earth shall not produce good in great quantities till much preparatory labour and ingenuity has been exercised upon its surface." The creator could have provided food "without the assistance of those little bits of matter, which we call seed, or even without the assisting labour and attention of man," Malthus explained, but instead she willed that cultivation should be the means of humankind realizing its full potential.[6]

Agriculture was nothing less than the wellspring from which human reason came into being. "The processes of ploughing and clearing the ground, of collecting and sowing seeds, are not surely for the assistance of God in his creation, but are made previously necessary to the enjoyment of the blessings of life, in order to rouse man into action, and form his mind to reason," according to the Malthusian universe spelled out in the *Essay.* How else could reason emerge, if food was plentiful without effort? In a somewhat surprising prefiguring of Marx and very much like the Physiocrats of France, labor generated its own unique form of value for Malthus. In human history, cultivation of the earth was linked to motivation and action not present in the story of Edenic existence. Yet the yoke of subjugation to such overpowering commands became essential as a subsequent goad to human realization and improvement: this tendency, he argued, was part of divine "general laws" as "absolutely necessary" and constant as any other aspect of nature. To modern eyes, the unstated assumptions of a division of labor render this moralism somewhat hypocritical, but the eighteenth century's notion of stewardship released Malthus and his fellow propertied contemporaries from any obligation to perform the actual labor of cultivation with their own hands.[7]

In remote locations, the act of cultivation gave occasion for a kind of universal conscription according to a hierarchy based on social difference. As Anthony Pagden has argued, such justifications were "not simply [about] improvement"; at stake was the very identity of the claimant of the soil.

> A crucial part of what it is to be human is the drive to actualize nature's potentiality, an obligation "imposed upon man by nature." Those, by implication all Native Americans other than the Aztecs and the Inka, who fail to fulfil this obligation do not merely choose one, albeit inferior, means of subsistence over another. They fail "in their duty to themselves" as men, something which, since it clearly constitutes a violation of the law of nature, makes them less than human, creatures who are a threat to the race as a whole and who, in common with

> Aristotle's natural slaves, may be regarded as indistinguishable from wild animals.

Enlightenment thinkers had already examined New World peoples in a search for qualities that distinguished their humanity from the animal world: sensory capacities (according to Lockean principles), reason, and powers of foresight came under scrutiny in their universal studies of food-getting. The rude nations came up short: they provided ample material for the study of the state of nature and, as scholars of political theory have shown, also for arguments on behalf of slavery.[8]

As Locke wrote in his *Second Treatise*, "God gave the World to Men in Common; but . . . it cannot be supposed he meant it should always remain common and uncultivated. He gave it to the use of the Industrious and Rational (and *Labour* was to be *his Title* to it)."[9] Comparison with the subsistence labor of Indigenous peoples of the New World, as we have seen, aided the case for the British formula for improvement. According to David Armitage, Locke's involvement in colonial matters in Carolina while formulating his theory of property indicates that he knew exactly what he was doing when he carefully worded the *Second Treatise* on matters of property and authority. "Locke's argument from divine command to cultivate . . . '*great Tracts*' of unappropriated land became the classic theoretical expression of the agriculturalist argument for European *dominium* over American land." This reasoning provided the "best justification that could be given for dispossession after arguments from conquest and from religion had been gradually abandoned."[10]

Malthus's pronouncements found distant kinship to an identifiably British way of thinking about biblical creation: popular understanding of Genesis 1:23, "Be fruitful and multiply and replenish the earth," rendered the verse as a reference to the act of cultivation, not, in the first instance, to human reproduction. According to Patricia Seed, the biblical passage "was used strictly for rendering land fertile," an application she argued was unique to Britain. Adopted into English folklore, phrases of the verse were "invoked in rituals to render soil fertile for grazing and harvesting." The connection between Genesis and the yield of the soil repeatedly appeared in sermons and homilies. Its foundational assumption—that humanity carried an obligation to till the land—also found expression in the claims of possession made by British explorers around the globe. In one of the early forays to the Falkland Islands, for example, a British surgeon set seeds into the ground as his ship left port, an act of cultivation subsequently cited as proof of British entitlement to the territory. According to legend, "the settlement of Australia was begun by planting the famous '9 acres in corn' at Sydney in July 1788." Such behavior abroad signified a deep cultural consensus about what constituted rightful use of land.[11]

Whether according to biblical dictates or technical prowess, the first and particularly the second editions of *Essay on the Principle of Population* presumed that the objective of tilling the fields fixed contemporary arrangements of rank, race, and culture by locking them into a mandate of unquestionable right and duty. Within this hierarchy, hunger played an essential role in securing human beings in their allotted places in a society of orders. Hunger constituted a simple sensation located in a lower region, the belly, an organ common to all brute creation, but as a form of appetite, it was deemed simpler and lower than almost all other appetites in humans. While comparable to the sex drive, the hunger for food had a widely recognized potential to inspire fine distinctions at one end of the human spectrum and abstract comparisons and objectification at the other. The ambivalent nature of hunger offered an adaptable litmus test of rank and sensibility. As Joseph Townsend put it in his caustic commentary on the Poor Laws, hunger seemed to be the only thing that taught "decency and civility, obedience and subjection, to the most brutish, the most obstinate, and the most perverse" members of society.[12]

This essential link between food-getting and human categories became amplified by enlightened stadial histories, which focused on the "savage state" observed in the Americas to prove that when gratification of very basic appetites governed "the mind of man," "the intellectual powers are extremely limited in their operations." There, humans were given to "the thoughtless levity of children, or the improvident instinct of animals." And where food could be obtained without much effort, an "aversion to labour" set in and, with it, an indifference to future happiness or danger.[13] As Malthus gleaned from Robertson's *History*, the people of America depended primarily upon hunting and fishing for their subsistence, activities that he understood to be inactive and parasitic in relation to nature. Such passivity left the productive potential of the land untapped and therefore reflected the ignorance and laziness of primitive peoples. "As savages are wonderfully improvident, and their means of subsistence always precarious," Malthus explained in the expanded 1803 edition of the *Essay*, loosely quoting Robertson, "they often pass from the extreme of want to exuberant plenty, according to the vicissitudes of fortune in the chace, or to the variety in the productions of the seasons."[14] In South America, Robertson had pointed out, the overwhelming bounty of fish made the project of subsistence so easy that "hunting seems not to have been the first employment of men, or the first effort of their invention and labour to obtain food."[15]

This was important information for readers educated in stadial history, yet it transmitted a blinkered point of view in relation to environmental adaptations of Indigenous subsistence practices. Robertson perceived fishing as an indolent sport prior to hunting, so he (and subsequently, Malthus) failed to comprehend the intentionality of seasonal migration of fish, even though his own words betrayed the cerebral skills necessary in capturing such bounty:

> The lakes and marshes, formed by the annual overflowing of the waters, are filled with all the different species, where they remain shut up, as in natural reservoirs, for the use of the inhabitants. They swarm in such shoals, that in some places they are catched without art or industry. In others, the natives have discovered a method of infecting the water with the juice of certain plants, by which the fish are so intoxicated that they float on the surface, and are taken with the hand. Some tribes have ingenuity enough to preserve them without salt, by drying or smoking them upon hurdles over a slow fire.

Nevertheless, Robertson explained that without the "exertions of activity, or talents," the people of South America "possess neither the same degree of enterprise nor ingenuity" as those who have passed through a hunting stage. In fact, the fishing peoples were "manifestly the most inactive and least intelligent of all Americans."[16]

Hunting, the noble pursuit of the British aristocracy, offered more promise of a cerebral performance to Enlightenment writers, and the Americas did not disappoint in this regard. No doubt through a process of identification, male writers expressed obvious admiration in recounting the evidence gathered from new sources. For Robertson, the magic of the hunt in the wilds of the Americas "called forth strenuous exertions of courage, of force, and of invention, [and] it was deemed no less honorable than necessary," he enthused, embellishing his account with rhetorical color. The men "shake off the indolence peculiar to their nature, the latent powers and vigour of their minds are roused, and they become active, persevering, and indefatigable." He told of ingenious methods of poisoning the tips of arrows, "secrets" that do "great execution among the birds and beasts which abound in the forests of America." Some tribes required a test of hunting skills before allowing young men to marry, further proof of the superior mental capacities developed by hunting nations.[17]

Yet none of these achievements in the hunt actually succeeded in raising the activity from its low status in the history of modes of subsistence owing to seasonal patterns of want. Robertson, like Locke, deemed cultivation the true sign of possession of the land; he argued that "[a]s long as hunting continues to be the chief employment of man to which he trusts for subsistence, he can hardly be said to have occupied the earth."[18] Locke's own assessment of New World subsistence had shown a similar form of blindness with regard to the territories in which Indigenous people obtained game and provender. "He regarded the forest that stretched from the eastern seaboard to the Ohio valley as a commons (like the oceans) and did not recognize that the Amerindians regarded these regions as hunting grounds or that they labored to maintain these forests by, for example, burning underbrush."[19] Such activity fell outside accepted formulae representing an ecological relationship to the earth.

Robertson's presentation of North American subsistence labor transmitted what might have been considered state-of-the-art knowledge of economic history in real time. As the principal of Edinburgh University, he frequented learned circles discussing the ideas of the day and his role as a reviewer for the

Edinburgh Review called upon such common knowledge. Notes taken in 1762–63 by a student at Glasgow University on Adam Smith's lectures on jurisprudence reflect a similar body of knowledge. Excerpts offer important indications of attitudes toward activities that were seen to precede cultivation, along with the vocabulary that would inform and educate Malthus as he drew from Scottish authors:

> If we should suppose 10 or 12 persons of different sexes settled in an uninhabited island, the first method they would fall upon for their sustenance would be to support themselves by the wild fruits and wild animals which the country afforded. Their sole business would be hunting the wild beasts or catching the fishes. The pulling of a wild fruit can hardly be called an imployment. The only thing amongst them which deserved the appellation of a business would be the chase. This is the age of hunters. In process of time, as their numbers multiplied, they would find the chase too precarious for their support. They would be necessitated to contrive some other method whereby to support themselves.

Smith must have repeated the ancient presuppositions of classifying such activities as discrete and uncompromised by additional means of support. When he mentioned "North American Indians," he noted with evident ambivalence that they had "some notion of agriculture." Most likely drawing information from the Spanish Jesuit José Gumilla, on whom Robertson depended for descriptions of Indigenous agriculture, Smith erroneously undervalued the significance of maize-growing. "Their women plant a few stalks of Indian corn at the

The Plan of Civilization, unknown artist, circa 1800. The painting presents an idealized sense of the willing subordination of the Creeks, who were experienced cultivators, to the directives of people of European descent. (Oil on canvas, 35 7/8 × 49 7/8 inches. Purchased by the Greenville County Museum of Art, South Carolina, with funds from the Museum Association's 1990 and 1991 Collectors Groups and the 1989, 1990, and 1991 Museum Antiques Shows, sponsored by Elliott, Davis & Company, CPAs)

back of their huts. But this can hardly be called agriculture," he asserted in the same lecture. "This corn does not make any considerable part of their food; it serves only as a seasoning or something to give a relish to their common food; the flesh of those animalls they have caught in the chase." Inevitably, Smith declared, "when a society becomes numerous," subsequent activities with "herds and flocks" would necessarily be abandoned in order to reach for an eventual "Age of Agriculture."[20]

The objective of agriculture was to bring natural plants and creatures under the sway of human power through a process of domestication; in a struggle for survival, humans must wage a kind of war against them all, subjugating them to their will. Cultivation was a "peacetime counterpart to virtuous exertion on the field of battle," lending literalism to the idea of turning swords into plowshares. For this reason, cultivation was accorded "the highest moral value in ancient Greek societies."[21] Robertson's *History* saw the same ancient and biblical arc encompassing the Americas: agriculture remained "a work of great labour; and it is with the sweat of his brow that [man] renders the earth fertile." Significantly, the notion of fertility was stripped from nature and became linked to human effort, despite plentiful evidence that abundance existed apart from human habitation. Agriculture was "the ultimate civilized art," the performance of human *techne,* which proved that humans could reshape animal life and land into value-laden domesticated possessions.[22]

The "Plan of Civilization" in the newly created United States employed many of the assumptions of Locke, Smith, and Malthus: teach the Indians "civilization" in the form of permanent settlements, cultivation, and animal husbandry. George Washington and an important cultural missionary, Colonel Benjamin Hawkins (1754–1816), initiated the project, illustrated by a painting by an unknown artist called "The Plan of Civilization" around 1800. The men knew perfectly well that cultivation was just one tool necessary to solve a specific "Indian problem" in Georgia, a contest for territorial supremacy among Georgian frontiersmen, the Creek tribes, and the national government. Scholars have since noted the arrogance of the "experiment," pointing out that the Creeks had participated in the "Mississippian Stage" of agriculture, which originated in the southern states around 700 CE and peaked between 1200 and

1400. During that time, North America witnessed extensive cultivation of maize, including the use of tools, fertilizer, and irrigation, supplemented by hunting, fishing, and gathering. Evidence indicates that as much as 75 percent of the diet of North American Indigenous tribes came from "horticultural products." Hawkins nevertheless sought to reorder many aspects of Creek subsistence labor, including the work of women. In a complex program of reeducation, he "used his North Carolina slaves to show the Indians how the white man farmed." All these efforts came to naught when warfare flared in 1813–14 and led to the removal of Creeks from all their tribal land east of the Mississippi. In the final instance, swords prevailed when persuasion and plowshares failed to establish settler supremacy.[23]

The agricultural arguments of Malthus, Robertson, and Locke prefigured what we now refer to as the Old World Neolithic Revolution, when humans began the exhaustive project of "direct control and exploitation of many species for the sake of one: *Homo sapiens.*"[24] The process continued for much of human history. Alfred W. Crosby's account of Europeans' relentless "conscription" of flora and fauna across the Atlantic in the sixteenth and seventeenth centuries brings to light the adversarial nature of this same historical process. His list of victims of the press gang of human colonizers includes "wheat, barley, peas, lentils, donkeys, sheep, pigs, and goats," along with hardy outliers who "maintained their independence for a few more million years," namely, cattle, camels, and horses. Assigning credit for bringing all these resources under human control presented chroniclers of origin stories with revealing dilemmas. In the Book of Job, Crosby pointed out, "Jehovah claimed full credit for the horse himself," but a "millennium later, Sophocles, who did not have to live with a single omnipotent god and was freer in his praise of humanity, did declare that one of man's greatest accomplishments was the taming of 'the wild horse, windy-maned.' " Crosby's wry humor helps to demystify this important construct of human dominion, part of the wellspring of European ascendancy, over plant and animal kingdoms around the world.[25]

It comes as no surprise that the rise of settled cultivation has suffered the same fate of narrative confusion. No "big bang" of cultivation occurred in one place at a particular moment. For millennia, the earliest forms of cultivation existed alongside other food-getting arrangements. As Colin Tudge put it, "people did not invent agriculture and shout for joy; they drifted or were forced into it, protesting all the way." Human actors saw value in other modes of subsistence and may have actively avoided the eventual physical and political submission demanded by sedentary agriculture. Ultimately, however, humans were willing to trade variety and quality of nutrients in the wild for reliability of returns under domestication. Over a very long duration, regularly cultivated crops like wheat became dominant in parts of the Mediterranean and Europe owing to characteristics that enabled easier transport and storage. Growing a crop required battling the very environment that both harbored and challenged plant survival. It is unclear exactly when Europeans began to understand the environment as something objectively separate from the resources they strove to claim and subdue. Yet the human struggles going on in the areas that Europeans claimed as their margins belong to the broader set of arguments having to do with the history of the natural environment and its degradation.[26]

Historical developments appear to follow the outlines of this ambitious, rather hubristic mandate: with the benefit of hindsight, historians have traced the process of "cerealization" visible in Europe from the tenth century.[27] From the High Middle Ages, Europeans worked toward the formation of a dominant form of agriculture constituted as large-scale production of grain and meat for the market. Grain-growing regions across western and central Europe expanded under manorialism, aiming to supply cities and towns. New settlers and heavier plows altered what had been a variegated terrain, where subsistence required a combination of cultivation, grazing, foraging, fishing, and trapping. "The face of Europe was transformed as wood and scrub were cleared, marsh drained and polder reclaimed from the sea." Robert Bartlett's account of the transformation of the European continent underscored this "highly particular form of land use" involving "a more densely populated monoculture." He described this as "a step away from the human ecology that could support only a sparse population but exploited a large variety of natural resources such as fish, honey and game, as well as livestock and cultivated crops." Over time, those activities would come to represent less prestigious forms of food procurement, seen as alternative or extraneous until agricultural depressions forced them out of the margins and into lucrative channels to urban markets.[28]

More organized states and constant warfare accompanied the settlement of large swaths of arable land, given that "settled people were easier to tax, and states needed soldiers, labor, and money."[29] James Scott's examination of the spread of grain-growing alongside the earliest formation of state systems revealed exactly this pattern of gradual domination: grain provided "an ideal tax and subsistence crop," given its ability to be divided up, stored, and transformed into food when needed. Hunting, fishing, and pastoralism, Scott argued, "were fiscally sterile; they could not repay the cost of controlling them." Given the mobility and dispersal of "non-grain peoples," they "often came to be seen as a different kind of people," characterized by what they ate, that is, "dairy products and meat and not, as Romans did, grain." The Mesopotamians defined themselves as different from their "barbarian" neighbors, the Amorites, in just this way. Herding and foraging people of the margins stubbornly resisted giving way to enriched and fortified sedentary cultivators.[30]

Historians have applied different descriptors to the European era stretching from roughly 1050 to 1300 and characterized by the extension of grain cultivation. Marc Bloch's term was "the Great Age of Clearing," and other national histories adopted the phrase "because of its aptness." C. T. Smith referred repeatedly to the process as "internal colonization." From the perspective of Hungarian, Spanish, and Irish historians writing about the High Middle Ages in a later era, their regions had undergone "Europeanization" at this time. Medieval historian Robert Bartlett translated this observation simply by pointing out that "certain social and cultural features" were "expanding into the surrounding regions." For historians of economic life, such shifts forecast an important turn toward supplying towns and cities with grain.[31]

Though not solely responsible for such complex changes, the expanding Christian church acted as a veritable propaganda machine for bread and new approaches to the land. From the fourth century, religious ritual and iconography disseminated the primacy of bread, as images of the Last Supper lent bread a visual reality. "The spread of cult and the spread of cultivation went hand in hand." Orderic Vitalis demonstrated a typical narrative style of an almost ritualistic reorganization: "Monks and clerks bear witness to this, for they cut down dense woods, and now give praise in high-roofed monasteries and spiritual places built there, chanting to God with peace of mind in places where formerly robber outlaws used to lurk and perform evil deeds." Writing from the frontiers, prolix monks produced a rash of literature depicting remote and marginal peoples as primitive and lazy; Christian chroniclers "saw themselves as bringing productive labour and arable technology to an idle people and an undercultivated land." Such commentary would be repeated later in the context of civilizing missions taking place in the New World. In the meantime, sowing wheat became a widely popular practice, even by Germanic "barbarians."[32]

The transition to grain cultivation on a larger scale constituted a "revolutionary change" from what had gone on before the eleventh and twelfth centuries in Europe. A substantial expanse of forests, ringed by scrublands, marshes, and pasture, had supported a population of small homesteads dependent on a mixed regimen of activities, including hunting, foraging, and gardening. Rivers and streams supplied additional nourishment. Inhabitants shifted locations at regular intervals when the land showed exhaustion from cultivation. "The chronology of cerealization, both uneven in itself and unevenly recorded," emerged from years in which famines racked areas of Carolingian Europe and monks took charge of land management. Greater productivity was the result, along with the establishment of tithes and considerable social conflict over paying them.[33]

The "final phase of what has been called the 'great domestication' " became evident from roughly 1650, when grain agriculture advanced on a global scale. C. A. Bayly defined this trend around the world as "human beings . . . moving from nomadism, foraging, and shifting with small-scale agriculture, to regular, intensive agrarian exploitation."[34] Agriculture required control of tremendous resources: land, water supply, tools like plows and hoes, technical know-how, and of course labor. Human resources fell within a larger category of cultural capital, which included the social values that supported labor and sustained communities, encouraging the sharing of resources for survival of the greatest possible number. A spectrum of differing arguments explaining why domestication in Europe took place in this way enables us to see Malthus's theory of population within a larger framework of analysis. His emphasis on a constantly expanding population as a motor of change suggested that agricultural development proceeded from the center to the margins as a logical response to the need for food. According to this theory, Malthus could argue, the earth's surface (and optimal zones) would inevitably face depletion. As a story of "scarcity and stress," the account presents particular humans (chosen cultivators) as their own saviors against the pressures of the environment and a threatening form of nature.

Malthus's tale of pressure on resources, springing from a British mind in the 1790s, saw Britain as a kind of second Mesopotamia, the wellspring of intelligent life on the path to progress. But in truth, his origin story obscures as much as it illuminates. The archeological record, first of all, tells a different story about resources and human subsistence activity. Recent research points out that the origins of agriculture arose out of abundance rather than scarcity. In tidal shoals and riverbeds, scholars argue, plants flourished in seasonal and periodic shifts in the environment, enabling human settlements to take advantage of and learn how to improve upon the output of wild plants. Floods acted as "nature's plow," revealing rich alluvial soils and hospitable environments for cultivated plants.[35] Recent excavations have uncovered multiple sites of civilizational settlement and agriculture, forcing scholars to amend age-old narratives of origins. Humans in several different settings, in fact, were taking their cue from nature, adapting in ways that enabled them to respond to ecological conditions, seasonal fluctuations, and native populations of plants and animals. Management of the environment came on gradually and with a spectrum of different techniques, some of them more cooperative than others in enhancing tendencies already present in nature. The key historical question then becomes one of dating particular attitudes toward mastery of environmental conditions.

Anthropological theorists have looked to psychological and cultural elements within prehistory to explain the forceful management of the earth's resources at the behest of political powers. Rather than emphasizing scarcity and stress, newer arguments highlight "an abundance of resources" that "ignites a basic human predisposition for acquisition and social competition."[36] Self-aggrandizement provides another helpful concept: "domestication is a direct consequence of a conceptual shift in mankind's mental template from one that saw humans as part of nature to one that cast humans in a dominant position, now free to manipulate and transform nature to their liking. This profound and irreversible transformation in the way that humans saw themselves in relation to nature, codified in religious ideology, found expression in concrete ways: in art, household and community structure, and the domestication of plants and animals."[37]

This is not to say that all humans joined in the pragmatic and scientific approach to manipulating nature. Various actions that displayed a willingness to work alongside nature continued to flourish out of necessity: they were often born of a lack of capital or a complete separation from spaces where, to borrow Crosby's notion of conscription, the press gangs of European colonial powers were at work. Attention to the margins at any point of the *longue durée* of agricultural history exposes just how wide a cast of human beings was entangled with nature, but very few of them would be found after the Last Great Domestication occurring during Malthus's lifetime.

6

In the Margins

Civilization and Nature in Lapland

The concept of civilization was strategically important to Malthus's argument in the *Essay*, even as it stood for many things: an advanced stage of economic development, including a capitalist system of property ownership in agriculture; a commercial economy that provided desirable goods for the wealthy while generating employment for the laboring classes; and, especially, for Malthus, a system of paternalistic relations dedicated to the cultivation of grain. Civilization stood as the endpoint of human history; it was the bulwark separating humanity from the vicissitudes of punishing natural forces. The divide between these realms, for Malthus, was categorical and insuperable. Activities on either side of this divide, which was both conceptual and temporal, appeared incompatible. To us, such limitations set forth important material for analysis because they suggest ways in which the passage of time lends strength to definitions shaped by powerful modernizing forces like trade and capital concentration. The meaning and plausibility of productive life beyond the boundary of civilization are at stake in this process, as the stronger forces can simply fail to recognize and sustain those outside the system. Each erasure signals a challenge to the notion of bringing different productive systems into the same conceptual world.

How much did Malthus know about other forms of productive life? Thus far, we have constructed a context of knowledge embraced by political and economic writers of the Enlightenment, who strove to place hunting and herding within a historical continuum leading to contemporary civilization. Within the pages of the *Essay,* Malthus aligned his history of humankind with these same principles, reoriented as a warning of the peril associated with primitive existence. It was precisely this transcendence of nature, according to Malthus, that revealed the special endowment of contemporary Europeans. So it should be of interest to us to consider his personal contact with humans living "inside" the forces of nature, the legendary Sami reindeer herders in northern Norway. While touring Scandinavia in 1799, Malthus and his companion sought out a visit to an encampment of Sami herders, then called Lapps, considered one of the world's most primitive and therefore fascinating tribes of humanity. Through his diary entries, we can see how he viewed the experience as a trip across a divide between civilization and a region of otherness or alterity, where people dwelled in nature in ways he would attempt to comprehend.

In proposing this investigation, I may be charged with engaging in what anthropologists would easily dismiss as a blatant nature-culture dualism, a shorthand of western ways of knowing the world. According to this view, "nature" presents itself as something outside human existence, a set of forces in opposition to human survival. This separation, in itself, is obviously a human construction belonging to a particular context (modern western thought) at a particular time (roughly the seventeenth to the twentieth centuries). Even the concept of hunter-gatherer is rooted in a specific historical period, understood as a "late eighteenth century invention." I invoke the dualism as a tool, one that helps us think, insofar as it sheds light on limitations framing the work of Malthus when he approached unfamiliar settings of subsistence production.

In his greatly expanded edition of the *Essay on the Principle of Population* of 1803, Malthus made no mention of the Lapps and he also excluded more conventional Norwegian pastoral production, regarding the cattle he saw there as belonging to a primitive stage of economic life. Beyond that, he was not able to recognize "hunter-gatherer" techniques and tools as evidence of knowledge-gathering of any value; he looked upon the unfamiliar environment as merely barren, with nothing to teach him. His remoteness from Indigenous knowledge and local strategies of combining various forms of subsistence activities meant that he could only categorize them as desperate measures, "eking out the deficiencies of one of them by another," as Aristotle had described them.[1]

The first edition of the *Essay* had cried out for more evidence, something Malthus felt compelled to gather from direct observation as well as from written sources. Urged on by two friends from his Cambridge years, William Otter and Edward Daniel Clarke, Malthus agreed to accompany them on a trip to Scandinavia. As one of his most ardent supporters, Otter felt the timing was right and favorable, especially with help coming from Clarke, an experienced tutor and companion of young Britons seeking the Grand Tour. Given the impossibility of traveling to the Continent during the Napoleonic Wars, Clarke mapped out an itinerary that would benefit the budding population theorist but also offer a serious investigation of geography and agronomy to his latest twenty-year-old charge, John Marten Cripps. Clarke shared an intellectual stake in the journey: he would make serious observations of the terrain and win considerable attention writing about his travels. Something of a bon vivant, Clarke would part company with Malthus and Otter once the party reached Lake Wenner in Sweden in order to follow a different itinerary with his well-to-do pupil. From that point, he would guide Cripps through Russia, Tartary, Turkey, and the Middle East for three and a half years, gathering considerable mineralogical and archeological booty. Following their return to England, Clarke was named the first professor of mineralogy at Cambridge in 1808. Cripps the horticulturalist would claim the distinction of introducing kohlrabi into English farming.[2]

With its legendary challenges of climate and terrain, the region promised Malthus the prospect of witnessing nature in a dramatically direct relationship to human society. With "eight months of winter and four of bad weather," peasant life in Norway and Sweden also provided a suitable arena for demonstrating how human convention could trump the powers of nature. Much later, Otter suggested that the official population records of the region, among the most advanced banks of statistics in Europe, had drawn their attention, particularly that of his friend Malthus, the noted theorist on the subject. Yet, as scholars have shown, statistical resources were never central to Malthus's approach. Ultimately, he relied on an eccentric assortment of interviews and selective, mostly obsolete statistics to support his arguments about Norway and Sweden in Book II of the second edition. More interested in the imposition of human will over nature, Malthus would assimilate the experiences of his journey and deploy their impact in more indirect ways.[3]

Malthus embarked on his trip equipped with a list of contacts, several blank notebooks, and two thermometers, all part of an approach he believed would serve him well in his wish to expand the *Essay.* In particular, his own understanding of his methodology helps to situate his visit to an encampment of Sami people, typical of the time, within a venerable history of such expeditions, particularly in the natural sciences. As Mary Terrall explains in her study of the French philosopher Pierre Louis Maupertuis, writers on scientific subjects can be investigated in their "movements and choices" in part as a means of tracing their bids for "fame and reputation" but also, just as importantly, as a way of revealing their intellectual affinities. As she shows in her examination of Maupertuis's celebrated trip to Lapland, enchanted and, at times, untamed nature provided a means by which the scientist's own rationality could locate its parameters.[4]

In popular as well as higher literary culture, the northern herders occupied a firm place in proverbial understandings of primitive ways of life. Lapland was a locus of the uncanny in literature: Shakespeare deployed "Lapland sorcerers" in his *Comedy of Errors*, and Milton's *Paradise Lost* featured "Lapland witches." Malthus's reading of Bishop Pontoppidan's *Natural History of Norway* would have reminded him of Tacitus's depiction of ancient peoples, whose habitations were reportedly exactly like those of the Lapps. It was commonly held that the northern nomads were simply frozen in time, reenacting the primitive past on a modern stage. Pontoppidan insisted that the "Finlaplanders" constituted "quite a distinct nation from the Norwegians," carrying out their hunting activities "in the woods, and on the barren tops of the mountains." In an unusual diversion from the Greek template of the pastoral nomad, the Lapps, Pontoppidan had also noted, sometimes cleared trees in order to sow rye, but he criticized this as doing "their country a good deal of damage . . . for many fine woods are destroyed by them." It was hard to avoid castigating the Lapps, Pontoppidan seemed to say, noting without comment that the Norwegians "command them like slaves, and treat them with such contempt, as in other countries the people do the Jews."[5]

Malthus would assiduously record his observations of the physical features, family composition, diet, dress, and behavior of the Lapps, along with their time-consuming demonstration of reindeer-herding and dairying. It is worth asking why, given the copious and detailed notes that he compiled, Malthus did not discuss their mode of survival in a comparative or critical way. Philosophers before him had featured Lapland as a netherworld of arduous subsistence-gathering in their accounts of the history of economy and society. And as his reading of stadial histories would have shown, Lapland served as a notable frontier of human development in the nomadic or pastoral phase. Kames, for one, devoted attention to the impact of the northern climate on the Laplanders, who were "chained to the shepherd-state, and can never advance to be husbandmen," owing to the unfitness of the terrain for growing grain. For Malthus, who was deeply interested in the impact of environmental conditions and natural resources on human populations, the omission seems particularly noteworthy. He was to draw examples of "prudential restraint," the key concept of the second edition, from the neighboring regions of Norway, data he would marshal with great confidence. What follows is an attempt to place that argument in juxtaposition with his close encounter with a living example of a herding population.[6]

In certain respects, Malthus's "Scandinavian Journal" appears as a rather jejune exercise in the discourse of travel, punctuated with pronouncements of "sublime" vistas and personal reactions to accommodations, service, and food. The reader cannot mistake the fact that this was Malthus's first experience of travel outside England, especially given the way in which he relied on texts in order to comprehend what he was seeing. It is unlikely that Malthus considered publishing the volumes of notes that he accumulated during his travels; by lending them to Edward Daniel Clarke for use in Clarke's own published work, he forfeited any claim to the originality and usefulness of his observations. (Clarke died while in possession of two of the diaries, which Malthus apparently failed to recover.) Certain subjects discussed in these journals of Scandinavia reflect Malthus's prior reading of Archdeacon William Coxe's *Travels into Poland, Russia, Sweden and Denmark* (4th edition, 1792) and Bishop Pontoppidan's *Natural History of Norway* (1755).[7] The latter volume included an earnest investigation of mermaids and mermen, which signaled the author's attachment to a somewhat credulous approach to natural history. Malthus, in his own way, seemed to believe much of what he was told; the reader is struck by how quickly he draws sweeping conclusions from conversations with a very select group of informants. Covering May 25 to August 2, 1799, the diaries nevertheless demonstrate alertness to behavior, living arrangements, manners of dress, and occupational activities, observations which at times make him sound more like an ethnographer than the political economist he was in the process of becoming.

The four men must have realized that they were embarking on a route through renowned sites of scientific tourism in the eighteenth century, rendered legendary by the famous Swedish naturalist Carl Linnaeus. Ever the publicist, Clarke wrote that the northern regions were "seldom seen by literary men" at the time, an odd remark, given that many men in pursuit of political economy were followers of Linnaeus and likely also travelers to Scandinavia. Moreover, Malthus certainly knew of Mary Wollstonecraft's *Letters Written During a Short Residence in Sweden, Norway, and Denmark* (1796), given that a copy existed in his library, and he had read Godwin's *Memoirs* of Wollstonecraft. (He also shared a publisher with the then-notorious author of *A Vindication of the Rights of Woman.*) As the homeland of Linnaeus, the region had been traversed by a

Carolus Linnaeus. In his Lapland Dress, mezzotint by Henry Kingbury, after a painting by Martin Hoffman, 1737 (Uppsala University Library)

multitude of Europeans and would see many more.[8] Readers of natural history would have assimilated the basic facts of northern Scandinavia, known generally as Lapland, from any one of several accounts recycled in widely popular works, such as Oliver Goldsmith's *History of the Earth, and Animated Nature* (1774). Perhaps Clarke's comment was an indirect reference to the kind of armchair travel that so often informed writers of the period.

Linnaeus's own famous tour of Lapland in 1732 had resulted in a virtual publicity program for the ecological, economic, and dietary characteristics of the region. In a stroke of flagrant self-promotion, Linnaeus had himself painted in what he wished to advertise as Lapp costume; in fact, he was wearing the summer hat of a Sami woman and "reindeer leather boots . . . of a type the Sami manufactured for export and did not wear themselves." As Lisbet Koerner mordantly observes in her revealing biography of Linnaeus, the botanist was intent on constructing a peculiar, hyperbolic authenticity in the picture: "his shaman's drum—an artifact illegal to own in Lapland itself—had been presented to him by an Uppsala professor as he packed for Holland." Maupertuis, who also immortalized himself in a portrait in Lapp costume, went one step further: he brought two Lapp women (actually the daughters of a Swedish grocer) back to Paris in 1737. Ralph Beilby and Thomas Bewick's immensely popular *General History of Quadrupeds* (1790) effectively disseminated knowledge of the region to a broad audience with a predilection for animals. Their richly illustrated volume included a winning image of the reindeer, supplemented by text pirated from Johannes Shefferus, an Alsatian philologist and author of the well-known *Lapponia* (1673; English translation, 1674), and Bishop Olaus Magnus, whose *Description of the Northern Peoples* enjoyed a long life after its publication in 1555.[9]

HISTORY OF QUADRUPEDS. 127

THE REIN-DEER.

(*Cervus Tarandus*, Lin.—*Le Renne*, Buff.)

This extraordinary animal is a native of the icy regions of the North; where, by a wise and bountiful dispensation, which diffuses the common goods of nature over every part of the habitable globe, it is made subservient to the wants of a hardy race of men inhabiting the countries near the pole, who would find it impossible to subsist among their snowy mountains without the aid of this most useful creature.

Page from Ralph Beilby's *A General History of Quadrupeds* (sixth ed., 1811), illustrated by Thomas Bewick. First published in 1790, these volumes enjoyed wide acclaim as instructive records of the natural world. The reindeer, a legendary animal of wonder, occupied a place in print culture from the sixteenth century. (Columbia University Rare Book and Manuscript Library)

Eighteenth-century Sweden and (by implication) northern Norway, in Koerner's words, offered "a holiday land for the ethnographic tourist and a natural utopia," particularly "post-Linnaean Lapland," which "became an exotic stage set for Romantic travel and for antics and jokes." As a prime example, she has noted that when Malthus's friend Clarke "met his first Sami, an old woman in Lulea, he promptly kissed her." The account appears, with an attempt at humor ("ugly as she was, we even ventured to kiss her"), in Clarke's volume on Scandinavia, published posthumously in 1824. Interest in the area and its fauna must have been considerable by then, judging from the fact that a Haymarket theater proprietor enlisted Thomas Dibdin in writing a play called "The Laplanders" around that year. The proprietor had demanded a script that called for a live herd of reindeer, but the attempt to stage the play failed when the imported animals died before the performance date.[10]

Malthus approached the journey with less experience and more gravitas. The entries of his *Travel Diaries*, in turn eclectic, empirical, and candidly naïve, are those of a young man working hard to master the correct distance from what he was seeing. An eagerness to record significant detail resulted in a rather clinical tone, interrupted at times by confessions of being "rather diverted" or mystified by the unfamiliar. As his lexicon of geography and settings expanded, Malthus proved to be a reliable recorder of flora and fauna, initially measured in relation to what he knew of English natural life. He often applied decidedly English visual calipers to alien vistas: "A branch of the river only runs by Tangberget, & is then contracted, to the breadth of the Thames at Putney," he recorded about seventy-five miles north of Oslo. (The mannerism of using the Thames at various landmarks along its course appears repeatedly in Coxe's five volumes.) "We passed no Towns or even what could be called villages; but clusters of houses, three or four together (tho not joined)," he noted, indicating that cottages were "more frequent . . . than in most parts of England." Perhaps Malthus was imitating the style of contemporary travel writers who spoke to an English audience; yet the repeated use of England as a yardstick for places unknown limited the likelihood that this new territory would ever stand on its own merits.[11]

Certain aspects of the environment, indisputably incommensurate with things British, nevertheless gave him a marked sense of seeing something new and potentially significant. The most striking segment of his journal reports his visit to a temporary settlement of "Lapfins," a purposeful detour during their travels through Norway and Sweden. Hints in the text indicate that Malthus anticipated with excitement the prospect of coming into contact with the migratory herders; certainly he and Otter went to considerable trouble to arrange the encounter. In letters of introduction to the director of copper mines near Roraas, in the northern part of their itinerary, "it had been mentioned that we wished very much to see the Laplanders," he reported. The director in turn gave them a letter to "a gentleman at Tolgen about 4 miles from Roraas who would probably be able to direct us where to find them," but, they were told, the Laplanders "remained for so short a time in the same place during the summer that it was difficult to catch them." Malthus's choice of verb revealed his categorical understanding of the Lapps, whom he regarded as wild and unattached to the forces of civilization. He believed that the "wandering Laplanders" were unlikely to be glimpsed at the end of July: "In winter they sometimes come down into the villages to sell their skins & buy a little grain," he noted; "but in the summer they are seldom seen or heard of except now & then by the peasants who are with their cattle at Saters [upland pastures]." In truth, the Lapps maintained regular relations with local markets and had been the target of missionary work, somewhat forcibly, since the seventeenth century. The contact at Tolgen sent Malthus's party another mile into the mountains, where they could gain "intelligence of the Laplanders, or Lap fins as they are called, sleep there, & the next morning go in pursuit of them." The expedition required a servant, acting as interpreter, and "a peasant on foot," guiding them across the varied landscape of hills, barren land, and forests.[12]

The elusive nature of the Lapps was matched by their environment. By this time in his journey, Malthus was accustomed to seeing houses topped with grass, but earlier, the sight of peasants mowing their roofs, or allowing their sheep and goats to graze there, went down in his diary as a remarkably odd sight. At the hamlet of his host, he noted that the "environs [were] in general extremely barren," but on "the tops of the houses the hay was in cock." Malthus took measure of the markedly different terrain of northern Norway and recorded taking comfort in the safety of dwellings, which his hosts confirmed would provide protection from wild animals. "In so wild & distant a situation we enquired about the bears & the wolves; & were told that the wolves did much mischief; but that the bears were of the small kind & seldom killed any cattle." Accommodation proved as melded with nature as the setting: the travelers "could get nothing to eat but very coarse oaten cake & milk." With only one bed for the two men, and "one sheet & a quilt made of cows' skins," Malthus chose to sleep on the dresser in the room, spreading a cow's skin and "a great coat over it." The party arose by "half past 3" and, after more milk and oat cake, "mounted . . . horses in pursuit of the Lapfins."[13]

Their expedition to see the Lapps wedded Malthus and Otter to a centuries-long fascination with the semi-nomadic people of northern Scandinavia. Believed to have migrated to the region from Finland or possibly as far as Central Europe, the Sami were seen as ethnically and culturally distinct from other Scandinavians, marked by distinctive languages, clothing, and means of subsistence. They spoke Finno-Urgric (Uralic) languages, which at least one early modern commentator, a seventeenth-century Jesuit named Sainovits, recognized as related to Hungarian. Johannes Schefferus posited in 1673 that the "Lapps derive without doubt their origin from the Finns, were born among them, but had been driven away and exiled from Finland." (It is now established that their presence in Finland dates from the Stone Age six thousand years ago.) In the earliest sources, they were called "Fenni" and were generally understood to reside in "Finnmark." With the establishment of Norwegian counties in 1634, "Lappland" came into being, though even today, "Finnmark" is used to refer to the northern regions of Norway. The profusion and confusion of nomenclature was an essential part of their eighteenth-century identity, a kind of proximate exoticism in a region that was quite literally off the map.[14]

Educated men like Malthus and Otter approached their Lapp encounter armed with classification tools derived from stadial history, which registered the Lapps as the remnant of ancient northern barbaric peoples. In his influential account of the northern tribes (likely part of required reading during the early studies of Malthus), Tacitus had established a profile of Lapland inhabitants in the first century. "The Fenni are astonishingly wild and horribly poor," he wrote in *Germania.* Seen as a race apart, the northerners migrated constantly and appeared wholly adapted to a way of life without fixed property or abode. "They have no arms, no horses, no homes. They eat grass, dress in skins and sleep on the ground," he reported. They lived in perilous proximity to nature. "The only way they can protect their babies against wild beasts or foul weather is to hide them under a makeshift network of branches. This is the hovel to which young men come back; this is where the old must die.

And yet they count their lot happier than that of others who groan over field labor, sweat over house building, or hazard their own or other men's fortunes in the wild lottery of hope and fear." Olaus Magnus's *Historius de gentibus septentrionalibus* [*History of the Northern Peoples*] (Rome, 1555; English translation, 1658) added many ethnographic details, but the thrust remained the same despite the passage of over fourteen centuries: the northern tribes, Laplanders among them, led rude and peculiar lives, forced by nature and custom into close proximity with wild beasts in unfathomable climatic conditions.[15]

Even though New World Indigenous tribes had displaced these northern pastoral nomads as the "ultimate barbaric type," a firsthand view of the Lapps presented Malthus and Otter with an extraordinary opportunity. The two men would expect to see humans who were as close to animal creation as they could have imagined; indeed, Malthus would record the experience in his journal as "our Laphunting day." Like Gibbon, Malthus probably assumed that "like the animals of prey, the savages, both of the Old and the New World, experience the alternate vicissitudes of famine and plenty." As Malthus was to argue in the revised edition of the *Essay*, "an insufficient supply of food to any people, does not shew itself merely in the shape of famine, but in other more permanent forms of distress, and in generating certain customs, which operate sometimes with greater force in the suppression of a rising population, than in its subsequent destruction."[16] Fluctuations of food supplies signaled the close association between herding activities and the seasonality of the natural world; thus, the considerable *techne* involved in successful dairying (particularly with restive mammals like horses or deer) would suffer erasure. Owing to climate and location as well as residual customs, the Sami could be viewed as imprisoned in nature, with little of the intellectual powers needed to achieve conquest over its forces.

Reindeer and sled from *A Winter in Lapland and Sweden* (1827) by Arthur de Capelle Brooke (Butler Library, Columbia University)

In recording his encounter with the Lapps, Malthus indicated from the start that he had ventured across the divide separating a relatively civilized peasantry from the wilderness. As his party approached the borderland where the Lapps had been sighted, he noted the presence of the telltale "rein deer moss," the well-known dietary staple of herds, in the "extremely barren" area, which sat in "strong contrast" with the "beauty and fertility of the vallies." Everything about the area suggested that its human inhabitants were hostages of nature. Along with his worry about wolves, Malthus noted that the house providing shelter for the night made no eggs available for breakfast; perhaps chickens were as much at risk as he himself felt. Even the cattle took their cues from nature, not humans: because of recent temperatures, they were currently grazing at a distance, where the grass was good, not in the nearby saeters.[17]

The two young English gentlemen were not above making sport of the occasion on that early summer morning. Malthus and Otter made a wager while they searched for their human prey: six pence to the man who first spotted them. Malthus claimed the reward when he "saw a she Lap peep out" from behind the flap of a skin-covered hut that appeared in the distance. The introduction did not disappoint: once they were invited into the shelter, the Englishmen were immediately privy to a numerous family (seven to ten people) emerging from under deerskins, the children naked and the young women in a partial state of undress, displaying no modesty. Female clothing had fascinated Malthus throughout his Scandinavian travels, and here he observed the familiar scant layering of tunics and shifts among the Lapp women. He revealed his own sensibility by registering several facts that surprised him, including "finding the smell very little offensive on account of fire, & opening at the top of the hut for smoke."[18] Taking note of the face-washing that went on, he believed it was not the Lapps' usual practice but more likely a "compliment to us." The fact that the "mother of the whole party" welcomed them in and spoke Norse "tolerably well" should have elicited more curiosity.

Malthus seems to have resisted comprehending that the Lapps were hardly isolated nomads but were instead currently subject to Christianizing efforts, laws, and commercial relations coming from Norwegians from the valleys below. His limited exposure to Scandinavian nomenclature was evident in the fact that he was unable to translate the names of his hosts into proper spellings (the ubiquitous patronym "-dottir" had escaped his notice); he recorded being "rather diverted at hearing" the matriarch's name, which he transcribed as "Maria Sophia Anders daughter." The patriarch became simply "Jonas Anderson."[19]

Malthus does not report money changing hands, though he later disclosed that they had presented the family with

"2 pound of tobacco & 2 bottles of brandy." It is likely that their guide also offered payment to the Lapps and that the family had some experience in hosting travelers and interacting with people from foreign countries. The fact that the visitors were quickly served a substantial breakfast of "very fine looking trout" and two kinds of reindeer cheese suggests that the family was ready to oblige its guests, though the guests themselves were not entirely pleased. Malthus thought little of the reindeer cheese ("I eat [*sic*] a bit of both the sorts . . . by way of curiosity; but it had not any predominant taste that I can describe"), and he turned down the plate of fish. He was not taken in by how "very neatly" it had been set out on a trencher; he had noticed that the woman had torn apart the trout with her fingers, sucking her fingertips while she worked, and when he told this to Otter, who had eaten a little, Otter "was almost sick afterwards with the idea."[20]

Genealogical information, along with physical characteristics, mattered to Malthus, and he recorded every fact he could obtain. His host family was of considerable size: the couple "had had 13 children, 7 of which were dead & 6 alive . . . who all lived in the family," including "the Son in-law who was married to one of the daughters & had 3 children." The patriarch of this household was 62, the "old woman" only 52, though Malthus commented that she looked a good deal older. "She had however a very good set of teeth," a characteristic that Linnaeus had also regularly noticed in his dealings with Lapps earlier in the century. (This fact helped convince the Swedish botanist that the dietary habits of the Lapps presented a unique menu for optimal health.) Blood relations between the son-in-law and both the old man and old woman made them related to each other, and to Swedish Lapps, in several ways. Malthus found this interesting, having learned that the governments of Sweden and Norway had attempted to control movement across the border. Malthus could not have been surprised to find that the patriarch was notably short, given how every description of the Lapps included reference to their small stature: he reckoned a precise 4 feet, 10 inches tall, while "the other men were 2 or 3 inches taller." He had determined enough about Lapp society to adopt an idea of an archetype: the patriarch was the "most complete [Lap]fin of the party," with "characteristic features of the Laplanders, high cheek bones, hollow cheeks, a prominent chin, & small flat eyes."[21]

Malthus's careful account of "the business of milking" recognized that this was clearly "a work of considerable time & trouble." With characteristic precision, he inadvertently generated one of the most detailed historical accounts of reindeer management extant. Reindeer herding presented a confounding mix of elements to the observer: the animals were usually not tame like domesticated cattle and goats, yet herders claimed rights over large numbers (herds averaged five hundred deer) through constant supervision by several people assisted by several dogs. The animals grazed mostly on moss across vast expanses of forest and tundra, changing location according to the season and depending on conditions. In order to milk them from spring to late autumn, skilled keepers would drive deer into carefully designed enclosures with broad entrances made of branches stuck into the ground. As Malthus witnessed, the activity proved challenging and laborious. Females did not submit easily and needed to be lassoed by their legs, necks, or horns and tied up for each session. Their yield was far less than what a cow or goat might provide, a stark reminder of how the elaborate system of herding originated in the fundamental fact of necessity. Deer were free and numerous but, in effect, were only borrowed from nature, on terms as much determined by the deer as their herders.[22]

The legendary creatures presented a marvelous sight to the visitors. "[W]e went out, & luckily the deer were just then coming home, & looked with their branching horns like a moving forest," Malthus related with a poetic touch. The Englishmen were kept back until the last of the roughly six hundred deer had entered the pen; many immediately lay down so that "the bottom of the pen was almost entirely covered with them." The experience of walking "among so many large branching horns, which we were sometimes obliged to push aside to get along," Malthus found "rather formidable at first." "[B]ut they were all perfectly quiet & did not shew the least disposition to butting." The sometime hunter competed with Malthus's other self, interested in the natural wonder of an unfamiliar species:

> They were fat & in fine order, & appeared to me about the size of the red deer. I measured two of the largest with my stick, & should conjecture that they were about 3 feet 6 inches high. The horns are nearly a yard high from the head besides the great circle that they make. They are covered with a skin & soft hair which gives them a very novel appearance, & the branches immediately over the forehead are varied in almost every deer.

According to his hosts, around one hundred of the six hundred deer were in milk at the moment, so the process of milking, done mainly by the women, lasted longer than the two remaining hours of the visit. At most, each doe gave "about a pint of milk," though over time, the "quantity soon falls off," they were told. The average yield was probably closer to "half a pint a piece." Young deer were prevented from nursing overnight by little sticks inserted into their mouths at the evening milking session. But by day, the little ones had their fill, which left only enough milk "for coffee or tea" by the late afternoon. Malthus and Otter found this last point humorous, perhaps because they saw incongruity in an apparently civilized habit in the midst of life in the wild.[23]

With the wisdom of hindsight, we might indict Malthus for a sin of omission at this moment in his narrative. Other Lapland travelers saw fit to taste and describe reindeer milk; Clarke would arrive a few weeks later and make a point of it in his own account. Malthus appears to have hung back from drinking the hard-won liquid, perhaps because, as he took pains to point out, "A good deal of hair generally gets into the milk, & to get rid of this they strain it thro a wooden cullender covered with a little wisp of hay." Clarke's less fastidious personality was in evidence throughout his recollections. "[T]he women presented us with the milk, warm: it was thick, and sweet as cream," he reported; "we thought we had never tasted any thing more delicious: but it is rather difficult of digestion, and apt to cause head-ache in persons unaccustomed to it, unless it be mixed with water." Here, Clarke was transmitting the ancient belief that bodies of refined people would have had difficulty consuming the crude dairy products of wild animals, a vestige of Galenic principles that matched dietary habits to bodily types according to social rank. Yet his description was nonetheless full and affirmative. He took careful note of curds of cheese drying on a "platform raised between two trees," an area which he rewarded with the title of dairy, a term missing from Malthus's account.[24]

Despite the seeming overwhelming strangeness of the scene of reindeer and humans in close communion, Malthus and Otter resisted being transported by the experience. Their curiosity and hunger for information continued unabated, but apparently not in an entirely empathic direction. Eventually, they found, their servant "thought so many questions trifling & foolish & shewed a little unwillingness to repeat them." It is possible that Malthus's empirical bent began to grate on his

Lapp woman with child, illustration from Edward Clarke, *Travels in Various Countries in Scandinavia* (1838). Clarke and Malthus shared a fascination with Lapp women, their mode of dress, and their behavior. This illustration is taken from the final volume of a series, finished after Clarke's death in 1822, which incorporated notes from Malthus's journal. (Columbia University Rare Book and Manuscript Library)

hosts. On their return journey, they attempted to take an eagle's nest but found the tree "so very rotten that we did not chuse to venture up." They also spotted a "large snipe of Linnaeus flying round us & . . . sometimes perching on a tree, as if it had a nest somewhere near." Malthus added, "We lamented much that we had not a gun." This reminded him, in his journal-keeping, that "when we were with the laps we saw a gun, & would have borrowed it to shoot the eagle; but they refused to lend it, saying that it was a bird which often took revenge." Their outlook remained firmly entrenched in that of gentlemen hunters rather than curious travelers or respectful naturalists.[25]

The opposing world views could not have been more pronounced at this moment. Anthropologist Tim Ingold's analysis of this dualism highlights the possessiveness involved in the hunter's perspective: "In social terms, an essential characteristic of the hunting economy is that animals do not constitute objects of property until they have been brought down, whereas in the pastoral economy the living animals belonging to each individual and household represent a store of wealth 'on the hoof.' " Lapland visitors sometimes failed to calculate the value, in Lapp terms, of the animals and animal products that they encountered. (Characteristically unconcerned, Linnaeus went down on record as eating the last piece of reindeer cheese belonging to a "destitute old Sami woman.") Malthus, ever the accountant, wished to comprehend the value of reindeer meat; he even recorded that when the Lapps killed deer and sold venison, "the finest haunch [sold] for six shillings," a considerable amount. But the distinction between human predation and the ecological relationship established by the Lapps with reindeer herds had not entered his consciousness. Malthus's diary recorded a long day of "little or nothing" to eat, erasing from memory his sampling of reindeer cheese. Turning down "milk & oat bread" at midday, he noted "a great craving for something more solid than milk." Malthus had no desire to follow an abbreviated nomadic diet. His account of his evening meal that day illustrated this and seemed to put a final stop to the adventure:

> At half past seven we sat down to some trout & a piece of Reindeer venison, which we thought a very lucky finishing to our Laphunting day. It was very tender, & not badly flavoured; but had no fat, & no very high or marked taste. We understood that it was a young one. Our host told us that we should take some with us cold the next day; but we were so hungry with our long expedition that we left very little remainder.

In a celebratory diary entry, Malthus barely distinguished between the Sami people he had observed that morning and his dinner menu of trout and reindeer. Though the intensely physical encounter with alien humans and beasts had startled him, his intellectual orientation remained intact. The Lapps and their animals, engaging in a vivid display of interspecies industry, remained safely categorized in a netherworld of prehistory. For the remainder of his Scandinavian tour, Malthus would focus on settled agriculture with an unswerving though hardly surprising conviction that the future lay in the dominion of humans over nature.[26]

Malthus hoped that his revisions of 1803 would address one of the principal objections to the first *Essay:* that it was "a specious argument inapplicable to the present state of society." The new edition would thus apply "the principle directly and exclusively to the existing state of society," using "the best authenticated accounts that we have of the state of other countries."

Book II, "Of the Checks to Population in the Different States of Modern Europe," began with a discussion of nations with notable caches of statistical records, Norway and Sweden. But Malthus deployed the available statistics in a selective and even misleading manner. He drew from statistical sources in German and French, one of which had been translated from the original Danish, but otherwise he relied heavily on chance impressions he gathered from his travels and from "such leading figures of Norwegian society as he happened to meet." As Michael Drake has painstakingly demonstrated, Malthus chose to omit the fertility rate calculated by Danish statistician Frederick Thaarup, most likely because it implied that the population of Norway would double in the lamentably short span of seventy-seven years. He also cited mortality rates that applied only to the years 1775–84. As a result, Malthus was able to argue that southern Norway, decidedly distinct from Lapland, was characterized by low mortality and fertility and therefore deserved special attention as a nation exercising exemplary restraint. Since E. F. Heckscher's early critique of 1943, scholars have generated considerable commentary on the peculiar use of Norway (and Sweden, seen as deplorably prolific and indigent) in the *Essay*, and yet they have not discussed precisely how and why Malthus would have chosen to do so.[27]

In the opening chapter of Book II, Malthus presented Norway as a mirror image of what he had witnessed among the Lapps: here was a society of stationary people, a condition he favored (and also exaggerated) in his search for a social organization that promoted prudential restraint. "Unless . . . an opportunity of foreign emigration offer [*sic*], the Norwegian peasant generally remains in the village in which he was born; and as the vacancies in houses and employments must occur very slowly, owing to the small mortality that takes place, he will often see himself compelled to wait a considerable time, before he can attain a situation which will enable him to rear a family." Against the Lapps' economy, in which "their reindeer formed their riches," Malthus adhered steadfastly to a belief in land, "incontrovertibly the sole source of all riches." A faithful allegiance to a relatively closed system of private property worked to the benefit of any population, Malthus believed; yet he never explicitly commented on the significant differences between a true peasantry (which he observed in Norway) and the very different, more unequal organization of landholding in his native England. For Malthus, land meant farming and farming meant grain, just as it did for Gibbon and Herodotus. Scholars of economic thought familiar with true mixed economies would add game to the list of provender forgotten in the *Essay.*[28] But in the *Essay* and its models of economic success, the larger goal of prosperity was inexorably linked to the cultivation of wheat: like the ancient figure of speech, *synecdoche,* the idea of grain stood for the larger reality of private property.

A landed system of property and agriculture of course meant much more than a staple food: with both came a cadre of cultural and moral superintendents who might guide their social inferiors toward a particular collective good. What separated civilized peoples from the uncivilized was an ability to project into the future. Malthus believed that this was already happening in the settled parts of Norway, where laws had imposed patience on the people and stopped them from procreating. Mandatory military service required of all males stood in the way of early marriages, while inheritance laws encouraged family-owned allotments and close control over a servant class. The region offered little by way of commerce and presented nowhere else to go, apart from fishing villages on the coast, which Malthus presented as "very poor and wretched; and, beyond comparison, in a worse state, than the peasants in the interior of the country." Even as some arrangements went into abeyance and Norwegians were now more "at liberty," their age-old customs, Malthus believed, favored restraint. A large servant class, as a result, seemed to exhibit those habits of sexual abstinence that Malthus dreamed of; this was his own version of utopia that he posed in opposition to that of Godwin. The fact that the soil and climate were uncooperative only proved how nature could collude to prevent the population from multiplying in an undesirable way. Other cultural factors contributing to this apparent homeostasis did not interest Malthus, whose English yardstick remained the principal tool of comparison.[29]

Malthus's greatest compliment to the Norwegians was his willingness to deem them participants in what Peter Mandler has called "the civilizational model" of the late eighteenth century. According to this view of progress, all nations were located within a historical continuum along the way to an ideal state of civilization; "fortified by the aftermath of the French Revolution," the overarching (anti-democratic) design provided part of the bedrock of Christian political economy in the nineteenth century. Rather than seeing rural Norwegians as simply different from English people, Malthus was ready to embrace their economic life as part of a universal model of development. An important aspect of advancement toward the highest expression of civilization entailed a mastery of nature and a progressive form of agriculture, which also included dominion over animals. The possessive individualism embedded in private property extended outward to the natural world. Unlike the Linnaean system, which recognized equilibrium within nature and embraced science as a technological means of entering into a relationship with it, the Malthusian approach led to a separation of society from nature and an objectification of its provender. As John Stuart Mill posed the problem some years later, "The ways of nature are to be conquered, not obeyed."

For Malthus, shored up by the dichotomies he had witnessed in Norway, this meant that herding reindeer had no place in modern political economy.[30]

We know that Malthus saw more in Norway than what he chose to discuss in the first chapter of Book II in the 1803 edition of the *Essay.* Everything was relative in the history of humankind, and the territory of Lapland, just beyond the far edge of cultivated land, loomed as an undeniable reminder of that fact. Neighboring Norwegians who engaged in herding dairy cows and cattle inhabited a proximate category: even with their belief in property and a demonstrated patience, Malthus presented them as somewhat retarded in their progress toward a truly civilized condition. "The Norwegians, though not in a nomadic state, are still in a considerable degree in the pastoral state, and depend very much upon their cattle," he admitted. "The high grounds that border on the mountains, are absolutely unfit to bear corn, and the only use to which they can be put, is to pasture cattle upon them for three or four months during the summer." Telltale dependency on animals threw up a red flag in any informed account of the history of civilization. Malthus chose not to mention the actual nomadic state situated beyond the border, in the adjacent mountains. There, the relationship to animals went beyond familiar dependency on cattle, a tribe of fully domesticated beasts, to a fitful relationship with semi-wild reindeer. He had observed the Lapp household system of labor and reproduction, tasted some of the homemade cheese, and even heard a snatch of Lapp flute music as he left the encampment. All of this apparently served to enforce his sense of boundaries. The non-nomadic pastoral state was as far as he would go.[31]

Malthus nevertheless wished to preserve what he could of his Scandinavian example, despite noting more than once that most of the country was "absolutely incapable of bearing corn." Even for such a backward agricultural state, hope glimmered on the horizon:

> Notwithstanding, however, all these obstacles, there is a very considerable capacity for improvement in Norway, and of late years it has been called into action. I heard it remarked by a professor at Copenhagen, that the reason why the agriculture of Norway had advanced so slowly, was, that there were no gentlemen farmers who might set examples of improved cultivation, and break the routine of ignorance and prejudice in the conduct of farms, that had been handed down from father to son for successive ages. From what I saw of Norway, I should say that this want is now, in some degree, supplied. Many intelligent merchants and well-informed general officers are at present engaged in farming.

An English model of agricultural development aided Malthus as he mapped out a future for Norway. Armed with a mentality of possessive individualism in a comparatively small setting, Norway was "almost the only country in Europe where a traveller will hear any apprehensions expressed of a redundant population," which might spoil the "happiness" achieved by such careful shepherding of the population.[32]

Should we wonder about the disappearance of reindeer in Malthus's account of Scandinavia? Despite the rich data present in the diary, the animal figured in none of Malthus's calculations, neither as a source of provender nor as a monitory or even didactic sign of a nomadic herding economy. Of course, few if any animals appear anywhere in the *Essay on Population*, a remarkable omission in an age attuned to creatures in pronounced and popular ways; they nevertheless proved superfluous to the nascent political economist. This was not merely because sensitivity to animals belonged to the romantic sensibility of a poet like Thomson or a social critic like Shelley. Reindeer prove to be an effective litmus test in another regard: their biological and ecological identities, troublesomely ambiguous, presented a complexity to the observer attuned to civilization. Keith Thomas has noted how Lapland herders, like most pastoral peoples, marshalled a wide spectrum of knowledge simply in classifying the colors of reindeer. This kind of mastery, quite distinct from the fading lexicon of any eighteenth-century English agriculturalist, no doubt came to the attention of Malthus on his trip to see the "Lapfins." Was his great refusal to mention reindeer related to a similar deficit of comprehension?[33]

A firm believer in the civilizational model would attribute such elisions to the price of escape from an archaic past. But our thoughts on the matter need not stop there. The seemingly obvious transition from a herding to a pastoral economy, as anthropology has taught us, can throw up a barrage of complexity. In the former setting, as exhibited by eighteenth-century Lapps, reindeer were not passive objects roped into an exploitative relationship by human captors. In fact, the animals achieved an ambiguous status as "quasi-persons": under constant supervision and always in danger of defecting to the wild, they behaved not as "objects" of consumption but rather as laborers, servants, or quasi-slaves in an economic system. The Lapps had introduced a number of features drawn from presumably more advanced pastoral society, most important, the activity of milking reindeer. The complicated adaptations taking place before Malthus's eyes in fact presented a confusing mix of both nomadic and pastoral systems.[34]

On top of this, Malthus witnessed traces, everywhere present, of curious forms of reindeer agency. Significantly, the animals were in charge of their own reproduction, and their unclassifiable behavior—sometimes tame, sometimes wild—demanded a careful negotiation that the Lapps were willing to engage in and accommodate. No wonder that English literary conventions retained a hold on the magical nature of the reindeer, opening up a space for something that might not be already "known" in the continuous human evolution taking place alongside and with animals. The long list of resources claimed from the reindeer (as Olaus Magnus had documented in the sixteenth century) did not include mastery of the creature itself. A reindeer economy instead represented a kind of contractual arrangement, a relationship with a defined set of adaptations and concessions. The human–reindeer–nature connection was an eccentric demonstration of social and technological constraints, but not the kind that interested Malthus. That he failed to see them became obvious each time he longed for his gun.

7
Malthus and the Margins
Rethinking the Paradigm of Limited Resources

An extraordinarily revealing account of agrarian production in postcolonial settings—the later location of Malthusian margins—emerged from the work of Danish economist Ester Boserup. As an independent western researcher in a decolonizing world, Boserup enjoyed unusual freedom to theorize from the ground up. Living in India and traveling extensively in South-Saharan Africa, she "became skeptical of the prevailing development theory" and acquired a transformative appreciation for cultural factors shaping economic life. Combining field observation with intense comparative study, she came to understand a wide array of Indigenous methods and their impact on environments across Africa, Latin America, India, and China. During the 1950s and 1960s, while western policy experts fastened their attention on the connection between food and population growth, Boserup found herself disagreeing with many widely held assumptions. Most western researchers held the view that the potential for agricultural growth in postcolonial settings had been exhausted and that population control—a signifier for limited reproduction—was too slow in the Global South to prevent massive starvation. Boserup saw that more intensive strategies emerged from precisely the situations where increased numbers of inhabitants made them possible. She observed that in many cases, more people meant a greater per capita food supply.[1]

As Boserup recalled years later, she chose to swim against "the Malthusian currents . . . considered a sort of basic truth" at the time. It was clear to her that problems lay in the framework of analysis, which began with Malthus himself. "Malthus knew nothing about agriculture, people always died from hunger, and so on. That's why he only grasped a small corner of the total picture and blew it up," she pointed out in an interview in the early 1990s. Her first book, *The Conditions of Agricultural Growth: The Economics of Agrarian Change Under Population Pressure* (1965), demonstrated how Malthus's assumptions were backward in their logic. Increased population did not follow a rise in agricultural productivity; on the contrary, an increase in numbers of people usually led to greater rural productivity. Boserup methodically examined the varied circumstances in which human ingenuity evolved in relation to the environment and the available workforce. As a result of painstaking study, her conclusions were complex. "It is incorrect to say that I turned Malthus on his head," she noted, not out of modesty, but with a wish for accuracy. "That would have been just another simplification."[2]

Trained in comparative agrarian technology, Boserup focused on very specific methods of land use particular to each location. By looking at "the whole group of activities that are needed in a given system of agriculture," she paid attention to existing local knowledge of the terrain and its role in a larger picture of land use and allocation of labor power. She was not put off by digging sticks and ash fertilization. Greater intensity of cultivation, either by more frequent cropping or by techniques that fortified the environment, proved capable of increasing output in ways unanticipated by classical economists. By bringing into the picture "fallow land, pasture, hunting ground," and other pursuits besides cultivation, Boserup reintegrated the types of subsistence work that had been eliminated by modern agricultural methods. Judgments drawn from the European agricultural revolution, as well as the Enlightenment's stadial historians, appeared awkwardly irrelevant in environmental settings far from Scotland and England. Boserup respected the fact that every productive decision made by local inhabitants sprang from knowledge gained through generations of experience with the land and its idiosyncrasies. Highly different climatic conditions and terrain demanded their own custom-made arrangements, an approach later recognized as sustainable and beneficial to the global environment. Finally, all economic activities within a locale required careful consideration as integral contributions to the overall success of a village economy. Not surprisingly, Boserup observed and credited the myriad productive capacities of women in postcolonial spaces. Her next book would present groundbreaking arguments that paved the way for a re-evaluation of women's work across all forms of modern economic production, including at the heart of the European industrial revolution.[3]

Seizing the Malthusian bias by the throat, Boserup pointed to the inflexible models often imposed on divergent settings. Starting with land use and the modern western notion of a "permanent field," she systematically critiqued the insistence on a landscape comparable to that of European regions. Rather than seeing the characteristics of land as "immutable natural conditions" (meaning typical in all settings and untouched by human actions), Boserup embraced a more environmental view that recognized the presence and impact of humans on the entire landscape over the course of decades, centuries, and, in some instances, millennia. European colonial settlers failed to recognize forest and bushlands as serviceable long-fallow areas and simply "expropriated" such areas "for the use of European settlers or plantation companies or they were declared restricted forests where natives were not allowed to clear plots for cultivation." Such interference severed the important connection between land under tillage and areas set aside for other uses, creating a rift that would have negative consequences later in the histories of colonized nations.[4]

A tragic irony lay in the sequence of strategies imposed on colonial agricultural sites. Without reference to the ideologically charged term of the commons, Boserup explained how a "certain amount of uncultivated land" was set aside for the local population, "meant as an area for the collection of fuel and other materials and for the expansion of cultivation in case the population should increase." Here was the English model, *redivivus*, but in contexts obviously different from the English village of the past. The strategy proved harmful to Indigenous populations, who were then prevented from accessing lands that had once functioned in their "long-fallow rotations." The new restrictions ultimately led to the exhaustion of "native reserves," supplying further proof to neo-Malthusian western critics that native populations could not properly manage their own resources. "[C]omplaints of the natives eventually opened the eyes of many Europeans to the existence of the systems of long-fallow cultivation and these have since been the subject of studies by many economists, agronomists and social anthropologists," Boserup reported.[5]

Boserup discerned the disrespect for Indigenous populations that underlay many of these strategies, bolstered by neo-Malthusian assumptions. Her diplomatic approach aimed to present both sides of the argument. Yes, one might find examples of Indigenous failure to use land in the best manner (described as "spoiling the land"), but other instances demonstrated success, particularly in an age equipped with increasing knowledge of methods of land preservation. But in the eyes of policy experts, who overlooked evidence of productive adaptation, the Global South was stymied by what was then spoken of as "primitive agriculture."

> Malthus thought that the increase of population to a level beyond the carrying capacity of the land must lead to the elimination of the surplus population either by direct starvation or by other positive checks which in his opinion could be traced back to the insufficiency of food supplies as the basic cause. The new version of Malthusian theory is based on the idea that the increase of population leads to the destruction of the land; and that people, in order to avoid starvation, move to other land which is then destroyed in its turn. The neo-Malthusians collect all the evidence on the misuse of land and paint a picture of the world as a place where growing populations are pressing against a food potential which not only is incapable of increase but is even gradually reduced by the action of these growing populations.[6]

These pessimistic and often racist views lacked important information and failed to recognize the "practical implications" of strategies, including decisions having to do with intelligent applications of labor and the increase of land fertility by realizable means. Hunting, fishing, and gathering were discounted as productive uses of time. Repeatedly, assessments of what native populations were doing were skewed by the assumption that they were ignorant, lazy, and lodged in a primitive stage of development.[7]

As a conclusion to my reappraisal of Malthus's impact, I want to use the central insight of Boserup—the value of intensification understood in terms of local practices—to reopen a consideration of European agricultural history. As one historian recently acknowledged, successive periods of agricultural intensification across the European continent proved that feeding growing populations there "turned out to be more Boserupian in shape than Malthusian." Measures of agricultural output reveal that the relationship between food and population was moving in a direction opposed to a dire outcome in the early nineteenth century. "How this productivity breakthrough was actually achieved leaves plenty of room for research and debate," Peter M. Jones acknowledged in a recent study of the "Agricultural Enlightenment" of the period. As far as Malthus's predictions went, Jones noted that "[w]ith the benefit of hindsight it is apparent that his theory was in the process of being invalidated even as he was formulating it." Different approaches to the land made this possible: in Zeeland and East Flanders, small farmers "generate[d] high yields, albeit at the price of very high labour inputs." Jones expressed skepticism about the ability of peasant polyculturalists to act as "agents of modernization," yet he also construed the benefits of "stabilizing rural social structures" as part of the reason for their success. The diversity of components contributing to the food supply stands out as the most significant factor involved in the success of sustainable food production.[8]

If we turn back to early nineteenth-century Britain, there is no question that Malthus was wrong in warning of population outstripping food supply in the era of industrialization.[9] Wartime shortages in England caused dearth and high prices around 1800, but these emergency conditions only prompted the Board of Agriculture to advise (contrary to Malthus's desiderata) "the import of rice and the cultivation of substitute crops such as the potato." By 1813, a "bumper harvest" brought down grain prices "by more than half between January 1813 and December 1815." The main cause was "over-production," owing to the fact that farmers had placed "more land under wheat."[10]

This is not to say that concerns about the food supply vanished. The next year (1816–17) witnessed what has been called "the last subsistence crisis" in western Europe, largely a case of harvest failure due to "climatic irregularities" brought about by volcanic activity. These events only encouraged an expansion of potato cultivation, an ominous turn, given what we now know of the blight looming on the horizon. Paradoxically, as the allure of the Malthusian ratio and its integral components won over adherents, food supplies continued to negate his predictions. In fact, Europe would witness even greater increases of food production in the next half-century, given that the "extensification of agriculture had not yet run its course" and "[i]ntensification, moreover, was waiting in the wings."[11]

But by 1815, the conceptual toolkit of Malthusian analysis (not quite the Malthus zombie) had begun its corrosive career. Even as articulate critiques captured attention, a foreboding sense of rising pauperism preoccupied the public arena. A full-blown economic and social crisis rolled forward at the end of the Napoleonic Wars, as "the reduction of government expenditure aggravated a cyclical depression, while demobilization released thousands onto a glutted labour market." Cornerstones of the public sphere were suddenly subject to debate—the Corn Laws, monetary supplements for the poor, the advantages of free trade—shading into even larger issues of "the reform of Parliament or of society." The expansion of the pauper population had reached "especially shameful" proportions even by

1803, when Malthus published his much augmented edition of the *Essay.* From the late 1790s to the early 1820s, relief had skyrocketed to historically high levels.[12] Over the following years, the case for abolishing the Old Poor Laws won adherents, though not precisely along the lines of Malthus's vision of a favored rural sector. Ricardian economics had helped to persuade the public that capital accumulation placed elsewhere would eventually improve the lot of the poor. The general aim of poor law reform after 1815 was to remove direct support of the poor and to impose the necessary discipline of the market and the workhouse upon the "surplus population." Under the new system, "economic society was subjected to laws which were not human laws" but rather "the grim realities of Nature," as Karl Polanyi memorably put it.[13]

The early Malthus had presented human life as subject to unchanging natural laws and scientific truth; the later Malthus ultimately modulated this view to accommodate the rules of the market as established by the laws of political economy that had been built around him. He provided the reasoning for a picture of scarce resources and the natural competitive struggle necessary to survive, while other political economists supplied self-regulating markets, the overarching structure of order. The social system that emerged from this evolution rested on what were described as the laws of nature. Malthus's *Essay* provided a key bulwark of support for this construct, which represented a significant shift in attitude. As Gertrude Himmelfarb explained, "it was under the aegis of Malthus and Ricardo that political economy freed itself from its ties to moral philosophy and emerged in the guise of a natural science—a 'natural economics,' one might say, which professed to be nothing more than the application to the economy of the simple, inviolable laws of nature."[14] Such a strategy effectively removed economic life from "specific social, cultural, historical and moral factors."

Like his predecessor, Joseph Townsend, the notoriously candid critic of the Old Poor Law, Malthus had captured the imagination of powerful elites and shaped their anxieties according to a fictive world of bestial struggle in nature. By waving the flag of alimentary economics, he encouraged propertied Britons to imagine a human free-for-all, infused with assumptions about the laborers expected to do the work of production. Scarcity was intrinsic to the allocation of both labor and resources.[15]

Earnest Evangelicals, recognizing the need to revise the now obsolete optimism of William Paley, embraced the ideas of Malthus and popularized them with a religious twist. Endorsing his views, they made Malthus seem as if he were reading God's design for humanity. Thus, Malthus became understood as a devoted man of faith. In an "Age of Atonement," fulsomely captured by Boyd Hilton, Anglicans resuscitated a robust version of human depravity and placed it at the center of a tumultuous environment of social and economic struggle. Moral restraint, including sexual abstinence, played a central role in this drama. This was social identity writ small, engraved into the individual heart or, put another way, the "ecological trap to stimulate rational thought" that would ultimately distinguish "between the savage and the civilized." While the message resonated in the first half of the nineteenth century, later theologians and political economists together were forced to work hard to "repair the damage" wrought by Malthus's unconventional arguments. Even they were uncomfortable with the fact that "the dismal science's picture of the world seemed to suggest that . . . God was mad, bad, and dangerous." Their successful realignment can be traced forward through Gladstonian liberalism as part of the conscience that fueled Victorian economics through the end of the century.[16]

The moral arguments of Malthus, pointing to the natural indolence of the lowest categories of society, deflected attention from the crucial departure from Adam Smith accomplished by

Malthusians. As Gareth Stedman Jones emphasized in his trenchant historical analysis of poverty, Malthus achieved his argument through a sleight of hand, as he promoted a distinctly different view of the laborer than that of a former age. "Smith accepted as a truism that 'the demand for men, like that for any other commodity, necessarily regulates the production of men; quickens it when it goes too slowly and stops it when it goes too fast.' But this did not mean that the poor only worked when pushed by 'necessity.' " Smith was able to recognize that the laborer was capable of "natural talent" and feeling "the hope of bettering his condition." In fact, he believed that the "differences between the philosopher and the street porter were 'much less than we are aware of' and were, for the most part, the effect rather than the cause of the division of labour." While Malthus reiterated the vulgar view of the laboring classes as indolent, Smith "never employed the notion of 'indolence' in connection with the laboring poor—this he reserved for depictions of the landed classes and the established clergy," an irony written out of political economy. The power of categorical thinking, which operated along a continuum with racial categories, deflected attention from the originating sources of poverty. The reactionary decades after the French Revolution silenced a generation of critical voices. Not until the Irish Famine would public debate question these issues and then only in relation to the concept of property.[17]

The case of Ireland at mid-century provided the laboratory and test case of Malthusian concepts of labor and food, amplified by the crucial turn to free trade in grain. The stewardship of property, in this case, was far from exemplary. Ireland's great landlords consolidated ownership to an extreme degree and then turned over administration of the land to a parasitic class of middlemen. A system of subdivisions and short-term leases with ever-rising rents created a unique form of peasant immiseration. Landless laborers struggled to afford a pig or a cow on small plots of land, dividing their labor between wage work for landlords and their own tiny holdings, which yielded bare subsistence in the form of potatoes. When the potato blight of 1845 triggered the disastrous years of famine lasting until mid-century, the most notorious application of theory came to roost: that is, the British government's inaction in the face of catastrophic food shortages and starvation. Both Liberals and Tories had aligned their policies with liberal principles of free trade, so when government action finally came in the form of shipments of wheat at reduced prices, such aid did nothing to relieve the situation. "Cheaper corn could not help those on the bottom rung of the agricultural ladder . . . because they normally functioned outside the market economy, growing their subsistence and paying their rent with labor."[18]

The tightening vice of free trade principles coupled with the Malthusian principle of population made room for the rampant growth of racist views of the Irish. After decades of discussion of Malthus's ideas about the laborer's responsibility for his own condition, such assumptions slid easily into place. British publications purveyed images that rendered the Irish "indolent, improvident, alcoholic, ignorant, and superstitious," and, as *Punch* added, "the missing link between the gorilla and the Negro." Catastrophic famine, high mortality, and massive emigration appeared to vindicate the principle of population in the short run. Yet this historic moment of mass starvation had more to do with larger structures of power and their theoretical scaffolding than with the alleged behavior of peasants. It was now clear that a chief source of famine lay in Malthusian thinking, not the other way round.[19]

At the center of poverty and scarcity lay the entwined understandings of land stewardship and racial superiority in the British empire. As Thomas Holt showed in his study of the circulation of British power throughout the Atlantic world, land policy exposed key dynamics of domination in settings as different as Ireland, Jamaica, and India. Through the post-Famine debate that mobilized Irish radicals and British Liberals, including John Stuart Mill, property rights for disenfranchised peoples elsewhere emerged as the important factor in their economic survival. Mill's arguments in favor of Irish land reform, evident in his *Principles of Political Economy* and vocalized after his election to Parliament in 1865, rendered visible many aspects of Malthusian thinking that had been broadly accepted by landed interests. The early nineteenth-century political economists had enshrined absolute rights of private property, citing Adam Smith as their origin, but Mill repudiated this stance and argued that land stood as an exception to the rule. Calling the prevailing notion of property rights a "superstition" belonging to the English, Mill declared that the inhabitants of the land should be the determinants of how it was used, presumably for the benefit of all. In a direct reference to Malthus's "mighty feast," he asserted:

> No man made the land. It is the original inheritance of the whole species. Public reasons exist for its being appropriated. But if those reasons lost their force, the thing would be unjust. . . . [I]t is some hardship to be born into the world and to find all nature's gifts previously engrossed, and no place left for the new-comer. To reconcile people to this, after they have once admitted into their minds the idea that any moral rights belong to them as human beings, it will always be necessary to convince them that the exclusive appropriation is good for mankind on the whole, themselves included. But this is what no sane human being could be persuaded of,

> if, the relation between the landowner and the cultivator were the same everywhere as it is in Ireland.

This argument held radical potential not just for the future of Ireland but also for colonial possessions everywhere in the nineteenth century.[20]

The strange career of Malthusian theory should help us grasp the importance of the issue of property and land use in a global context. If we remind ourselves that "'property' was a concept that fired imaginations in the late eighteenth and early nineteenth century as never before," we can map colonial stewardship with its Malthusian assumptions across diverse landscapes. In examining land claims and Indigenous dispossession in the Caribbean and North America, Allan Greer pointed out how "William Blackstone's hyperbolic view of property as 'that sole and despotic dominion which one man claims and exercises over the external things of the world, in total exclusion of the right of any other individual in the universe,'" helped to erase the ambiguities of customary rights of land use inherited from the past. Malthusian assumptions rested on centuries, if not millennia, of food history that became condensed within a patriotic notion of "agricultural improvement" and land acquisition in North America, the Caribbean, and South Asia. This all-important act of condensation carried implicit assumptions about stewardship and the correct use of property. It is no coincidence that the debate over population and assistance from the Poor Laws of Britain occurred just as the British state aimed to establish clearer rights of ownership of agricultural land across its own global network. During Malthus's lifetime, "the setting of universal standards for the holding of property was one of the most important changes of the whole era."[21]

Property and land policy require the vantage point of deeper history encompassing centuries before the age of

Malthus. The threats posed by consolidation of land had been evident since the sixteenth century, as the demands of the woolen industry had paved the way for state support for enclosure. Where areas of manorial lands had passed into the hands of small landowners, a gradual erosion of their numbers intensified between 1688 and 1750, most notably, across "the best corn-growing regions." Indebtedness drove many small farmers to the brink and taxation added yet another burden they could hardly afford. "The engrossing of holdings proceeded apace and many merchants and town dwellers became [rural land] owners" in places like Buckinghamshire during that time. The classic conception of the agricultural revolution across the southern regions produced "a more recognisably modern conception of land as a basis for secure entitlements."[22]

For justifiable reasons, historians have focused on rural resistance to enclosure, seen as the vanguard of consciousness in a classic moment of economic transition. Yet as we reconsider the lasting impact of Malthus's ideas on the countryside, more needs to be said about those who survived the waves of social and economic winnowing through means other than those identified as improvement. Pockets of small farmers held out against the powerful encroachments of the emerging property rights regime. They were able to survive because they combined tillage with a host of other income-producing activities, a fact forgotten because our way of understanding this period of history causes us to overlook the variability of rural activity. Even as the age of classical political economy gathered strength and bolstered the view that liberal economic theory had won the day, areas outside the improvers' grasp had something to say about the ecological transitions taking place. A fresh look at the margins enables us to write a rural history according to "moral ecologies" of a different sort, relationships founded on alternative methods of extracting a living from the land.[23]

It is worth our while to revisit this terrain in all its variety as it competed with enclosure, especially as elite observers may not have registered the long-term significance of all there was to see. Detailed archival excavation by agricultural historians often presented a more complex picture of the rural past than was relayed by our simplified assumption about a shift to modern agriculture. Involved in a network of lesser crop activities carried on in the interstices of the market, rural producers tapped into many other plant and animal sources, creating a wide range of ancillary commodities, which often failed to register within the categories supplied by the state and improvers. Collectors of tithe at the local level might detect money-making in their neighborhood and uncover marginal sources of income from apple-harvesting, small-scale dairying, or woad- or madder-growing. As late as the 1880s and 1890s, such tensions became evident between the church and owners of "small peasant farms" in Wales. Booms and slumps in the economy, particularly at the end of the nineteenth century, exposed these activities to view, revealing how they could flourish during agricultural depressions. At other times, such marginal activities withered when local pressures altered the terms of access to land.[24]

These arrangements often developed in regions long accustomed to combining a variety of cottage industries with agricultural production. The fact that these activities remained largely unseen calls to mind the pattern of development outlined by James Scott in *Seeing Like a State* (1998): governmentality determined what rural activities mattered and even "what count[ed] as agriculture" in borderlands, wastes, and other marginal areas on the periphery. As Gillian G. Tan summarized this process, "improvement" aimed to bring about "organized nature, permanent settlements, maximized production, and social engineering."[25] In the eyes of the state, fully acknowledged crops might receive assistance and protection for the sake of industriousness, while monetary exchanges and profit occurring outside endorsed employments would attract less supportive forms of investigation. Local records reveal just how acutely rural people registered awareness of such policies and resisted their control.[26]

Special characteristics distinguished this world of the margins from more conventional agrarian life: people pursuing alternative activities drew from varied and sometimes unauthorized stores of knowledge, including practical experience, and sought to create their own distinct markets. An analogy today might be the start-up economy, with its openness to self-taught expertise, along with new risks, including unknown potential markets. Their main asset was self-employment and unlimited hours of self-imposed labor that could pivot quickly, adapting to demands that shifted from year to year. But the analogy holds true for only so long, because the social spectrum populating rural margins in the early modern period was much broader than the bit economy today. Time and again, foods like potatoes, beans, onions, hops, flax, herbs of all kinds, and turnips produced income for smallholders, whose combined activities resembled gardening on a slightly larger scale. Seventeenth-century writers on agriculture had reflected on the productivity and success of deep-digging small crops on small pieces of ground, and several wondered if "dividing our lands into very small farms for the ease both of oversight and amendment" promised a better outcome than large-scale grain agriculture. "The firm knowledge that husbandmen could live on smaller units of land, using gardening methods" persisted as a principle of popular knowledge from the time of the Civil War, surfacing in print periodically as tracts dating from the earlier decades were reprinted. Such a close relationship with the environment and its uses for "special crops" would recede from view during periods of land consolidation, only to return for consideration during later agricultural recessions.[27]

Charting the food security of the nation through the price of grain represents a market-oriented, partial, and even prejudicial view of what sustained people living on the land. Measurements have usually been urban oriented, predicated on continual rural depopulation, and they are therefore likely to identify age-old "traditional" activities as desperate measures rather than active choices. With access to land, as food historians have long shown, rural people relied on household crops like potatoes, leeks, and fruit from orchards, which proved valuable without being tremendously profitable, and legumes and pottage provided numerous meals without ever registering as market purchases related to the price of wheat. We do know that local interest in botanical information from all over the world merged with customs of scouring hedgerows for bounty and experimenting with plant life for taste and even appetite suppression. "Harnessing local wisdom from the past" was popular in the seventeenth and eighteenth centuries as well as today; the Royal Society sponsored many such trials with plants that promised to feed people in "scarce times." These instances of elite excitement over eccentric knowledge drew evidence from steadily retreating marginal lands, where a wide variety of wild plants had once been found.[28]

Modern-day studies of "famine foods" point out the obstacle of using that very term. Many instances of such food sources, pressed into service during times of need, are actually familiar "marginally used species" that "provide excellent sources of protein, minerals and vitamins" even under normal circumstances. Food classifications have always been subject to modification, as we know from the current world of "ancient grains" and plant milks. The occurrence of extreme weather in the past brought to the fore strategies that depended on adaptable plants, which only small farmers and cottagers could turn to quickly and know how to grow and use. In present-day markets, such food sources stand a chance of establishing a commodity chain that produces profit and attracts publicity. But in the eighteenth century, such foods remained under the radar, so to speak, and often out of widespread market activity. Occasionally, tithe collectors called attention to profit-making in the margins, detectable today in the archives. One must look closely (and optimistically) to see the modulation of foodways responding to shortages and other pressures.[29]

Even while grain-growing remains the gold standard of agricultural modernization in surveys of European history, we don't have to view the potential of a variegated countryside as a counterfactual argument unworthy of attention. After all, alternative paths favoring the "peasant polyculturalist" presented a viable economic model across the Channel in France. Such an arrangement inserted itself into critical narratives of persistent regional identities linked to ecologies and climatic conditions, peasant-style independence, and popular insurrection. On a trip to France in the early 1790s, agrarian writer Arthur Young commented that he would not have imagined such a system, "spread with a sort of cultivation I had never seen before, a mixture of vineyard[,] . . . garden, and corn. A piece of wheat; a scrap of lucerne; a patch of clover or vetches; a bit of vines; with cherry, and other fruit-trees scattered among all, and the whole cultivated with the spade." Were the "scrap" and scatter meant to disparage the polymorphous nature of the homestead? Alexis de Tocqueville would take note of Young's amazement at "the infinite subdivision of land among the peasantry" and see it as evidence of the uniquely French basis for attachment to rights (and revolt) in rural districts. No such subdivision remained anywhere else by this point, according to de Tocqueville. Property consolidation—the march of enclosure familiar to so many students of history—was even by then part of the convention, what Engels would call "the corrosive logic" of property itself.[30]

Across Europe, a delicate and largely invisible negotiation had taken place between a dominant culture of grain-growing and "alternative agriculture." As Joan Thirsk explained in her study of the phenomenon in England, "Certainly no one in the seventeenth century used the term," but at times contemporaries "came close to describing it as agricultural diversification." During periods when land was plentiful and labor was in short supply, grain agriculture wasn't lucrative enough to support the occupants of smaller tracts of land. Such people seldom left a record of quotidian assessments of their situation, captured in the words of a French peasant: "it profits us nothing to grow grain." Local alternatives were known to generate profitable commodities and thus sporadic income: harvesting food from vines, trees, forests, and animals enabled smallholders to take other products to the market. Available pastures presented a worthwhile horizon of potential: cows, goats, sheep, and rabbits figured as food and commercial resources. Many marginal industrial crops, such as woad and madder, had potential for larger-scale enterprise. The Civil War period in England provided a moment when spatial distinctions and land use acquired both productive and political meaning, as in the case of "chalk" and "cheese" in the "great stretch of chalk downland, from the South Downs in the east, through Salisbury Plain, to the Dorset Downs in the west." Autonomy in economic pursuits allied with political affiliations, in this case, as opposition to royalism.[31]

A host of trades based on commodities drawn from pastoral and wooded hinterlands throughout Europe—wool, animal skins, and well-crafted dairy products, to name just a few—represented important sources of commercial wealth and commanded respect. Though evidence may not be available to show this, such suppliers could have carried on food-producing activities as part of a mixed economic strategy. Certain elements of these economies of the margins, like furs and precious metals, constituted commodities signaling power and prestige. Examples could be found along the forests and streams of Scandinavia: advertised in the fashionable beaver hats and upmarket marten pelts of Netherlandish portraiture, urban elites of Renaissance Europe craved such resources. Tradesmen drew from a wide spectrum of products that provided lucrative sources of income to inhabitants of borderlands and margins. Malthus was unaware that he brought a limited measure to Scandinavia, where he searched for models familiar to his British eye. The first aim of his theory, the procurement of foodstuffs, imposed its own hierarchies on rural diversity, leaving much of value outside the purview of an up-and-coming English political economist. In more modern times, such commodities acquired a markedly exotic and even primitive aura colored by ever-shifting judgments rendered by the metropole and powerful commercial states.[32]

Microhistories of resistance to enclosure, such as Steve Hindle's portrait of the forested areas of Geddington Chase, show how marginal communities found ways around the supposed lockstep march to modernized forms of property regulation. In the early modern period, the Geddington poor who accepted loaves of bread as charitable gifts needed to demonstrate "deference and respectability" as part of the exchange. Those who fell into this category were stigmatized as "bread people." The endowed charity, with its "monopolistic pretensions of the trustees and parish officers," ensured that the local population would use every available stopgap resource in order to avoid dealing with the alternatives of the parish. Hindle's study documented how the term "economy of makeshifts" failed to take account of "the highly diversified economies of those parts of England which failed to conform to the arable regime of sheep-corn country." A better description, he suggested, would be "an 'economy of diversified resources,' an economy whose products arrived just as regularly and seasonally, if less visibly in the historical record, as corn, sheep and cattle."[33]

Ecologically attuned history requires a reorientation of perspective. Early studies of enclosure included many suggestive insights into the unexpectedly large number of smallholders who retained some use of the commons through the eighteenth century. Describing them "reluctantly, but necessarily" as peasants, Jeanette Neeson painted them as independent agents within a larger network of economic relationships. "In reality, on the ground, the range of common produce was magnificently broad, the uses to which it was put were minutely varied, and the defence of local practice was determined and often successful." These rural inhabitants occupied a social spectrum of considerable breadth ranging from simply poor to modestly prosperous. Their diversity therefore acts as a vivid indicator of the often overlooked fact that rural survival was intimately related to environment, which required attention to specific features of the land shaped by the action of climate and social change. Within this context, those who forged precarious economic lives "are better understood disaggregated" from the larger histories of environment and land use. The lived experiences of those who forged paths apart from modernized agriculture may produce their own distinct environmental history.[34]

Perhaps no one will ever slay the "Malthus zombie," which enables simple equations to replace careful and complex consideration of the dynamic interplay of land, nature, and human survival. But seeing Malthus the author more clearly, as a narrow theorist who mobilized a narrow framework for British economic strategies and social categories, may offer a way of undercutting his power. While his intellectual life drew inspiration from the formative influences of the British Enlightenment, he inaugurated a new sensibility that marked the century that followed him. Malthus introduced a combative repudiation of an era of social responsibility that had characterized preindustrial England. His neat negative coupling of food and population forced the discussion of a just and flourishing society into a controlled laboratory, isolated from the complex array of factors understood to be part of food production and the interdependent relationships that made up the actual social world of 1798. While his arithmetical formula appealed to a society enamored with reason and scientific method, such simplification obscured the real workings of property and power across time and space.

Abbreviations

BLMC	British Library Manuscripts Collection
DF	Edward Gibbon, *The History of the Decline and Fall of the Roman Empire* (Basel, 1787–89)
DNB	*Oxford Dictionary of National Biography*
Essay (1798)	*Essay on the Principle of Population* (Harmondsworth: Penguin, 1982)
Essay (1803)	*Essay on the Principle of Population: The 1803 Edition*, ed. Shannon C. Stimson (New Haven: Yale University Press, 2018)
HA	William Robertson, *History of America* (London, 1777)
JCOL	Jesus College Old Library, Cambridge University
P&P	*Past and Present*
TD	*Travel Diaries of Thomas Robert Malthus*, ed. Patricia James (Cambridge: Cambridge University Press, 1966)
UP	*T. R. Malthus: The Unpublished Papers in the Collection of Kanto Gakuen University*, ed. John Pullen and Trevor Hughes (Cambridge: Cambridge University Press, 1997)

Notes

1
Immortal Malthus

1. For a helpful discussion of the emergence of factors contributing to food deserts, see Michaela DeSoucey, *Contested Tastes: Fois Gras and the Politics of Food* (Princeton: Princeton University Press, 2016); Raj Patel, *Stuffed and Starved: The Hidden Battle for the World Food System* (New York: Melville House, 2012); Dipesh Chakrabarty, *The Climate of History in a Planetary Age*, rev. ed. (Chicago: University of Chicago Press, 2021).

2. *Essay on the Principle of Population* (London: J. Johnson, 1798; Harmondsworth: Penguin, 1982), 70, 74–77. Citations to the first *Essay* refer to the Penguin edition throughout.

3. Malthus used this phrase three times in three paragraphs within the preface to the second edition of the *Essay.*

4. John Bohstedt, *The Politics of Provisions: Food Riots, Moral Economy, and Market Transition in England, c. 1550–1850* (Burlington, VT: Ashgate, 2010); Michael Braddick and John Walter, eds., *Negotiating Power in Early Modern England* (Cambridge: Cambridge University Press, 2001); Buchanan Sharp, *Famine and Scarcity in Late Medieval and Early Modern England: The Regulation of Grain Marketing, 1256–1631* (Cambridge: Cambridge University Press, 2016).

5. On the Poor Laws, see J. M. Poynter, *Society and Pauperism: English Ideas on Poor Relief, 1795–1834* (Melbourne: Melbourne University Press, 1969), still not superseded; for a generous and insightful survey of Malthus's ideas across two centuries of discussion, see Robert J. Mayhew, *Malthus: The Life and Legacies of an Untimely Prophet* (Cambridge, MA: Harvard University Press, 2014); on colonial famine and economic policy, see Mike Davis, *Late Victorian Holocausts: El Niño and the Making of the Third World* (London: Verso, 2001).

6. Recent scholars have come to realize that trade in grain acted as an important driver of British history since the Middle Ages. See Steve Hindle and Jane Humphries, "Feeding the Masses: Plenty and Want and the Distribution of Food and Drink in Historical Perspective," *Economic History Review*, New Series 61, no. S1 (2008): 1–4 and the essays that follow; see also Frank Trentmann, *Free Trade Nation: Commerce, Consumption, and Civil Society in Modern Britain* (Oxford: Oxford University Press, 2008), and most recently, James Stafford, *The Case of Ireland: Commerce, Empire, and the European Order, 1750–1848* (Cambridge: Cambridge University Press, 2022).

7. Eric B. Ross, *The Malthus Factor: Poverty, Politics, and Population in Capitalist Development* (New York: Zed Books, 1998), 32–34, 60.

8. Josué de Castro, *The Geography of Hunger* (Boston: Little, Brown, 1952), quoted in Alex de Waal, *Mass Starvation: The History and Future of Famine* (Cambridge: Polity Press, 2018), 47; Amartya Sen, *Poverty and Famines: An Essay on Entitlement and Deprivation* (Oxford: Clarendon Press, 1981), 1.

9. De Waal, *Mass Starvation*, 37, 39.

10. De Waal, *Mass Starvation*, 45.

11. D. L. LeMahieu, "Malthus and the Theology of Scarcity," *Journal of the History of Ideas* 40, no. 3 (1979): 467–474; J. M. Pullen, "Malthus' Theological Ideas and Their Influence on His Principle of Population," *History of Political Economy* 13, no. 1 (1981): 39–54; A. M. C. Waterman, *Revolution, Economics, and Religion: Christian Political Economy, 1798–1833* (Cambridge: Cambridge University Press, 1991).

12. R. L. Meek, "Malthus—Yesterday and Today," in *Thomas Robert Malthus: Critical Assessments*, ed. John Cunningham Wood (London: Croom Helm, 1986), vol. 1, 175–197; Donald Winch, *Riches and Poverty: An Intellectual History of Political Economy in Britain, 1750–1834* (Cambridge: Cambridge University Press, 1996); Donald Winch, "Mr. Gradgrind and Jerusalem," in *Economy, Polity, and Society: British Intellectual History, 1750–1950*, ed. Stefan Collini et al. (Cambridge: Cambridge University Press, 2000), 243–266; and Winch's contribution to the Past Masters series, *Malthus* (Oxford: Oxford University Press, 1987).

13. Mayhew, *Malthus;* Brian Cooper, *Family Fictions and Family Facts: Harriet Martineau, Adolphe Quetelet, and the Population Question in England, 1798–1859* (London: Routledge, 2007); Catherine Gallagher, *The Body Economic: Life, Death, and Sensation in Political Economy and the Victorian Novel* (Princeton: Princeton University Press, 2006) and "The Body Versus the Social Body in the Works of Thomas Malthus and Henry Mayhew," in *The Making of the Modern Body*, ed. Catherine Gallagher and Thomas Laqueur (Berkeley: University of California Press, 1987), 83–106; Brian Dolan, ed., *Malthus, Medicine, and Morality: 'Malthusianism' After 1798* (Amsterdam: Rodopi, 2000).

14. Murray Milgate and Shannon C. Stimson, *After Adam Smith: A Century of Transformation in Politics and Political Economy* (Princeton: Princeton University Press, 2009); Mark Skousen, *The Making of Modern Economics: The Lives and Ideas of the Great Thinkers,* 2nd ed. (Armonk, NY: M. E. Sharpe, 2009).

15. Gail Bederman, "Sex, Scandal, Satire, and Population in 1798: Revisiting Malthus's First *Essay,*" *Journal of British Studies* 47 (2008): 768–795; Lisa Forman Cody, "The Politics of Illegitimacy in an Age of Reform: Women, Reproduction, and Political Economy in England's New Poor Law of 1834," *Journal of Women's History* 11, no. 4 (2000): 131–156; Mervyn Nicholson, "The Eleventh Commandment: Sex and Spirit in Wollstonecraft and Malthus," *Journal of the History of Ideas* 51, no. 3 (1990): 406.

16. Alison Bashford and Joyce Chaplin, *The New Worlds of Thomas Robert Malthus: Rereading the Principle of Population* (Princeton: Princeton University Press, 2016); Robert J. Mayhew, ed., *New Perspectives on Malthus* (Cambridge: Cambridge University Press, 2016); Alison Bashford, Duncan Kelly, and Shailaja Fennell, eds., "Malthusian Moments: Introduction," *Historical Journal* 63, no. 1 (2020).

17. Fredrik Albritton Jonsson, "The Origins of Cornucopianism: A Preliminary Genealogy," *Critical Historical Studies* 1, no. 1 (2014), 151–168.

18. Leonard Schwarz, "Custom, Wages, and Workload During Industrialization," *P&P* 197 (2007): 143–175. The expression "rules of the game" is drawn from Eric Hobsbawm's essay on the same subject, "Custom, Wages, and Work-Load in Nineteenth-Century Industry," originally published in *Essays in Labour History in Memory of G. D. H. Cole,* ed. Asa Briggs and John Saville (London: Macmillan, 1960), 113–139.

19. Mayhew, *Malthus,* 133; for "definite ambivalence," see Poynter, *Society and Pauperism,* 110; Davis, *Late Victorian Holocausts.*

20. BLMC, Macintosh Papers (3rd series), vol. 22 A (f. 142).

21. Joan Thirsk, "Reply [to Jan de Vries]," following "Policies for Retrenchment in Seventeenth-Century Europe: A Review Article," *Comparative Studies in Society and History* 22, no. 4 (1980): 638; Peter M. Jones, *Agricultural Enlightenment: Knowledge, Technology, and Nature, 1750–1840* (Oxford: Oxford University Press, 2016), 224. For a clear example of loyalty to Malthus's framework of analysis, see R. I. Woods, "Review Article: Immortal Malthus," *Journal of Historical Geography* 14, no. 3 (1988): 298–300.

22. Thirsk, "Policies for Retrenchment," 626–633.

23. Robert Bartlett, "Heartland and Border: The Mental and Physical Geography of Medieval Europe," in *Power and Identity in the Middle Ages: Essays in Memory of Rees Davies,* ed. Huw Pryce and John Watts (Oxford: Oxford University Press, 2007), 31.

24. See *Marx and Engels on Malthus,* ed. Ronald L. Meek (London: Lawrence and Wishart, 1953); David Harvey, *Spaces of Capital: Towards a Critical Geography* (New York: Routledge, 2001), 61.

25. Eric J. Hobsbawm, *Industry and Empire* (Harmondsworth: Penguin, 1969), 98; R. A. Houston, ed. *Peasant Petitions* (New York: Palgrave Macmillan, 2014), especially chap. 1, "'Unimportant Minorities': The Landholding Peasantry of Britain and Ireland, c. 1600–1850," 3–4.

26. Harvey, *Spaces of Capital*, 222–223.

2
Nature's Mighty Feast

1. Boyd Hilton, *The Age of Atonement: The Influence of Evangelicalism on Social and Economic Thought, 1785–1865* (Oxford: Oxford University Press, 1988); Donald Winch, *Riches and Poverty: An Intellectual History of Political Economy in Britain, 1750–1834* (Cambridge: Cambridge University Press, 1996).

2. This observation was made by Gertrude Himmelfarb, *The Idea of Poverty* (New York: Knopf, 1984), 101; a more critical and informed analysis can be found in Gareth Stedman Jones, *An End to Poverty? A Historical Debate* (New York: Columbia University Press, 2004); Philipp Lepenies, "Of Goats and Dogs: Joseph Townsend and the Idealisation of Markets—A Decisive Episode in the History of Economics," *Cambridge Journal of Economics* 38, no. 2 (2014): 447–457; Hilton, *Age of Atonement*, 50.

3. Stedman Jones, *An End to Poverty?* chaps. 1–2; Emma Rothschild, *Economic Sentiments: Adam Smith, Condorcet, and the Enlightenment* (Cambridge, MA: Harvard University Press, 2001); Istvan Hont and Michael Ignatieff, eds., *Wealth and Virtue: The Shaping of Political Economy in the Scottish Enlightenment* (Cambridge: Cambridge University Press, 1983).

4. The "trio" included the queen, the king's mother, Princess Augusta, and the Earl of Bute, all of whom advanced the cause of botany and allied sciences at home and abroad. David Elliston Allen, *The Naturalist in Britain: A Social History* (Princeton: Princeton University Press, 1976), 27, 35, 37–38; for a discussion of Malthus's aspiration to be a natural philosopher, see Deborah Valenze, "The Tortoise and the Hare: Thomas Robert Malthus as Natural Philosopher," in *An Essay on the Principle of Population: The 1803 Edition*, ed. Shannon C. Stimson (New Haven: Yale University Press, 2018), 497–515.

5. Patricia James, *Population Malthus: His Life and Times* (London: Routledge, 1979), 5–13; Daniel Malthus to Jean-Jacques Rousseau, February 26, 1766. http://www.e-enlightenment.com.ezproxy.cul.columbia.edu/item/rousjeVF0280331a1c/?letters=corr&s=malthdanie023323&r=8, accessed February 13, 2022. See also Christopher Brooke, "Robert Malthus, Rousseauist," *Historical Journal* 63, no. 1 (2020): 15–31.

6. Henrietta Malthus was Daniel Malthus's second cousin; her sister's daughter, Georgina, would marry her eldest son, Sydenham. The Malthus,

Graham, and Dalton families intermarried several times over the course of a century. T. R. Malthus would marry his cousin, Harriet Eckersall, a descendant of the Dalton family. In addition to their seven children, the Malthus household also included an orphaned niece, Jane Dalton. James, *Population Malthus,* 9–15.

7. Daniel's encounter with Rousseau took place in the spring of 1764 in Môtiers-Travers; James, *Population Malthus,* 10–12; Daniel Malthus to Jean-Jacques Rousseau, January 16, 1766: http://www.e-enlightenment.com.ezproxy.cul.columbia.edu/item/rousjeVF0280194a1c; Daniel Malthus to Jean-Jacques Rousseau, January 16, 1766: http://www.e-enlightenment.com.ezproxy.cul.columbia.edu/item/rousjeVF0280194a1c/?letters=corr&s=malthdanie023323&r=2; Daniel Malthus to Jean-Jacques Rousseau, February 26, 1766. http://www.e-enlightenment.com.ezproxy.cul.columbia.edu/item/rousjeVF0280331a1c/?letters=corr&s=malthdanie023323&r=8, accessed February 13, 2022.

8. In June 1766, the family traveled to Derbyshire and botanized with Rousseau; it is unlikely that the baby traveled with them. James, *Population Malthus,* 11–12. On Malthus's disability, 2–3. James adds that she was "surprised to find so little evidence of Malthus's deformity" in the records of his life.

9. John Aitken, *Principles of Midwifery, or puerperal medicine,* 2nd ed. (Edinburgh, 1785), 202–203; Nicolas Andry de Bois-Regard, *Orthopaedia: or, the art of correcting and preventing deformities in children,* 2 vols. (London, [1743]), 1: 101–103.

10. James, *Population Malthus,* 13, 39. Daniel Malthus, according to his granddaughter, "was cold and reserved in his own family, except towards his eldest daughter, of whom he was very fond, and his youngest son [*sic*], whose talents probably early attracted his attention" (13).

11. James, *Population Malthus,* 18–19; David Oakleaf, "Graves, Richard (1715–1804), writer and translator," *DNB* (2004), accessed April 15, 2021. https://www-oxforddnb-com.ezproxy.cul.columbia.edu/view/10.1093/ref:odnb/9780198614128.001.0001/odnb-9780198614128-e-11313.

12. David Oakleaf, "Graves, Richard (1715–1804), writer and translator," *DNB* (2004), accessed April 15, 2021. https://www-oxforddnb-com.ezproxy.cul.columbia.edu/view/10.1093/ref:odnb/9780198614128.001.0001/odnb-9780198614128-e-11313. Graves became a friend of the Malthus family and composed an interesting poetic portrait of the parents, reproduced in James, *Population Malthus,* 15–16. Malthus's adoption of passages of Townsend's *Dissertation* and his *Travels Through Spain* suggest that Marx had a point; see Lepenies, "Of Goats and Dogs," 451–454; Oakleaf, "Graves."

13. Wakefield, *Memoirs of the Life of Gilbert Wakefield, B.A.* (London, 1792), 23–24; Malthus's mother, revealingly, did not wish for her son to go to university at all. The reasons for this are never stated but likely had to do with Robert's physical disability. Daniel Malthus to Malthus, April 21, 1784, *UP* 1: 25.

14. Richard Graves to Daniel Malthus, August 10, [1780?]; Richard Graves to Daniel Malthus, October 20, 1780, in *UP*, 1: 4–7; James, *Population Malthus*, 22; for Wakefield's stance as a pacifist during the Revolutionary decade, see Gilbert Wakefield, *The Spirit of Christianity compared with the Spirit of the Times in Great Britain* (London, 1794). Malthus had little contact with Wakefield during the last decade of Wakefield's life, and Otter's "Memoir of Robert Malthus" comments at length on the fact that "there seems to have been no great community of sentiment or opinion between" Malthus and Wakefield (xxiii–xxv).

15. In the more diplomatic words of Murray Milgate and Shannon C. Stimson, "Though not a consummate theorist, Malthus was consistently a reactive and critical thinker, and throughout his life the work of Smith remained vital and transformative to his enterprise." *After Adam Smith: A Century of Transformation in Politics and Political Economy* (Princeton: Princeton University Press, 2009), 122; D. L. LeMahieu, "Malthus and the Theology of Scarcity," *Journal of the History of Ideas* 40, no. 3 (1979): 467–474; LeMahieu, *The Mind of William Paley* (Lincoln: University of Nebraska Press, 1976), 117–122.

16. William Empson, "Life, Writings, and Character of Mr. Malthus," *Edinburgh Review* 64, no. 130 (January 1837), 496.

17. Malthus to Daniel Malthus, Cambridge, November 14, 1784, *UP*, 1: 29; Daniel Malthus to Malthus, December 19, 1785, *UP*, 1: 36; Malthus to Daniel Malthus, February 11, 1786, *UP*, 1: 41–42.

18. Malthus to Daniel Malthus, April 19, 1786, *UP*, 1: 47–48; LeMahieu, *The Mind of William Paley*, chap. 1.

19. Lady Theresa Lewis, ed., *Extracts of the Journals and Correspondence of Miss Berry* (3 vols., London, 1865), 2: 475, quoted in James, *Population Malthus*, 3; Harriet Martineau, *Autobiography*, 2nd ed. (3 vols., London, 1877), 1: 327–328, quoted in James, *Population Malthus*, 3; Maria Edgeworth to Mrs. Edgeworth, January 23, 1822, written while a guest at the Malthus home near the East India College; "Malthus' diary of a tour of the Lake District" in *UP*, 2: 29; see also 49.

20. The editors note that such slashes probably indicated pause marks but seem to think these indicated Malthus's deftness and care in the delivery of his sermons. *UP*, 2: 1.

21. Empson, "Life," 481; LeMahieu, "Malthus and the Theology of Scarcity"; J. M. Pullen, "Malthus' Theological Ideas and Their Influence on His Principle of Population," *History of Political Economy* 13 (1981): 39–54; Hilton, *Age of Atonement*, 49ff.

22. James, *Population Malthus*, 55.

23. Bederman, "Sex, Scandal, Satire, and Population in 1798: Revisiting Malthus's First *Essay*," *Journal of British Studies* 47 (2008): 778; see also Daniel Malthus to Malthus, April 14, [1796], in which he adds to the conclusion of

his letter, "I am sure [publishing your pamphlet] will never do you discredit, tho' I can not answer that it will get you a Deanery," *UP,* 1: 63; Daniel Malthus to Malthus, April 14, [1796], *UP,* 1:62.

24. Tim Fulford, "Apocalyptic Economics and Prophetic Politics: Radical and Romantic Responses to Malthus and Burke," *Studies in Romanticism* 40, no. 3 (2001): 345–368; Frank Prochaska, "English State Trials in the 1790s: A Case Study," *Journal of British Studies* 13 (1973): 64.

25. Prochaska, "English State Trials," 64; Otter, "Memoir of Robert Malthus," comments that the "natural good sense" of Malthus "happily protected him" from the "dangers" of contact with such men as Wakefield; T. R. Malthus, *Principles of Political Economy,* 2nd ed. (London 1836; New York: Augustus M. Kelley, 1951), xxiii-xxv.

26. Frances Ferguson, "Recent Studies in the Restoration and Eighteenth Century," *Studies in English Literature, 1500–1900* 54, no. 3 (2014): 730–731. See also Kenneth R. Johnston, *Unusual Suspects: Pitt's Reign of Alarm and the Lost Generation of the 1790s* (Oxford: Oxford University Press, 2013).

27. Edmund Burke, *Thoughts and Details on Scarcity, originally presented to the Right Hon. William Pitt, in the month of November, 1795* (London, 1800), vii, 2–3; Fulford, "Apocalyptic Economics," 346–352.

28. On the theoretical point of fitness within disability studies, see Rosemarie Thompson, "Misfits: A Feminist Materialist Concept," *Hypatia* 26, no. 3 (2011): 591–609; James, *Population Malthus,* 102; Gail Bederman, "Sex, Scandal, Satire, and Population," 768–795; Joan Thirsk, "Younger Sons in the Seventeenth Century," in *The Rural Economy of England: Collected Essays* (London: Hambledon, 1984), 338–339; Daniel's involvement is evident from the correspondence: for example, "There is no doubt you might have got it printed, there is still time to do it, & I shou'd be very willing to bear you harmless." He added, "I wish you had call'd upon your old friend Mr Wakefield." Daniel Malthus to Malthus, April 14, [1796], *UP,* 1: 62.

29. Bederman, "Sex, Scandal, Satire, and Population," 772; James, *Population Malthus,* 102.

30. E. A. Wrigley, "Malthus's Model of a Pre-Industrial Economy," in *Malthus Past and Present,* ed. J. Dupâquier, A. Fauve-Chamoux, and E. Grebenik (London: Academic Press, 1983), 114.

31. Fulford, "Apocalyptic Economics," 349; Marilyn Gaull, "Malthus on the Road to Excess," in *1798 The Year of the Lyrical Ballads,* ed. R. Cronin (London: Palgrave Macmillan, 1998), 93–94.

32. James, *Population Malthus,* 39; as Malthus had argued in his unpublished essay "The Crisis," Paley's *Principles of Moral and Political Philosophy* (1785) held an incorrect view of precisely when a society could claim to be happy with regard to population. Once the number of people in a nation was large, then happiness must be in the past, he believed. James, *Population Malthus,* 52.

33. Bederman, "Sex, Scandal, Satire, and Population"; James, *Population Malthus,* 102.

34. William Godwin, *An Enquiry concerning Political Justice* (London, 1793), 2: 871–872.

35. Godwin also discussed the incapability of present-day reason to imagine the inventive ways that subsistence might be satisfied in the future. *Political Justice,* 2: 861–872.

36. On the conventions of examinations at Cambridge in the era of Paley and Malthus, see LeMahieu, *The Mind of William Paley,* 6–8; see also Charles Henry Cooper, *Annals of Cambridge,* 5 vols. (Cambridge, 1852), vol. 4; Christopher Wordsworth, *Scholae Academicae: Some Account of the Studies at the English Universities in the Eighteenth Century* (Cambridge: The University Press, 1877), 78–81.

37. *An Essay on the Principle of Population: The 1803 Edition,* ed. Shannon C. Stimson (New Haven: Yale University Press, 2018), 409.

38. Paley, *Natural Theology,* quoted in LeMahieu, *The Mind of William Paley,* 82–83.

39. Milgate and Stimson, *After Adam Smith,* 129–130; see Townsend's *A Journey through Spain in the years 1786 and 1787,* 3 vols. (London, 1791), chap. 5.

40. Stedman Jones, *An End to Poverty?* 99. See also A. M. C. Waterman, *Revolution, Economics, and Religion: Christian Political Economy, 1798–1833* (Cambridge: Cambridge University Press, 1991), 106–112.

41. I owe these last points to Penny Ismay and to Stedman Jones, *An End to Poverty?* 107. See also LeMahieu, "Malthus and the Theology of Scarcity," 470.

42. *Essay on the Principle of Population* (1798; Harmondsworth: Penguin, 1982), 118–119.

43. *Essay* (1803), 425.

44. "Malthus' Diary of a Tour of the Lake District" makes this clear. *UP,* 2: 2–55. The Malthus library is notably lacking in theological texts; it includes two volumes of Paley's works, dated 1825 and 1828; Robert Wallace, *Dissertation on the Numbers of Mankind in Ancient and Modern Times* (Edinburgh, 1753), table on 4.

45. *Essay* (1798), 94, 98; E. A. Wrigley and Richard Smith, "Malthus and the Poor Law," *Historical Journal* 63, no. 1 (2020): 33–62.

46. Kenneth Curry, ed., *New Letters of Robert Southey,* 2 vols. (New York: Columbia University Press, 1965), 1: 326–327, 357, quoted in James, *Population Malthus,* 103, 111; "Mr. Malthus" quoted in Winch, *Riches and Poverty,* 294.

47. Empson, "Life," 472.

48. Letter from William Godwin to Thomas Robert Malthus, August 15, 1798, in *The Letters of William Godwin,* vol. 2, *1798–1805,* ed. Pamela Clemit, Oxford Scholarly Editions Online (March 2015), DOI: 10.1093/

actrade/9780199562626.book.1; letter from Malthus to Godwin, August 20, 1798, cited in James, *Population Malthus*, 68.

49. Dan LeMahieu, "Malthus and the Theology of Scarcity," 469.

50. William Otter, "Memoir of Robert Malthus," xxxi; the student's recollection comes from John Venn, quoted in James, *Population Malthus*, 323; Empson, "Life," 486.

51. These points are outlined in Bederman, "Sex, Scandal, Satire, and Population," 779.

52. *Essay* (1803), 417–418. Emphasis mine. In the original, Malthus underscored "right."

53. Margaret R. Somers and Fred Block, "From Poverty to Perversity: Ideas, Markets, and Institutions over 200 Years of Welfare Debate," *American Sociological Review* 70, no. 2 (2005): 270. They liken the adoption of Malthus's perspective to an "ideational regime change." See also Deborah Valenze, "Charity, Custom, and Humanity: Changing Attitudes Towards the Poor in Eighteenth-Century England," in Jane Garnett and Colin Matthew, eds., *Revival and Religion Since 1700: Essays for John Walsh* (London, 1993), 59–78.

54. Amartya Sen, *Poverty and Famines: An Essay on Entitlement and Deprivation* (Oxford: Clarendon, 1981), 3–8.

55. James, *Population Malthus*, 102. It was clear that the family was negotiating on behalf of Robert during the 1790s, but the rector in charge at the time lived until 1803.

56. For an insightful examination of this position, see Timothy L. Alborn, "From Boys to Men: Moral Restraint at Haileybury College," in *Malthus, Medicine, and Morality: 'Malthusianism' After 1798*, ed. Brian Dolan (Amsterdam: Rodopi, 2000), 33–56; Keith Tribe, "Professors Malthus and Jones: Political Economy at the East India College, 1806–1858," *European Journal of the History of Economic Thought* 2, no. 2 (1995): 333–335.

57. Malthus's own *Principles of Political Economy*, published in 1820, was written as a response to Ricardo and can be considered "an extended commentary upon problems in Smithian economics." At 522 pages, Tribe points out, it "suffered by its relative inaccessibility." He also notes that Malthus failed to incorporate work by Ricardo, James Mill, and McCulloch in any of the examination questions during his many years there, a fact that seems remarkable, given the development of the field of political economy during that time. "Professors Malthus and Jones," 335, 340–341.

58. James, *Population Malthus*, 384.

59. Gerald P. Tyson, *Joseph Johnson, a Liberal Publisher* (Iowa City: University of Iowa Press, 1995), 266n; William Godwin's Journal, http://godwindiary.bodleian.ox.ac.uk/index2.html. Empson, "Life," 477; Otter, "Memoir of Robert Malthus."

3
Rewriting the Agricultural Revolution

1. Catherine Gallagher, *The Body Economic: Life, Death, and Sensation in Political Economy and the Victorian Novel* (Princeton: Princeton University Press, 2006), 15. Donald Winch echoed this observation, pointing out that J. M. Keynes's Malthus was not the same as Malthus himself: *Riches and Poverty: An Intellectual History of Political Economy in Britain, 1750–1834* (Cambridge: Cambridge University Press, 1996), 26–27; Robert J. Mayhew, *Malthus: The Life and Legacies of an Untimely Prophet* (Cambridge, MA: Harvard University Press, 2014), 131, 167.

2. I owe much of this summary to Mayhew's *Malthus*, 133–134, 135, 137, 167. See also Brian Dolan, ed., *Malthus, Medicine, and Morality: 'Malthusianism' After 1798* (Amsterdam: Rodopi, 2000).

3. Conrad Leyser, Naomi Standen, and Stephanie Wynne-Jones, "Settlement, Landscape, and Narrative: What Really Happened in History," *P&P* 238, supplement 13 (2018): 257.

4. Tim Ingold, *Hunters, Pastoralists, and Ranchers: Reindeer Economies and Their Transformations* (Cambridge: Cambridge University Press, 1980), 9.

5. François Hartog, *The Mirror of Herodotus: The Representation of the Other in the Writing of History*, trans. Janet Lloyd (1980; Berkeley: University of California Press, 1988), 9, 375.

6. James C. Scott, *Against the Grain: A Deep History of the Earliest States* (New Haven: Yale University Press, 2017), 62; Leyser et al., "Settlement, Landscape, and Narrative," 232–233; D. Smail, "In the Grip of Sacred History," *American Historical Review* 110 (2005): 1337–1361; Deborah Valenze, *Milk: A Local and Global History* (New Haven: Yale University Press, 2011), 24–27.

7. Robert Bartlett, "Heartland and Border: The Mental and Physical Geography of Medieval Europe," in *Power and Identity in the Middle Ages: Essays in Memory of Rees Davies*, ed. Huw Pryce and John Watts (Oxford: Oxford University Press, 2007), 27.

8. Bartlett, "Heartland and Border"; John Patrick Montaño, *The Roots of English Colonialism in Ireland* (Cambridge: Cambridge University Press, 2011), 30–37.

9. Lauro Martines, *Power and Imagination: City-States in Renaissance Italy* (New York: Knopf, 1979), 72–73; John Hale, *Renaissance Europe: Individual and Society, 1480–1520* (1971; Berkeley: University of California Press, 1977), 173–174.

10. Scott, *Against the Grain*, 7, 221.

11. R. I. Moore, *The First European Revolution, c. 970–1215* (Oxford: Blackwell, 2000), 39–41; Fernand Braudel, *The Structures of Everyday Life: The Limits of the Possible*, trans. Siân Reynolds (New York: Harper & Row,

1981), 133; Sebastien Mercier, *Tableau de Paris* [1781–1788], cited in Braudel, *Structures of Everyday Life*, 133.

12. Braudel, *The Mediterranean and the Mediterranean World in the Age of Philip II*, trans. Siân Reynolds (1966; Berkeley: University of California Press, 1995), 735; David H. Fischer, *The Great Wave: Price Revolutions and the Rhythm of History* (New York: Oxford University Press, 1996).

13. Leyser et al., "Settlement, Landscape, and Narrative"; Fredrik Albritton Jonsson, *Enlightenment's Frontier: The Scottish Highlands and the Origins of Environmentalism* (New Haven: Yale University Press, 2013); Peter M. Jones, *Agricultural Enlightenment: Knowledge, Technology, and Nature, 1750–1840* (Oxford: Oxford University Press, 2016).

14. "Alimentation et categories de l'histoire," *Annales* 16: (1961) 723–728, quoted in Andrew Shryock and Daniel Lord Smail, *Deep History: The Architecture of Past and Present* (Berkeley: University of California Press, 2011), 148.

15. Shryock and Smail, *Deep History*, 148.

16. James Clifford, "On Collecting Art and Culture" in *The Predicament of Culture: Twentieth-Century Ethnography, Literature, and Art* (Cambridge, MA: Harvard University Press, 1988), 226; John J. Corso, "What Does Greimas's Semiotic Square Really Do?" *Mosaic* 47, no. 1 (2014): 70.

17. Gibbon, *DF*, vol. 1, chap. 9, 314; Robert Bartlett, *The Making of Europe: Conquest, Colonization and Cultural Change, 950–1350* (Princeton: Princeton University Press, 1993), 152. Final quote from Bartlett, "Heartland and Border," 37. The modernizing narrative of agriculture is an accurate representation of what appears in typical survey texts today.

18. Peter King, "Gleaners, Farmers, and the Failure of Legal Sanctions, 1750–1850," *P&P* 125 (1989): 116–150; Deborah Valenze, *The First Industrial Woman* (New York: Oxford University Press, 1995), 35–39; on the agricultural revolution, see Eric Kerridge, *The Agricultural Revolution* (London: Allen & Unwin, 1967).

19. James Stafford, "Political Economy and the Reform of Empire in Ireland, 1776–1845" (PhD diss., University of Cambridge, 2016), 11–15. Stafford points out that the "potato held the key to the cultivation of grain as a 'manufacture' " (15).

20. Andrew Lipman, *The Saltwater Frontier: Indians and the Contest for the American Coast* (New Haven: Yale University Press, 2015).

21. Scott, *Against the Grain*, 249ff.

22. Joan Thirsk has described this form of agriculture as "primarily concerned with the production of cereals and meat," foodstuffs in greatest demand by consumers who depended on the market after the Black Death. *Alternative Agriculture: A History from the Black Death to the Present Day* (Oxford: Oxford University Press, 1997), 7.

23. V. Gordon Childe, *What Happened in History* (1942; Harmondsworth: Penguin, 1961), 48. Peter Gathercole, "Childe, (Vere) Gordon (1892–1957),

prehistorian and labour theorist," *DNB* (2004), accessed June 17, 2022. https://www-oxforddnb-com.ezproxy.cul.columbia.edu/view/10.1093/ref:odnb/9780198614128.001.0001/odnb-9780198614128-e-32400. "Even where Childe has ceased to be referenced directly, the teleological premise of his argument—with history as a journey towards complex, urban civilization—continues to influence the way we reconstruct the global past." Childe remains "popular as a framework and straw man in archeological explanation." Leyser et al., "Settlement, Landscape, and Narrative," 233–234.

24. Scott, *Against the Grain*, 65 and passim; Gibbon, *DF*, vol. 1, chap. 9, 206.

25. Thomas Robert Malthus, *An Essay on the Principle of Population: The 1803 Edition*, ed. Shannon C. Stimson (New Haven: Yale University Press, 2018), 417–418. Emphasis added. Malthus's view of nature reaches across the centuries to a summary offered by Woody Allen: "Nature and I are two."

26. S. Eben Kirksey and Stefan Helmreich, "The Emergence of Multispecies Ethnography," *Cultural Anthropology* 25, no. 4 (2010): 545; Fredric Jameson, *The Political Unconscious*, quoted in Corso, "What Does Greimas's Semiotic Square Really Do?" 77.

27. Dorian Q. Fuller, "An Emerging Paradigm Shift in the Origins of Agriculture," *General Anthropology* 17, no. 2 (2010): 10.

28. Fuller, "An Emerging Paradigm Shift," 11. For an account of the impracticality of such a niche construction in the twenty-first century, see Isabella Tree, *Wilding: Returning Nature to Our Farm* (New York: New York Review Books, 2018), 34–39.

29. Ingold, *Hunters, Pastoralists, and Ranchers*.

30. Rachel Laudan, *Cuisine and Empire: Cooking in World History* (Berkeley: University of California Press, 2013), 80–81, 184; Lipman, *The Saltwater Frontier*, 27; Thomas M. Wickman, *Snowshoe Country: An Environmental and Cultural History of Winter in the Early American Northeast* (Cambridge: Cambridge University Press, 2018), 56–90.

31. John R. Gillis, *The Human Shore* (Chicago: University of Chicago Press, 2012), 86; he quotes Donna Merwick, who aptly called the Dutch "alongshore folk," traders who approached their settlements "with the eyes of a seaman," uninterested in gaining possession of and responsibility for land. *The Shame and the Sorrow: Dutch-Amerindian Encounters in New Netherlands* (Philadelphia: University of Pennsylvania Press, 2006), 53.

32. Thirsk, *Alternative Agriculture*, 64.

33. Thirsk, *Alternative Agriculture*, 9.

34. Thirsk, *Alternative Agriculture*, 39, 31, 66, 60, 64, 70, 69.

35. Thirsk, *Alternative Agriculture*, 65, 68–71, 195; Steven King and Alannah Tomkins, eds., *The Poor in England: An Economy of Makeshifts* (Manchester: Manchester University Press, 2003); John Emrys Morgan, "Poverty and Envi-

ronment in Early Modern England," in *Routledge History of Poverty, c. 1450–1800*, ed. David Hitchcock and Julia McClure (London: Routledge, 2020), 79–99.

36. John Bellamy Foster, *Marx's Ecology: Materialism and Nature* (New York: Monthly Review Press, 2000), 144–147.

37. John Bellamy Foster, "Marx's Theory of Metabolic Rift: Classical Foundations for Environmental Sociology," *American Journal of Sociology* 105, no. 2 (1999): 373; *Marx's Ecology*, 149–156, 165.

38. Carl J. Griffin, Roy Jones, and Iain J. M. Robertson, eds., *Moral Ecologies: Histories of Conservation, Dispossession, and Resistance*, Palgrave Studies in World Environmental History (London: Palgrave Macmillan, 2019). https://doi-org.ezproxy.cul.columbia.edu/10.1007/978-3-030-06112-8; and Tim Ingold, *The Perception of the Environment: Essays on Livelihood, Dwelling, and Skill* (London: Routledge, 2011), 11.

4
The Ignoble Savage

1. *Essay* (1798), 82–84.

2. J. G. A. Pocock, "Barbarians and the Redefinition of Europe," in *The Anthropology of the Enlightenment*, ed. Larry Wolff and Marco Cipolloni (Stanford: Stanford University Press, 2007), 45.

3. *Essay* (1798), 84.

4. Ann M. Blair points out that Gibbon was one of several writers in the eighteenth century to "[articulate] fantasies of destroying useless books to stem the never-ending accumulation" of information. *Too Much to Know: Managing Scholarly Information Before the Modern Age* (New Haven: Yale University Press, 2010), 5.

5. Hugh Goodacre, "The William Petty Problem and the Whig History of Economics," *Cambridge Journal of Economics* 38, no. 3 (2014): 563–583.

6. Ted McCormick, *William Petty and the Ambitions of Political Arithmetic* (New York: Oxford University Press, 2009), 212, 214.

7. Roxann Wheeler, *The Complexion of Race: Categories of Difference in Eighteenth-Century British Culture* (Philadelphia: University of Pennsylvania Press, 2000), 46, 190. "Given the way that four-stages theory explained England's special genius and the anatomy of its commercial greatness," Wheeler has argued, "it is surprising that it has not been widely treated as a racial ideology" (188).

8. The participation of exotic Others in reconstituting Britishness has been widely analyzed by eighteenth-century historians. See Kathleen Wilson, *The Island Race: Englishness, Empire, and Gender in the Eighteenth Century* (London: Routledge, 2003), chap. 2. Quotations are from 84–85.

9. Ronald L. Meek, *Social Science and the Ignoble Savage* (Cambridge: Cambridge University Press, 1976), 35, 176; Bashford and Chaplin, *The New Worlds of Thomas Robert Malthus: Rereading the Principle of Population* (Princeton: Princeton University Press, 2016), 39; Patricia James, *Population Malthus: His Life and Times* (London: Routledge, 1979), 25–34; Malthus to Daniel Malthus, April 17, 1788, *UP*, 1: 53.

10. Edward Gibbon, *DF*, vol. 4, chap. 26, 282–283.

11. Karen O'Brien, *Narratives of Enlightenment: Cosmopolitan History from Voltaire to Gibbon* (Cambridge: Cambridge University Press, 1997), 5–7.

12. Meek, *Ignoble Savage*, 174.

13. Meek, *Ignoble Savage*, 2.

14. Anthony Pagden, *European Encounters with the New World: From Renaissance to Romanticism* (New Haven: Yale University Press, 1993), 117; John Locke, *Two Treatises of Government* (London, 1689), Book II, chap. 5, section 49; Bashford and Chaplin, *New Worlds*, 30.

15. Meek, *Ignoble Savage*, 32; WorldCat: http://www.worldcat.org/identities/lccn-n79063793/; Wheeler, *Complexion*, 181.

16. An important exception is Brian Cooper, *Family Fictions and Family Facts: Harriet Martineau, Adolphe Quetelet, and the Population Question in England, 1798–1859* (London: Routledge, 2007); see also Margaret R. Somers and Fred Block, "From Poverty to Perversity: Ideas, Markets, and Institutions over 200 Years of Welfare Debate," *American Sociological Review* 70, no. 2 (2005): 260–287.

17. Malthus to Daniel Malthus, April 17, 1788, *UP*, 1: 53; Andrew Shryock and Daniel Lord Smail, *Deep History: The Architecture of Past and Present* (Berkeley: University of California Press, 2011), 9; Malthus to Daniel Malthus, April 17, 1788, *UP*, 1: 53.

18. Bashford and Chaplin, *New Worlds*, 136.

19. Wheeler, *Complexion*, 24.

20. Paul B. Wood, "The Science of Man," in *Cultures of Natural History*, ed. N. Jardine, J. A. Secord, and E. C. Spary (Cambridge: Cambridge University Press, 1996), 204–205; Anthony Pagden, *The Fall of Natural Man: The American Indian and the Origins of Comparative Ethnology* (Cambridge: Cambridge University Press, 1982), 13–14; Wheeler, *Complexion*, 293–295.

21. Wilson, *Island Race*, 64–65, 71, 230n.

22. Kate Fullagar, *The Savage Visit: New World People and Popular Imperial Culture in Britain, 1710–1795* (Berkeley: University of California Press, 2012), 4–8; Coll Thrush, *Indigenous London: Native Travelers at the Heart of Empire* (New Haven: Yale University Press, 2016), 129; Brian Cooper, *Family Fictions and Family Facts*, 2, 196–240.

23. Meek, *Ignoble Savage*, 71, 116.

24. J. G. A. Pocock, "Barbarians and the Redefinition of Europe: A Study of Gibbon's Third Volume," 37; see also Pocock, *Barbarism and Religion,* 6 vols. (Cambridge: Cambridge University Press, 1999–2015); Pocock, "Gibbon and the Shepherds: The Stages of Society in the *Decline and Fall,*" *History of European Ideas* 2, no. 3 (1981): 193–202 .

25. Pagden, *Fall of Natural Man,* 18–21.

26. Brent D. Shaw, " 'Eaters of Flesh, Drinkers of Milk': The Ancient Mediterranean Ideology of the Pastoral Nomad," *Ancient Society* 13/14 (1982/1983): 5–6.

27. Winfried Menninghaus, *Disgust: The Theory and History of a Strong Sensation* (Albany: State University of New York Press, 2003), 6; Robert Garland, *Daily Life of the Ancient Greeks* (Westport, CT: Greenwood Press, 1998), 76. Garland notes that " 'Typical' barbarian behavior included drinking neat wine, beer, and milk; wearing effeminate clothing; and circumcision." Wheeler, *Complexion,* 46. For deformity as a descriptor of nomadic peoples, see William Smellie, *Philosophy of Natural History,* 2 vols. (Edinburgh, 1790), 2: 159, 160, quoted in Wheeler, *Complexion,* 24.

28. Shaw, " 'Eaters of Flesh, Drinkers of Milk,' " 20. For an important and unmatched treatment of these ideas, see Meek, *Ignoble Savage;* Pagden, *Fall of Natural Man;* see also Tim Ingold, *Hunters, Pastoralists, and Ranchers: Reindeer Economies and Their Transformations* (Cambridge: Cambridge University Press, 1980), chap. 2. For a modern-day meditation on related issues, see Richard W. Bulliet, *Hunters, Herders, and Hamburgers: The Past and Future of Human-Animal Relationships* (New York: Columbia University Press, 2005).

29. Gibbon, *DF,* vol. 9, chap. 50, 91–92.

30. Gibbon, *DF,* vol. 1, chap. 9, 293–294.

31. Gibbon, *DF,* vol. 1, chap. 9, 293.

32. Thomas Robert Malthus, *An Essay on the Principle of Population: The 1803 Edition,* ed. Shannon C. Stimson (New Haven: Yale University Press, 2018), 60.

33. Bashford and Chaplin, *New Worlds,* 83, 87, 117, 120–122, 240. See also Fredrik Albritton Jonsson, "Island, Nation, Planet: Malthus in the Enlightenment," in *New Perspectives on Malthus,* ed. Robert J. Mayhew (Cambridge: Cambridge University Press, 2016), 134, for a discussion of "armchair science" in a similar vein.

34. Bashford and Chaplin, *New Worlds,* 120–121, 134ff. It is worth positing that Malthus selected these sources because of a personal ambition to write a bestseller of his own.

35. Shaw, " 'Eaters of Flesh, Drinkers of Milk,' " 28–29.

36. Jeffrey R. Smitten, "Robertson, William (1721–1793), historian and Church of Scotland minister," *DNB* (2004), accessed April 16, 2021. https://www-oxforddnb-com.ezproxy.cul.columbia.edu/view/10.1093/ref:odnb/9780198614128.001.0001/odnb-9780198614128-e-23817.

37. Jorge Cañizares-Esguerra, *How to Write the History of the New World: Histories, Epistemologies, and Identities in the Eighteenth-Century Atlantic World* (Stanford: Stanford University Press, 2001), 53. Robertson never visited the Americas and, indeed, never left Scotland, a fact that should enhance a sense of wonder at his intellectual indefatigability. Marvin Harris, *The Rise of Anthropological Theory* (New York: Crowell, 1968), 34; Meek, *Ignoble Savage*, 143; Smitten, "Robertson."

38. Robertson, *HA* (1777), 1: 341. Unless otherwise noted, all subsequent references to *The History of America* (*HA*) are to the 1777 edition.

39. Robertson, *HA* (1777), 1: 314.

40. Francisco de Vitorio, *De Indis et De Iure Belli* (1557), ed. Ernest Nys, trans. John Pawley Bate (Washington: Carnegie Institution, 1917), 161; Robertson, *HA* (1777), 1: 316.

41. Robertson, *HA* (1777), 1: 328–329.

42. *Essay* (1803), 41.

43. Robertson, *HA* (1777), 1: 331; *Essay* (1803), 33.

44. Robertson, *HA* (1777), 1: 330.

45. Robertson, *HA* (1777), 1: 329.

46. Malthus, *Essay* (1803), 40, does not copy verbatim. Text from Robertson, *The History of America* (1780 edition), 2: 490, note XXVIII; *The Journey of Álvar Núñez Cabeza de Vaca* (1542), trans. Fanny Bandelier (New York: Allerton Book Company, 1922), 90.

47. *Essay* (1803), 41.

48. *Essay* (1798), 82.

49. Bashford and Chaplin, *New Worlds*, 144; *Essay* (1803), 58–59.

50. *Essay* (1798), 254, 270–71, 354, 357.

51. Somers and Block, "From Poverty to Perversity: Ideas, Markets, and Institutions over 200 Years of Welfare Debate," 271, 276.

52. Malthus, *Principles of Political Economy*, 2nd ed. (London, 1836; New York: Augustus Kelley, 1951), 403.

Interlude

1. Florence Dupont, "The Grammar of Roman Dining," in *Food: A Culinary History from Antiquity to the Present*, ed. Jean-Louis Flandrin and Massimo Montanari (New York: Penguin Books, 2000), 126–127; Rachel Laudan, *Cuisine and Empire: Cooking in World History* (Berkeley: University of California Press, 2013), 84.

2. Massimo Montanari, "Production Structures and Food Systems in the Early Middle Ages," in *Food: A Culinary History*, 172–173; R. I. Moore, *The*

First European Revolution, c. 970–1215 (Oxford: Blackwell, 2000), 40; Stephen L. Kaplan, *The Bakers of Paris and the Bread Question, 1700–1775* (Durham, NC: Duke University Press, 1996), 27.

3. Thomas Moffet, *Health's Improvement: or, Rules Comprizing and Discovering the Nature, Method and Manner of Preparing all sorts of Foods used in this Nation* (London, 1746), 337; William Rubel, *Bread: A Global History* (London: Reaktion Books, 2011), chap. 2; David Gentilcore, *Food and Health in Early Modern Europe: Diet, Medicine, and Society, 1450–1800* (London: Bloomsbury, 2016), 58–63.

4. For an extended discussion of regional differences in bread in Britain, see Joan Thirsk, *Food in Early Modern England: Phases, Fads, Fashions, 1500–1760* (London: Hambledon Continuum, 2006), 46, 86, 167–168, 196–197, 217; J. C. Drummond and Anne Wilbraham, *The Englishman's Food: A History of Five Centuries of English Diet* (London: J. Cape, 1958).

5. Thirsk, *Food in Early Modern England,* 218; Earl of Sheffield, *Remarks on the Deficiency of Grain,* 2 vols. (London, 1799), 1: 108.

6. See Kaplan, *Bakers of Paris,* 26–28, 32, 597n, for a discussion of Simon-Nicolas-Henri Linguet, *Annales politiques, civiles et littéraires du XVIIIe siècle* (Brussels, 1777–92), vol. 5, 431–436.

7. Joan Thirsk, *Food in Early Modern England,* 217.

8. *Essay* (1798), 116; *Essay* (1803), 275.

9. William Buchan, M.D., *Domestic Medicine: or, a Treatise on the Prevention and Cure of Diseases by Regimen and Simple Medicines,* 15th ed. (Dublin, 1797), li, lv.

10. *Essay* (1803), 275.

11. Thomas Robert Malthus, *An Investigation of the Cause of the Present High Price of Provisions* (2nd ed., London, 1800), 12.

12. *Essay* (1798), 116–119.

5
A Natural History of Hunger

1. *An Essay on the Principle of Population* (1798; Harmondsworth: Penguin, 1986), 118.

2. Margaret Schabas, *The Natural Origins of Economics* (Chicago: University of Chicago Press, 2005), 108–109. See also James Stafford, *The Case of Ireland: Commerce, Empire, and the European Order, 1750–1948* (Cambridge: Cambridge University Press, 2022), chap. 5.

3. Fredrik Albritton Jonsson, "Island, Nation, Planet: Malthus in the Enlightenment," in *New Perspectives on Malthus,* ed. Robert J. Mayhew (Cambridge: Cambridge University Press, 2016), 136, 138.

4. Schabas, *Natural Origins of Economics,* 108. For Malthus's inability to "[grasp] how industrial technology would transform the nation in the long run," see Albritton Jonsson, "Island, Nation, Planet," 134.

5. *Essay* (1798), 70, 71–72.

6. *Essay* (1798), 204.

7. *Essay* (1798), 204–205.

8. Anthony Pagden, *Lords of All the World: Ideologies of Empire in Spain, Britain, and France c. 1500–1800* (New Haven: Yale University Press, 1995), 79. Inner quotes from Emeric de Vatell's *Le Droit de gens ou principe de la loi naturelle* (1758).

9. *Second Treatise,* section 34, in John Locke, *Two Treatises of Government,* ed. Peter Laslett (Cambridge: Cambridge University Press, 1988), 291.

10. David Armitage, "John Locke, Carolina, and the Two Treatises of Government," *Political Theory* 32 (2004): 618. For a more ambivalent account, see William Uzgalis, "John Locke, Racism, Slavery, and Indian Lands," *Oxford Handbook of Philosophy and Race,* ed. Naomi Zack (New York: Oxford University Press, 2017), 21–30.

11. Patricia Seed, *Ceremonies of Possession in Europe's Conquest of the New World 1492–1640* (Cambridge: Cambridge University Press, 1995), 34, 36, 36n. Notable from the perspective of today, the picture drawn by Malthus did not include the "ghost acres" of the British overseas empire or any mention of contributing acreage in Ireland. Stafford, *The Case of Ireland;* Fredrik Albritton Jonsson, "Island, Nation, Planet," 141–142.

12. The spatial terms of postcolonial theory are useful here, especially in relation to the longer historical impact of Malthusian thought. See, for example, Arjun Appadurai, "Theory in Anthropology: Center and Periphery," *Comparative Studies in Society and History* 28, no. 2 (1986): 356–361; Joseph Townsend, *A Dissertation on the Poor Laws* (London, 1786), 20–21. Historians have expanded on the importance of this complex feature of human commonality: see James Vernon, *Hunger: A Modern History* (Cambridge, MA: Harvard University Press, 2007), chap. 1, on our tendency to hold misleading views of hunger in the past; see also Nadja Durbach, *Many Mouths: The Politics of Food in Britain from the Workhouse to the Welfare State* (Cambridge: Cambridge University Press, 2020).

13. William Robertson, *HA* (1777), 1: 310, 312, 314, 315.

14. Malthus, *Essay* (1803), 33. A lengthy section is drawn mostly from Robertson without careful attribution and has a more censorious tone.

15. Robertson, *HA* (1777), 1: 306.

16. Robertson, *HA* (1777), 1: 325–326.

17. Robertson, *HA* (1777), 1: 326–328.

18. Robertson, *HA* (1777), 1: 337.

19. Uzgalis, "John Locke," 28.

20. Quoted in Ronald L. Meek, *Social Science and the Ignoble Savage* (Cambridge: Cambridge University Press, 1976), 117–118; see Robertson, *HA* (1777), 1: 335ff on the considerable degree of cultivation by Indigenous Americans.

21. Brent D. Shaw, " 'Eaters of Flesh, Drinkers of Milk': The Ancient Mediterranean Ideology of the Pastoral Nomad," *Ancient Society* 13/14 (1982/1983): 19–20.

22. Robertson, *HA* (1777), 1: 335; Shaw, " 'Eaters of Flesh, Drinkers of Milk,' " 20.

23. Jack D. L. Holmes, "Benjamin Hawkins and the United States Attempts to Teach Farming to Southeastern Indians," *Agricultural History* 60, no. 2 (1986): 224, 231.

24. Alfred W. Crosby, *Ecological Imperialism: The Biological Expansion of Europe, 900–1900* (Cambridge: Cambridge University Press, 1986), 21.

25. Crosby, *Ecological Imperialism,* 23.

26. Colin Tudge, *Neanderthals, Bandits, and Farmers: How Agriculture Really Began* (New Haven: Yale University Press, 1998), 3; James C. Scott, *Against the Grain: A Deep History of the Earliest States* (New Haven: Yale University Press, 2017), 8–12; Fredrik Albritton Jonsson, "The Origins of Cornucopianism: A Preliminary Genealogy," *Critical Historical Studies* 1 (Spring 2014): 151–168; Robert Bartlett, "Heartland and Border: The Mental and Physical Geography of Medieval Europe," in *Power and Identity in the Middle Ages: Essays in Memory of Rees Davies,* ed. Huw Pryce and John Watts (Oxford: Oxford University Press, 2007), 23–36.

27. Robert Bartlett, *The Making of Europe: Conquest, Colonization, and Cultural Change, 950–1350* (Princeton: Princeton University Press, 1993), 152–156.

28. Bartlett, *Making of Europe,* 152.

29. C. A. Bayly, *The Birth of the Modern World, 1780–1914* (Oxford: Blackwell, 2004), 50.

30. Scott, *Against the Grain,* 134–137.

31. C. T. Smith, *An Historical Geography of Western Europe Before 1800* (New York: Praeger, 1967), 163–165; Robert Bartlett, *Making of Europe,* 270.

32. Bartlett, *Making of Europe,* 153–155; Orderic Vitalis in R. I. Moore, *The First European Revolution, c. 970–1215* (Oxford: Blackwell, 2000), 38; see also 39–41; Massimo Montanari, "Romans, Barbarians, Christians: The Dawn of European Food Culture," in *Food: A Culinary History,* trans. Albert Sonnenfeld, ed. Jean-Louis Flandrin and Massimo Montanari (New York: Columbia University Press, 1999), 166; Rachel Laudan, *Cuisine and Empire: Cooking in World History* (Berkeley: University of California Press, 2013), 166–168.

33. Moore, *The First European Revolution,* 39–41.

34. Bayly, *Birth of the Modern World,* 49–50.

35. Richard Manning, *Against the Grain: How Agriculture Has Hijacked Civilization* (New York: North Point Press, 2004), 30.

36. Brian Hayden, "A New View of Domestication," in *Last Hunters, First Farmers,* ed. T. D. Price and A. B. Grebauer (Santa Fe, NM: School of American Researchers Press, 1995), 273–300, cited in Melinda A. Zeder, "Central Questions in the Domestication of Plants and Animals," *Evolutionary Anthropology* 15 (2006): 105–117.

37. Zeder, "Central Questions in the Domestication of Plants and Animals," 113, paraphrasing Jacques Cauvin in *The Birth of the Gods and the Origins of Agriculture* (Cambridge: Cambridge University Press, 2000).

6
In the Margins

1. Alan Barnard, "Hunting-and-Gathering Society: An Eighteenth-Century Scottish Invention," in *Hunter-Gatherers in History, Archaeology, and Anthropology,* ed. Alan Barnard (Oxford: Berg, 2004), 31; Tim Ingold, *The Perception of the Environment: Essays on Livelihood, Dwelling, and Skill* (Oxford: Routledge, 2011), 40; Aristotle's *Politics* as quoted in Mark Pluciennik, "Historical Frames of Reference for 'Hunter-Gatherers,'" in *The Oxford Handbook of the Archaeology and Anthropology of Hunter-Gatherers,* ed. Vicki Cummings, Peter Jordan, and Marek Zvelebil (Oxford: Oxford University Press, 2014), 59.

2. Patricia James, "Biographical Sketches," *TD,* 15–17; Gordon Goodwin and Elizabeth Baigent, "Cripps, John Marten (1780–1853), traveller and antiquary," *DNB* (2004), accessed April 7, 2021. https://www-oxforddnb-com.ezproxy.cul.columbia.edu/view/10.1093/ref:odnb/9780198614128.001.0001/odnb-9780198614128-e-6704.

3. Malthus noted this proverbial expression about Scandinavian weather after hearing it spoken in French while in Norway: *TD,* 92; William Otter, *Life and Remains of Edward Daniel Clarke,* 2nd ed., 2 vols. (London, 1825), 1: 440–443; see also Edward Daniel Clarke, *Travels in Various Countries of Europe, Asia, and Africa: Part the Third: Scandinavia* (London, 1823), 9: ix, 2. Population statistics, such as they were at the time he wrote, seemed to elude Malthus. E. A. Wrigley, "Malthus's Model of a Pre-industrial Economy," in *Malthus Past and Present,* ed. J. Dupâquier, A. Fauve-Chamoux, and E. Grebenick (London: Academic Press, 1983), 114; Michael Drake, "Malthus on Norway," *Population Studies* 20, no. 2 (November 1966); Brian Dolan also offers a helpful discussion of Scandinavian statistical history in "Malthus's Political Economy of Health: The Critique of Scandinavia in the *Essay on Population,*" in *Malthus, Medicine, and Morality,* ed. Brian Dolan (Amsterdam: Rodopi, 2000), 10.

4. Mary Terrall, *The Man Who Flattened the Earth: Maupertuis and the Sciences in the Enlightenment* (Chicago: University of Chicago Press, 2002), 7 and chap. 4 passim.

5. Both cited in Frank Edgar Farley, "Three 'Lapland Songs,'" *Publications of the Modern Language Association of America* 21, no. 1 (1906): 11–12; Erich Pontoppidan, *The Natural History of Norway,* 2 vols. (London, 1755), 2: 286.

6. Kames, *Sketches of the History of Man,* vol. 1, 79–81, quoted in Ronald L. Meek, *Social Science and the Ignoble Savage* (Cambridge: Cambridge University Press, 1976), 158; For discussion of Malthus's travels in Norway within the context of his life, see Patricia James, *Population Malthus: His Life and Times* (London: Routledge, 1979), 71–76.

7. What we know today as the "Travel Diaries" consists of four manuscript volumes transcribed by Patricia James after their recovery from a descendant of T. R. Malthus's older brother, Sydenham. They are now in the Malthus archive at Jesus College, Cambridge University. "Introduction," *TD,* xv; It is possible that Malthus brought along Coxe's and Pontoppidan's books on his journey. Indications of several overlapping descriptions are provided by Patricia James throughout the *Travel Diaries,* such as on 66, 76, 153–154.

8. Fredrik Albritton Jonsson, *Enlightenment's Frontier: The Scottish Highlands and the Origins of Environmentalism* (New Haven: Yale University Press, 2013), 61–65; Edward D. Clarke, *Travels in Various Countries,* 9: 2; Bederman, "Sex, Scandal, Satire, and Population in 1798: Revisiting Malthus's First *Essay,*" *Journal of British Studies* 47 (2008): 775–776; on Joseph Johnson, see James, *Population Malthus,* 55; Clarke himself implied that the region was well traveled, noting, for example, when encounters with other foreigners made the road congested. See Clarke, *Travels in Various Countries,* 9: 334.

9. Lisbet Koerner, *Linnaeus: Nature and Nation* (Cambridge, MA: Harvard University Press, 1999), 66; the Bewick volume went into seven editions, selling roughly 14,000 copies. Iain Bain, "Bewick, Thomas (1753–1828), wood-engraver," *DNB* (2004), accessed April 7, 2021. https://www-oxforddnb-com.ezproxy.cul.columbia.edu/view/10.1093/ref:odnb/9780198614128.001.0001/odnb-9780198614128-e-2334.

10. Koerner, *Linnaeus,* 174; Clarke, *Travels in Various Countries,* 9: 326; John Russell Stephens, "Dibdin, Thomas John (1771–1841), playwright and actor," *DNB* (2004), accessed April 7, 2021. https://www-oxforddnb-com.ezproxy.cul.columbia.edu/view/10.1093/ref:odnb/9780198614128.001.0001/odnb-9780198614128-e-7589.

11. As Clarke put it, his "companions were, for the most part, novices in such pursuits, but not a whit less ardent in the undertaking they had in view." He offered a puff for Malthus's second edition of the *Essay* in a footnote. *Travels in Various Countries,* 9: 43. An early entry during the German part of the trip reported, "The cattle appeared very small and poor. Sheep less than

the welsh breed & lambs very backward." However, he added, "The Viola tricolor, the viola Canina, the ranunculus aquaticus were larger & finer than they usually are in England." Patricia James notes another passage on a fruit tree, crossed out, that concluded (with suggestive syntax), "I believe we have it not in England." *TD*, 40–41, 125, 126; see also 128.

12. Malthus's use of the term "Lapfins" may derive from his reading of Pontoppidan. His contemporaries were much more likely to refer to the Sami as "Laplanders" or simply "Lapps." The group today is the only constituency formally identified as an Indigenous people on the European continent. Because "Lapp" has negative associations with a historical condition of oppression and control, as well as possible linguistic associations to derisive terms, it is now regarded as an appellation of disrespect. *TD*, 182, 185–187; Koerner, *Linnaeus*, 58–59; Åsa Nilsson Dahlström, *Negotiating Wilderness in a Cultural Landscape: Predators and Saami Reindeer Herding in the Laponian World Heritage Area* (Uppsala: Acta Universitatis Upsaliensis, 2003).

13. *TD*, 188.

14. William Coxe, *Travels into Poland, Russia, Sweden, and Denmark: Illustrated with Charts and Engravings*, 4th ed., 5 vols. (London, 1792), 4: 65; Noel D. Broadbent, *Lapps and Labyrinths: Saami Prehistory, Colonization, and Cultural Resilience* (Washington, D.C.: Smithsonian Institution Scholarly Press, 2010), 13–16. Twentieth-century science confirms that "their mtDNA and Y chromosomes indicate that they are an ancient European population" (Broadbent, *Lapps and Labyrinths*, 15). On Schefferus, see Barbara Sjoholm, "Lapponia," *Harvard Review* 29 (2005): 6–19; Allan Ellenius, "Johannes Schefferus and Swedish Antiquity," *Journal of the Warburg and Courtauld Institutes* 20, nos. 1-2 (1957): 59–74. Schefferus's name was Anglicized as "John Scheffer" in the English translation of his history of Lapland, *Lapponia* (Oxford, 1674).

15. Brent D. Shaw, "'Eaters of Flesh, Drinkers of Milk': The Ancient Mediterranean Ideology of the Pastoral Nomad," *Ancient Society* 13/14 (1982/1983): 20; Tacitus as cited in Broadbent, *Lapps and Labyrinths*, 14–15; Olaus Magnus, *A Compendious History of the Goths, Swedes, & Vandals and Other Northern Nations* (London, 1658).

16. Shaw, "'Eaters of Flesh, Drinkers of Milk,'" 28; for his Scandinavian longings for a gun, see *TD*, 195, 200, 219; Gibbon, *DF*, vol. 4, chap. 26, 279; Malthus, *Essay* (1803), 29–30.

17. *TD*, 187–189.

18. *TD*, 189–190.

19. *TD*, 192. Malthus was a notoriously bad speller, as his biographer pointed out and his correspondence with his father demonstrated, but the point here has to do with a significant aspect of Norwegian culture.

20. *TD*, 190–191, 194.

21. *TD*, 190–191.

22. *TD*, 192; Tim Ingold, *Hunters, Pastoralists, and Ranchers: Reindeer Economies and Their Transformations* (Cambridge: Cambridge University Press, 1980), chap. 2.

23. *TD*, 192–193.

24. *TD*, 193; Clarke, *Travels in Various Countries*, 9: 44. Scheffer described the milk as "fat and thick, and very n[o]urishing," an assessment repeated in later accounts. *History of Lapland*, 131.

25. *TD*, 195.

26. Ingold, *Hunters, Pastoralists, and Ranchers*, 5; Koerner, *Linnaeus*, 61; *TD*, 194, 196. The social interaction between humans and non-humans, according to recent anthropology, requires a distinct theoretical approach, described as "multispecies ethnography." According to Bruno Latour, "alterworlds" of animals only partly intersect with those of humans in the course of economic production. S. Eben Kirksey and Stefan Helmreich, "The Emergence of Multispecies Ethnography," *Cultural Anthropology* 25, no. 4 (2010): 553.

27. From his "High Price of Provisions," quoted in James Bonar, *Malthus and His Work* (London, 1885), 28; Michael Drake, "Malthus on Norway," *Population Studies* 20, no. 2 (1966): 176, 181; For Heckscher's critique, see "Malthus och den nordiska befolkningsutvecklingen under 1700-talet," *Ekonomisk Tidskrift* 45 (1943): 191ff, as discussed by Lars Magnusson, "Malthus in Scandinavia, 1799," in *Malthus and His Time*, ed. Michael Turner (London: Palgrave Macmillan, 1986), 60–70; see also Brian Dolan, "Malthus's Political Economy of Health" in *Malthus, Medicine, and Morality*.

28. *Essay* (1803), 151. "Their reindeer form their riches" is drawn from James Thomson's *The Seasons* (London, 1727) and is perhaps the most frequently quoted fact about Lapland existence in eighteenth-century literature on the subject. It is probably no coincidence that Malthus echoed the phrase in his account of nearby Norwegian peasants. Malthus owned a copy of the Thomson volume: see the *Malthus Library Catalogue: The Personal Collection of Thomas Robert Malthus at Jesus College, Cambridge* (New York: Pergamon Press, 1983), 170. The phrase on land is from Book III, chapter 8 of the 1803 edition of the *Essay* (342); Schabas, *The Natural Origins of Economics* (Chicago: University of Chicago Press, 2005), 108.

29. *Essay* (1803), 150, 152–153.

30. Peter Mandler, *The English National Character: The History of an Idea from Edmund Burke to Tony Blair* (New Haven: Yale University Press, 2006), 28, 30–32; John Stuart Mill, "On Nature" in *Collected Works of John Stuart Mill*, vol. 10, *Essays on Ethics, Religion, and Society* (Toronto: University of Toronto Press, 2006), 380–381; Koerner, *Linnaeus*, 29–31.

31. *Essay* (1803), 156.

32. *Essay* (1803), 153, 156–157.

33. Keith Thomas, *Man and the Natural World: A History of the Modern Sensibility* (New York: Pantheon, 1983), 70.

34. Ingold, *Hunters, Pastoralists, and Ranchers*, 10; Kirksey and Helmreich, "Emergence of Multispecies Ethnography," 562–566.

7
Malthus and the Margins

1. Ester Boserup, *My Professional Life and Publications, 1929–1998* (Copenhagen: Museum Tusculanum Press, 1999), 15–27.

2. Boserup provided candid assessments in a series of interviews in the early 1990s. Jon Mathieu, " 'Finding Out Is My Life': Conversations with Ester Boserup in the 1990s," in *Ester Boserup's Legacy on Sustainability: Orientations for Contemporary Research*, ed. Marina Fischer-Kowalski, Anette Reenberg, Anke Schaffartzik, and Andreas Mayer (Dordrecht: Springer, 2014), 15.

3. Ester Boserup, *The Conditions of Agricultural Growth: The Economics of Agrarian Change Under Population Pressure* (Chicago: Aldine, 1965), 13–14. It is difficult for students today to comprehend the need to establish recognition for women workers and their distinct contributions of labor. See Boserup, *Woman's Role in Economic Development* (London: George Allen and Unwin, 1970). Both works have been reprinted. See also *Ester Boserup's Legacy on Sustainability: Orientations for Contemporary Research*, ed. Marina Fischer-Kowalski et al.

4. Boserup, *Conditions*, 13, 18.

5. Boserup, *Conditions*, 18.

6. Boserup, *Conditions*, 21–22.

7. Boserup, *Conditions*, 44, 54–55.

8. Peter M. Jones, *Agricultural Enlightenment: Knowledge, Technology, and Nature, 1750–1840* (Oxford: Oxford University Press, 2016), 134, 223–224.

9. As Pierre Goubert put it, "Something had changed [after 1750], whether in the nature, level, yield, or cost of production, the speed or cost of transportation, the resources of the consumer, or perhaps in government policy." *The Ancien Regime*, trans. Steve Cox (London: Weidenfeld and Nicolson, 1973), 41, quoted in John D. Post, *The Last Great Subsistence Crisis in the Western World* (Baltimore: Johns Hopkins University Press, 1977), xiv.

10. Jones, *Agricultural Enlightenment*, 55–56.

11. Post, *The Last Great Subsistence Crisis*, xii, 25–26, 66; Jones, *Agricultural Enlightenment*, 192.

12. J. R. Poynter, *Society and Pauperism: English Ideas on Poor Relief, 1795–1834* (London: Routledge & Kegan Paul, 1969), 189, 223–224, 242–243.

13. Karl Polanyi, *The Great Transformation: The Political and Economic Origins of Our Time* (Boston: Beacon Press, 1957), 125. On Polanyi, see Margaret R. Somers and Fred Block, "In the Shadow of Speenhamland: Social Policy and the Old Poor Law," *Politics and Society* 31 (2003): 283–323; Margaret R. Somers and Fred Block, "From Poverty to Perversity: Ideas, Markets, and Institutions over 200 Years of Welfare Debate," *American Sociological Review* 70, no. 2 (2005): 260–287.

14. Himmelfarb, *The Idea of Poverty* (New York: Knopf, 1984), 101.

15. Philipp H. Lepenies, "Of Goats and Dogs: Joseph Townsend and the Idealisation of Markets—-A Decisive Episode in the History of Economics," *Cambridge Journal of Economics* 38, no. 2 (2014): 455. Marx charged Malthus of writing "a schoolboyish, superficial plagiary" that "copies whole pages" from Townsend (quoted in Lepenies, "Of Goats and Dogs," 452). For alimentary economics, see Alex de Waal, *Mass Starvation: The History and Future of Famine* (Cambridge: Polity Press, 2018), 39.

16. Boyd Hilton, *The Age of Atonement: The Influence of Evangelicalism on Social and Economic Thought, 1785–1865* (Oxford: Oxford University Press, 1988), 50, 78–79.

17. Gareth Stedman Jones, *An End to Poverty? A Historical Debate* (New York: Columbia University Press, 2004), 97–98, 227.

18. Thomas C. Holt, *The Problem of Freedom: Race, Labor, and Politics in Jamaica and Britain, 1832–1938* (Baltimore: Johns Hopkins University Press, 1992), 320.

19. *Punch* quoted in Holt, *The Problem of Freedom*, 319; E. A. Wrigley and Richard Smith, "Malthus and the Poor Law," *Historical Journal* 63, no. 1 (2020), 33–62.

20. John Stuart Mill, "What Is to Be Done with Ireland?" [1848], quoted in Holt, *The Problem of Freedom*, 324; Mill, *Principles of Political Economy with Some of Their Applications to Social Philosophy* (London, 1848), 272–273.

21. Allan Greer, *Property and Dispossession: Natives, Empires, and Land in Early Modern North America* (Cambridge: Cambridge University Press, 2018), 389–390; see also John Patrick Montaño, *The Roots of English Colonialism in Ireland* (Cambridge: Cambridge University Press, 2011); C. A. Bayly, *The Birth of the Modern World, 1780–1914* (Oxford: Blackwell, 2004), 49–51, 112.

22. Joan Thirsk, "Seventeenth-Century Agriculture and Social Change," in Thirsk, *The Rural Economy of England* (London: Hambledon Continuum, 1984), 192; A. H. Johnson, *The Disappearance of the Small Landowner* (Oxford: Clarendon Press, 1909); Nicholas Blomley, "Making Private Property: Enclosure, Common Right, and the Work of Hedges," *Rural History* 18, no. 1 (2007): 2; Mark Overton, *Agricultural Revolution in England: The Transformation of the Agrarian Economy 1500–1750* (Cambridge: Cambridge University Press, 1996).

23. See Carl J. Griffin, Roy Jones, and Iain J. M. Robertson, eds., *Moral Ecologies: Histories of Conservation, Dispossession, and Resistance* (London:

Palgrave Macmillan, 2019), and Carl J. Griffin and Iain Robertson, "Moral Ecologies: Conservation in Conflict in Rural England," *History Workshop Journal* 82, no. 1 (2016): 24–49.

24. Joan Thirsk, *Alternative Agriculture: A History* (Oxford, 1997), 70, 82–83, 115–116. Much of the following discussion is derived from her unique grasp of local and broad contexts, argued in earlier essays, including "Seventeenth-Century Agriculture and Social Change." For a wealth of diverse examples, see *The Agrarian History of England and Wales*, vol. 5, part 2, *1640–1750: Agrarian Change*, ed. Joan Thirsk (Cambridge: Cambridge University Press, 1985), especially chapters 17–19; John Chartres and David Hey, eds., *English Rural Society, 1500–1800* (Cambridge: Cambridge University Press, 1990); Pamela Horn, *The Tithe War in Pembrokeshire* (Fishguard: Preseli, 1982).

25. James C. Scott, *Seeing Like a State: How Certain Schemes to Improve the Human Condition Have Failed* (New Haven: Yale University Press, 1998), 4–5; Gillian G. Tan, "Pastoralists by Choice," in *Frontier Tibet: Patterns of Change in the Sino-Tibetan Borderlands*, ed. Stéphane Gros (Amsterdam: Amsterdam University Press, 2019), 283, 285.

26. Thirsk, *Alternative Agriculture*, 115–116.

27. Thirsk, *Alternative Agriculture*, 41–42.

28. Thirsk, *Food in Early Modern England*, 93–94, 151–152, 155–157, 163–169, 174–175.

29. J. Hughes, "Just Famine Foods? What Contributions Can Underutilized Plants Make to Food Security?" *International Symposium on Underutilized Plants for Food Security, Nutrition, Income and Sustainable Development*, ed. H. Jaenicke, J. Ganry, I. Hoeschle-Zeledon, R. Kahane, eds. (Arusha, Tanzania, 2009), published as *Acta Horticulturae* 806: https://www.ishs.org/ishs-article/806_2; Jane Corbett, "Famine and Household Coping Strategies," *World Development* 16, no. 9 (1988): 1099–1112.

30. Arthur Young, *Travels, during the years 1787, 1788, and 1789, undertaken more particularly with a view of ascertaining the cultivation, wealth, resources, and national prosperity, of the kingdom of France* (London, 1792), 6–7; Alexis de Tocqueville, *The Old Regime and Revolution*, trans. John Bonner (New York: Harper & Brothers, 1856), 41. Liam Murphy and Thomas Nagel comment that "the conventional nature of property is both perfectly obvious and remarkably easy to forget." *The Myth of Ownership: Taxes and Justice* (New York: Oxford University Press, 2002), 8. For "corrosive logic," see Gareth Stedman Jones, "Malthus, Nineteenth-Century Socialism, and Marx," *Historical Journal* 63, no. 1 (2020): 99; *An End to Poverty*, 103-107.

31. Thirsk, *Alternative Agriculture*, 8, 43; David Underdown, "The Chalk and the Cheese: Contrasts Among the English Clubmen," *P&P* 85 (1979): 30.

32. Peregrine Horden and Nicholas Purcell, *The Corrupting Sea: A Study of Mediterranean History* (Oxford: Blackwell, 2000); Robert Bartlett, "Heartland

and Border: The Mental and Physical Geography of Medieval Europe," in *Power and Identity in the Middle Ages: Essays in Memory of Rees Davies,* ed. Huw Pryce and John Watts (Oxford: Oxford University Press, 2007), 23–36.

33. Steve Hindle, " 'Not by Bread Only'? Common Right, Parish Relief, and Endowed Charity in a Forest Economy, c. 1600–1800," in *The Poor in England, 1700–1850,* ed. Steven King and Alannah Tomkins (Manchester: Manchester University Press, 2003), 63, 65; J. Innes, "The 'Mixed Economy of Welfare' in Early Modern England: Assessments of the Options from Hale to Malthus (1683–1803)," in *Charity, Self-Interest, and Welfare in the English Past,* ed. Martin Daunton (London: Routledge, 1996), 104–134.

34. J. M. Neeson, *Commoners: Common Right, Enclosure, and Social Change in England, 1700–1820* (Cambridge: Cambridge University Press, 1993), 297, 313; John Emrys Morgan, "Poverty and Environment in Early Modern England," in *Routledge History of Poverty, c. 1450–1800,* ed. David Hitchcock and Julia McClure (London: Routledge, 2020), 82.

Bibliography

Early Works

Aitken, John. *Principles of midwifery, or puerperal medicine.* 2nd ed. Edinburgh, 1785.

Andry de Bois-Regard, Nicolas. *Orthopaedia: or, the art of correcting and preventing deformities in children.* 2 vols. London, 1743.

Bonar, James. *Malthus and His Work.* London, 1885.

Buchan, William, M.D. *Domestic Medicine: or, a Treatise on the Prevention and Cure of Diseases by Regimen and Simple Medicines.* 15th ed. Dublin, 1797.

Burke, Edmund. *Thoughts and Details on Scarcity, originally presented to the Right Hon. William Pitt, in the month of November, 1795.* London, 1800.

Cabeza de Vaca, Alvar Nuñez. *The Journey of Alvar Nuñez Cabeza De Vaca.* 1542. Translated by Fanny Bandelier. New York: A. S. Barnes, 1905. https://www.pbs.org/weta/thewest/resources/archives/one/cabeza.htm.

Clarke, Edward Daniel. *Travels in Various Countries of Europe, Asia, and Africa: Part the Third: Scandinavia.* London, 1823.

Cooper, Charles Henry. *Annals of Cambridge.* 5 vols. Cambridge, 1852.

Coxe, William. *Travels into Poland, Russia, Sweden, and Denmark: Illustrated with Charts and Engravings.* 4th ed. 5 vols. (London, 1792).

Empson, William. "Life, Writings, and Character of Mr. Malthus." *Edinburgh Review* 64, no. 130 (1837): 469–506.

Gibbon, Edward. *The History of the Decline and Fall of the Roman Empire.* 13 vols. Basel, 1787–89.

[Godwin, William.] *The Diary of William Godwin.* Edited by Victoria Myers, David O'Shaughnessy, and Mark Philp. Oxford: Oxford Digital Library, 2010. http://godwindiary.bodleian.ox.ac.uk/index2.html.

Godwin, William. *An Enquiry concerning Political Justice*. 2 vols. London, 1793.

Jevons, William Stanley. *The Coal Question*. London, 1865.

Kames, Henry Home. *Sketches of the History of Man*. 4 vols. London, 1788.

Lewis, Theresa, ed. *Extracts of the Journals and Correspondence of Miss Berry*. 3 vols. London, 1865.

Locke, John. *Two Treatises of Government*. London, 1689. Edited with an introduction and notes by Peter Laslett. Cambridge: Cambridge University Press, 1988.

Macintosh Papers. 3rd series. Vol. 22 A (f. 142).

Magnus, Olaus. *A Compendious History of the Goths, Swedes & Vandals and Other Northern Nations*. London, 1658.

Malthus, Daniel. *Letters*. In Electronic Enlightenment Scholarly Edition of Correspondence. Edited by R. V. McNamee. http://www.e-enlightenment.com.ezproxy.cul.columbia.edu/item/rousjeVF0280194a1c.

[Malthus, Thomas Robert]. *An Essay on the Principle of Population*. London: J. Johnson, 1798. Reprint, Harmondsworth: Penguin, 1982.

Malthus, Thomas Robert. *An Essay on the Principle of Population: The 1803 Edition*. Edited by Shannon C. Stimson. New Haven: Yale University Press, 2018.

———. *An Investigation of the Cause of the Present High Price of Provisions.* 2nd ed. London, 1800.

———. *The Pamphlets of Thomas Robert Malthus*. Reprints of Economic Classics. New York: Augustus Kelley, 1970.

———. *Principles of Political Economy*. 2nd ed. London, 1836. Reprint, New York: Augustus M. Kelley, 1951.

———. *The Travel Diaries of T. R. Malthus*. Edited by Patricia James. Cambridge: Cambridge University Press, 1966.

———. *The Unpublished Papers in the Collection of Kanto Gakuen University*. Edited by John Pullen and Trevor Hughes. 2 vols. Cambridge: Cambridge University Press, 1997.

Martineau, Harriet. *Autobiography*. 2nd ed. 3 vols. London, 1877.

Mercier, Sebastien. *Tableau de Paris*. Neuchâtel, 1781.

Mill, John Stuart. *Principles of Political Economy with Some of Their Applications to Social Philosophy*. London, 1848.

Moffett, Thomas. *Health's Improvement: or, Rules Comprizing and Discovering the Nature, Method and Manner of Preparing all sorts of Foods used in this Nation*. London, 1746.

Otter, William. *Life and Remains of Edward Daniel Clarke*. 2nd ed. 2 vols. London, 1825.

[Otter, William]. "Memoir of Robert Malthus." In T. R. Malthus, *Principles of Political Economy*, xiii–liv. London, 1836.

Pontoppidan, Erich. *The Natural History of Norway*. 2 vols. London, 1755.

Robertson, William. *The History of America*. 2 vols. London, 1777.

Scheffer, John [Johannes]. *The History of Lapland, Wherein Are shewed the Original, Manners, Habits, Marriages, Conjurations, &c. of that People*. Oxford, 1674.

Sheffield, John Holroyd, Earl of. *Remarks on the Deficiency of Grain*. 2 vols. London, 1799.

Smellie, William. *Philosophy of Natural History*. 2 vols. Edinburgh, 1790.

Thomson, James. *The Seasons*. London, 1727.

Tocqueville, Alexis de. *The Old Regime and Revolution*. Translated by John Bonner. New York: Harper & Brothers, 1856.

Townsend, Joseph. *A Dissertation on the Poor Laws*. London, 1786.

———. *A Journey through Spain in the years 1786 and 1787*. 3 vols. London, 1791.

Vattel, Emer de. *Le droit des gens ou principes de la loi naturelle*. Lyon, 1758.

Vitoria, Francisco de. *De Indis et De Iure Belli*. 1557. Edited by Ernest Nys. Translated by John Pawley Bate. Washington, D.C.: Carnegie Institution, 1917.

Wakefield, Gilbert. *Memoirs of the Life of Gilbert Wakefield, B.A.* London, 1792.

———. *The Spirit of Christianity compared with the Spirit of the Times in Great Britain*. London, 1794.

Wallace, Robert. *Dissertation on the Numbers of Mankind in Ancient and Modern Times: in which the superior populousness of antiquity is maintained*. Edinburgh, 1753.

White, Gilbert. *The Natural History of Selborne*. London, 1789.

Wordsworth, Christopher. *Scholae Academicae: Some Account of the Studies at the English Universities in the Eighteenth Century*. Cambridge: The University Press, 1877.

Young, Arthur. *Travels, during the years 1787, 1788, and 1789, undertaken more particularly with a view of ascertaining the cultivation, wealth, resources, and national prosperity, of the kingdom of France*. London, 1792.

Later Works

Alborn, Timothy L. *All That Glittered: Britain's Most Precious Metal from Adam Smith to the Gold Rush*. Oxford: Oxford University Press, 2019.

———. "From Boys to Men: Moral Restraint at Haileybury College." In *Malthus, Medicine, and Morality: 'Malthusianism' After 1798*, 33–56. Edited by Brian Dolan. Amsterdam: Rodopi, 2000.

Albritton, Fredrik Jonsson. "The Coal Question Before Jevons." *Historical Journal* 63, special issue 1 (2020): 107–126.

———. *Enlightenment's Frontier: The Scottish Highlands and the Origins of Environmentalism*. New Haven: Yale University Press, 2013.

———. "Island, Nation, Planet: Malthus in the Enlightenment." In *New Perspectives on Malthus*, 128–152. Edited by Robert J. Mayhew. Cambridge: Cambridge University Press, 2016.

———. "The Origins of Cornucopianism: A Preliminary Genealogy." *Critical Historical Studies* 1, no. 1 (2014): 151–168.

Allen, David Elliston. *The Naturalist in Britain: A Social History*. Princeton: Princeton University Press, 1976.

Appadurai, Arjun. "Theory in Anthropology: Center and Periphery." *Comparative Studies in Society and History* 28, no. 2 (1986): 356–361.

Armitage, David. "John Locke, Carolina, and the Two Treatises of Government." *Political Theory* 32, no. 5 (2004): 602–627.

Bain, Iain. "Bewick, Thomas (1753–1828), wood-engraver." *DNB*. September 23, 2004. https://www-oxforddnb-com.ezproxy.cul.columbia.edu/view/10.1093/ref:odnb/9780198614128.01.0001/odnb-9780198614128-e-2334.

Barnard, Alan. "Hunting-and-Gathering Society: An Eighteenth-Century Scottish Invention." In *Hunter-Gatherers in History, Archaeology, and Anthropology*, 1–14. Oxford: Berg, 2004.

Bartlett, Robert. "Heartland and Border: The Mental and Physical Geography of Medieval Europe." In *Power and Identity in the Middle Ages: Essays in Memory of Rees Davies*, 23–36. Edited by Huw Pryce and John Watts. Oxford: Oxford University Press, 2007.

———. *The Making of Europe: Conquest, Colonization, and Cultural Change, 950–1350*. Princeton: Princeton University Press, 1993.

Bashford, Alison, and Joyce Chaplin. *The New Worlds of Thomas Robert Malthus: Rereading the Principle of Population*. Princeton: Princeton University Press, 2016.

Bashford, Alison, Duncan Kelly, and Shailaja Fennell, eds. "Malthusian Moments." *Historical Journal* 63, no. 1 (2020).

Bayly, C. A. *The Birth of the Modern World, 1780–1914*. Oxford: Blackwell, 2004.

Bederman, Gail. "Sex, Scandal, Satire, and Population in 1798: Revisiting Malthus's First *Essay*." *Journal of British Studies* 47, no. 4 (2008): 768–795.

Berg, Maxine. *The Age of Manufactures, 1700–1820*. London: Routledge, 1994.

Blair, Ann M. *Too Much to Know: Managing Scholarly Information Before the Modern Age*. New Haven: Yale University Press, 2010.

Blomley, Nicholas. "Making Private Property: Enclosure, Common Right, and the Work of Hedges." *Rural History* 18, no. 1 (2007): 1–21.

Bohstedt, John. *The Politics of Provisions: Food Riots, Moral Economy, and Market Transition in England, c. 1550–1850*. Burlington, VT: Ashgate, 2010.

Boserup, Ester. *The Conditions of Agricultural Growth: The Economics of Agrarian Change Under Population Pressure*. Chicago: Aldine, 1965.

———. *Woman's Role in Economic Development*. London: George Allen and Unwin, 1970.

Braddick, Michael, and John Walter, eds. *Negotiating Power in Early Modern England*. Cambridge: Cambridge University Press, 2001.

Braudel, Fernand. "Alimentation et categories de l'histoire." *Annales* 16, no. 4 (1961): 723–728.

———. *The Mediterranean and the Mediterranean World in the Age of Philip II*. Paris: Armand Colin, 1949. Translated by Siân Reynolds. Berkeley: University of California Press, 1995.

———. *The Structures of Everyday Life: The Limits of the Possible*. Paris: Armand Colin, 1979. Translated by Siân Reynolds. New York: Harper & Row, 1981.

Broadbent, Noel D. *Lapps and Labyrinths: Saami Prehistory, Colonization, and Cultural Resilience*. Washington, D.C.: Smithsonian Institution Scholarly Press, 2010.

Brooke, Christopher. "Robert Malthus, Rousseauist." *Historical Journal* 63, no. 1 (2020): 15–31.

Bulliet, Richard W. *Hunters, Herders, and Hamburgers: The Past and Future of Human-Animal Relationships*. New York: Columbia University Press, 2005.

Cañizares-Esguerra, Jorge. *How to Write the History of the New World: Histories, Epistemologies, and Identities in the Eighteenth-Century Atlantic World*. Stanford: Stanford University Press, 2001.

Castro, Josué de. *The Geography of Hunger*. Boston: Little, Brown, 1952.

Cauvin, Jacques. *The Birth of the Gods and the Origins of Agriculture*. Cambridge: Cambridge University Press, 2000.

Chakrabarty, Dipesh. *The Climate of History in a Planetary Age*. Chicago: University of Chicago Press, 2021.

———. *Provincializing Europe: Postcolonial Thought and Historical Difference*. Princeton: Princeton University Press, 2000.

Chartres, John, and David Hey, eds. *English Rural Society, 1500–1800*. Cambridge: Cambridge University Press, 1990.

Childe, V. Gordon. *What Happened in History*. Baltimore: Penguin, 1961.

Clemit, Pamela, ed. *The Letters of William Godwin*. Vol. 2, *1798–1805*. Oxford Scholarly Editions Online (March 2015), DOI: 10.1093/actrade/9780199562626.book.1.

Clifford, James. *The Predicament of Culture: Twentieth-Century Ethnography, Literature, and Art*. Cambridge, MA: Harvard University Press, 1988.

Cody, Lisa Forman. "The Politics of Illegitimacy in an Age of Reform: Women, Reproduction, and Political Economy in England's New Poor Law of 1834." *Journal of Women's History* 11, no. 4 (2000): 131–156.

Cooper, Brian. *Family Fictions and Family Facts: Harriet Martineau, Adolphe Quetelet, and the Population Question in England, 1798–1859*. London: Routledge, 2007.

Corbett, Jane. "Famine and Household Coping Strategies." *World Development* 16, no. 9 (1988): 1099–1112.

Corso, John J. "What Does Greimas's Semiotic Square Really Do?" *Mosaic* 47, no. 1 (2014): 69–89.

Crosby, Alfred W. *Ecological Imperialism: The Biological Expansion of Europe, 900–1900*. Cambridge: Cambridge University Press, 1986.

Curry, Kenneth, ed. *New Letters of Robert Southey*. 2 vols. New York: Columbia University Press, 1965.

Dahlström, Åsa Nilsson. *Negotiating Wilderness in a Cultural Landscape: Predators and Saami Reindeer Herding in the Laponian World Heritage Area*. Uppsala: Acta Universitatis Upsaliensis, 2003.

Davis, Mike. *Late Victorian Holocausts: El Niño and the Making of the Third World*. London: Verso, 2001.

DeSoucey, Michaela. *Contested Tastes: Fois Gras and the Politics of Food*. Princeton: Princeton University Press, 2016.

Dolan, Brian, ed. *Malthus, Medicine, and Morality: 'Malthusianism' After 1798*. Amsterdam: Rodopi, 2000.

Drake, Michael. "Malthus on Norway." *Population Studies* 20, no. 2 (1966): 175–196.

Durbach, Nadja. *Many Mouths: The Politics of Food in Britain from the Workhouse to the Welfare State*. Cambridge: Cambridge University Press, 2020.

Ellenius, Allan. "Johannes Schefferus and Swedish Antiquity." *Journal of the Warburg and Courtauld Institutes* 20, nos. 1-2 (1957): 59–74.

Farley, Frank Edgar. "Three 'Lapland Songs.'" *Publications of the Modern Language Association of America* 21, no. 1 (1906): 11–12.

Ferguson, Frances. "Recent Studies in the Restoration and Eighteenth Century." *Studies in English Literature, 1500–1900* 54, no. 3 (2014): 730–731.

Fischer, David H. *The Great Wave: Price Revolutions and the Rhythm of History*. New York: Oxford University Press, 1996.

Fischer-Kowalski, Marina, Anette Reenberg, Anke Schaffartzik, and Andreas Mayer, eds. *Ester Boserup's Legacy on Sustainability: Orientations for Contemporary Research*. Dordrecht: Springer, 2014.

Foster, John Bellamy. *Marx's Ecology: Materialism and Nature*. New York: Monthly Review Press, 2000.

———. "Marx's Theory of Metabolic Rift: Classical Foundations for Environmental Sociology." *American Journal of Sociology* 105, no. 2 (1999): 366–405.

Fulford, Tim. "Apocalyptic Economics and Prophetic Politics: Radical and Romantic Responses to Malthus and Burke." *Studies in Romanticism* 40, no. 3 (2001): 345–368.

Fullagar, Kate. *The Savage Visit: New World People Popular and Imperial Culture in Britain, 1710–1795*. Berkeley: University of California Press, 2012.

Fuller, Dorian Q. "An Emerging Paradigm Shift in the Origins of Agriculture." *General Anthropology* 17, no. 2 (2010): 1–12.

Gallagher, Catherine. *The Body Economic: Life, Death, and Sensation in Political Economy and the Victorian Novel.* Princeton: Princeton University Press, 2006.

———. "The Body Versus the Social Body in the Works of Thomas Malthus and Henry Mayhew." In *The Making of the Modern Body*, 83–106. Edited by Catherine Gallagher and Thomas Laqueur. Berkeley: University of California Press, 1987.

Garland, Robert. *Daily Life of the Ancient Greeks.* Westport, CT: Greenwood Press, 1998.

Gathercole, Peter. "Childe, (Vere) Gordon (1892–1957), prehistorian and labour theorist." *DNB.* September 23, 2004. https://www.oxforddnb.com/view/10.1093/ref:odnb/9780198614128.001.0001/odnb-9780198614128-e-1001997.

Gaull, Marilyn. "Malthus on the Road to Excess." In *1798: The Year of the Lyrical Ballads*, 93–107. Edited by R. Cronin. London: Palgrave Macmillan, 1998.

Gillis, John R. *The Human Shore.* Chicago: University of Chicago Press, 2012.

Goodacre, Hugh. "The William Petty Problem and the Whig History of Economics." *Cambridge Journal of Economics* 38, no. 3 (2014): 563–583.

Goodwin, Gordon, and Elizabeth Baigent. "Cripps, John Marten (1780–1853), traveller and antiquary." *DNB.* September 23, 2004. https://doi-org.ezproxy.cul.columbia.edu/10.1093/ref:odnb/6704.

Goubert, Pierre. *The Ancien Regime.* Translated by Steve Cox. London: Weidenfeld and Nicolson, 1973.

Greer, Allan. *Property and Dispossession: Natives, Empires, and Land in Early Modern North America.* Cambridge: Cambridge University Press, 2018.

Griffin, Carl J., and Iain J. M. Robertson. "Moral Ecologies: Conservation in Conflict in Rural England." *History Workshop Journal* 82, no. 1 (2016): 24–49.

Griffin, Carl J., Roy Jones, and Iain J. M. Robertson, eds. *Moral Ecologies: Histories of Conservation, Dispossession, and Resistance.* London: Palgrave Macmillan, 2019.

Grove, Richard. *Green Imperialism: Colonial Expansion, Tropical Island Edens, and the Origins of Environmentalism, 1600–1860.* New York: Cambridge University Press, 1995.

Harris, Marvin. *The Rise of Anthropological Theory.* New York: Crowell, 1968.

Hartog, François. *The Mirror of Herodotus: The Representation of the Other in the Writing of History.* Translated by Janet Lloyd. Berkeley: University of California Press, 1988.

Harvey, David. *Spaces of Capital: Towards a Critical Geography*. New York: Routledge, 2001.

Hayden, Brian. "A New View of Domestication." In *Last Hunters, First Farmers*. Edited by T. Douglas Price and Anne Birgitte Gebauer. Santa Fe, NM: School of American Research Press, 1995.

Heckscher, Eli F. "Malthus och den nordiska befolkningsutvecklingen under 1700-talet." *Ekonomisk Tidskrift* 45, no. 3 (1943): 191–214.

Hilton, Boyd. *The Age of Atonement: The Influence of Evangelicalism on Social and Economic Thought, 1785–1865*. Oxford: Clarendon Press, 1988.

Himmelfarb, Gertrude. *The Idea of Poverty*. New York: Knopf, 1984.

Hindle, Steve. " 'Not by Bread Only'? Common Right, Parish Relief, and Endowed Charity in a Forest Economy, c. 1600–1800." In *The Poor in England 1700–1850: An Economy of Makeshifts*. Ed. Steven King and Alannah Tomkins. Manchester: Manchester University Press, 2003.

Hindle, Steve, and Jane Humphries. "Feeding the Masses: Plenty and Want and the Distribution of Food and Drink in Historical Perspective." *Economic History Review*, New Series 61, no. S1 (2008): 1–4.

Hobsbawm, Eric J. "Custom, Wages, and Work-Load in Nineteenth-Century Industry." In *Essays in Labour History in Memory of G. D. H. Cole*, 113–139. Edited by Asa Briggs and John Saville. London: Macmillan, 1960.

———. *Industry and Empire*. Harmondsworth: Penguin, 1969.

Holt, Thomas C. *The Problem of Freedom: Race, Labor, and Politics in Jamaica and Britain, 1832–1938*. Baltimore: Johns Hopkins University Press, 1992.

Hont, Istvan, and Michael Ignatieff, eds. *Wealth and Virtue: The Shaping of Political Economy in the Scottish Enlightenment*. Cambridge: Cambridge University Press, 1983.

Horden, Peregrine, and Nicholas Purcell. *The Corrupting Sea: A Study of Mediterranean History*. Oxford: Blackwell, 2000.

Horn, Pamela. *The Tithe War in Pembrokeshire*. Fishguard: Preseli, 1982.

Houston, R. A., ed. *Peasant Petitions*. New York: Palgrave Macmillan, 2014.

Hughes, J. "Just Famine Foods? What Contributions Can Underutilized Plants Make to Food Security?" *International Symposium on Underutilized Plants for Food Security, Nutrition, Income, and Sustainable Development*, 39–48. Edited by H. Jaenicke, J. Ganry, I. Hoeschle-Zeledon, R. Kahane. Arusha, TZ: Acta Horticulturae, 2009.

Ingold, Tim. *Hunters, Pastoralists, and Ranchers: Reindeer Economies and Their Transformations*. Cambridge: Cambridge University Press, 1980.

———. *The Perception of the Environment: Essays on Livelihood, Dwelling, and Skill*. London: Routledge, 2011.

Innes, J. "The 'Mixed Economy of Welfare' in Early Modern England: Assessments of the Options from Hale to Malthus (1683–1803)." In *Charity,*

Self-Interest, and Welfare in the English Past, 104–134. Edited by Martin Daunton. London: Routledge, 1996.

Ismay, Penelope. *Trust Among Strangers: Friendly Societies in Modern Britain*. Cambridge: Cambridge University Press, 2018.

James, Patricia. *Population Malthus: His Life and Times*. London: Routledge & Kegan Paul, 1979.

Jameson, Fredric. *The Political Unconscious: Narrative as a Socially Symbolic Act*. Ithaca: Cornell University Press, 1981.

———. *The Prison-House of Language: A Critical Account of Structuralism and Russian Formalism*. Princeton: Princeton University Press, 1974.

Johnson, A. H. *The Disappearance of the Small Landowner*. Oxford: Clarendon Press, 1909.

Johnston, Kenneth R. *Unusual Suspects: Pitt's Reign of Alarm and the Lost Generation of the 1790s*. Oxford: Oxford University Press, 2013.

Jones, Peter M. *Agricultural Enlightenment: Knowledge, Technology, and Nature, 1750–1840*. Oxford: Oxford University Press, 2016.

Kerridge, Eric. *The Agricultural Revolution*. London: Allen & Unwin, 1967.

King, Peter. "Gleaners, Farmers, and the Failure of Legal Sanctions, 1750–1850." *Past and Present* 125 (1989): 116–150.

King, Steven, and Alannah Tomkins, eds. *The Poor in England, 1700–1850: An Economy of Makeshifts*. Manchester: Manchester University Press, 2003.

Kirksey, S. Eben, and Stefan Helmreich. "The Emergence of Multispecies Ethnography." *Cultural Anthropology* 25, no. 4 (2010): 545–576.

Koerner, Lisbet. *Linnaeus: Nature and Nation*. Cambridge, MA: Harvard University Press, 1999.

Laqueur, Thomas. "The Places of the Dead in Modernity." In *The Age of Cultural Revolutions: Britain and France, 1750–1820*. Ed. Colin Jones and Dror Wahrman. Berkeley: University of California Press, 2002.

LeMahieu, D. L. "Malthus and the Theology of Scarcity." *Journal of the History of Ideas* 40, no. 3 (1979): 467–474.

———. *The Mind of William Paley*. Lincoln: University of Nebraska Press, 1976.

Lepenies, Philipp. "Of Goats and Dogs: Joseph Townsend and the Idealisation of Markets—A Decisive Episode in the History of Economics." *Cambridge Journal of Economics* 38, no. 2 (2014): 447–457.

Leyser, Conrad, Naomi Standen, and Stephanie Wynne-Jones. "Settlement, Landscape, and Narrative: What Really Happened in History." *Past and Present* 238, supplement 13 (2018): 232–260.

Lipman, Andrew. *The Saltwater Frontier: Indians and the Contest for the American Coast*. New Haven: Yale University Press, 2015.

Magnusson, Lars. "Malthus in Scandinavia, 1799." In *Malthus and His Time*, 60–70. Edited by Michael Turner. London: Palgrave Macmillan, 1986.

Malthus Library Catalogue: The Personal Collection of Thomas Robert Malthus at Jesus College, Cambridge. New York: Pergamon Press, 1983.

Mandler, Peter. *The English National Character: The History of an Idea from Edmund Burke to Tony Blair*. New Haven: Yale University Press, 2006.

Manning, Richard. *Against the Grain: How Agriculture Has Hijacked Civilization*. New York: North Point Press, 2004.

Martines, Lauro. *Power and Imagination: City-States in Renaissance Italy*. New York: Knopf, 1979.

Mathieu, Jon. "'Finding Out Is My Life': Conversations with Ester Boserup in the 1990s." In *Ester Boserup's Legacy on Sustainability: Orientations for Contemporary Research*, 13–22. Edited by Marina Fischer-Kowalski, Anette Reenberg, Anke Schaffartzik, and Andreas Mayer. Dordrecht: Springer, 2014.

Mayhew, Robert J. *Malthus: The Life and Legacies of an Untimely Prophet*. Cambridge, MA: Harvard University Press, 2014.

Mayhew, Robert J., ed. *New Perspectives on Malthus*. Cambridge: Cambridge University Press, 2016.

McCalman, Iain. *Radical Underworld: Prophets, Revolutionaries, and Pornographers in London, 1795–1840*. Cambridge: Cambridge University Press, 1988.

McCormick, Ted. *William Petty and the Ambitions of Political Arithmetic*. New York: Oxford University Press, 2009.

Meek, Ronald L. "Malthus—Yesterday and Today." In *Thomas Robert Malthus: Critical Assessments*. Vol. 1, 175–197. Edited by John Cunningham Wood. London: Croom Helm, 1986.

———. *Social Science and the Ignoble Savage*. Cambridge: Cambridge University Press, 1976.

Menninghaus, Winfried. *Disgust: The Theory and History of a Strong Sensation*. Albany: State University of New York Press, 2003.

Merchant, Carolyn. *The Death of Nature: Women, Ecology, and the Scientific Revolution*. New York: Harper & Row, 1982.

Merwick, Donna. *The Shame and the Sorrow: Dutch-Amerindian Encounters in New Netherlands*. Philadelphia: University of Pennsylvania Press, 2006.

Milgate, Murray, and Shannon C. Stimson. *After Adam Smith: A Century of Transformation in Politics and Political Economy*. Princeton: Princeton University Press, 2009.

Montanari, Massimo. "Romans, Barbarians, Christians: The Dawn of European Food Culture." In *Food: A Culinary History from Antiquity to the Present*, 165–167. Edited by Jean-Louis Flandrin and Massimo Montanari. Translated by Albert Sonnenfeld. New York: Columbia University Press, 1999.

Montaño, John Patrick. *The Roots of English Colonialism in Ireland*. Cambridge: Cambridge University Press, 2011.

Moore, R. I. *The First European Revolution, c. 970–1215*. Oxford: Blackwell, 2000.

Morgan, John Emrys. "Poverty and Environment in Early Modern England." In *Routledge History of Poverty, c. 1450–1800*, 79–99. Edited by David Hitchcock and Julia McClure. London: Routledge, 2020.

Muldrew, Craig. *Food, Energy, and the Creation of Industriousness: Work and Material Culture in Agrarian England, 1550–1780*. Cambridge: Cambridge University Press, 2011.

Murphy, Liam, and Thomas Nagel. *The Myth of Ownership: Taxes and Justice*. Oxford: Oxford University Press, 2002.

Neeson, J. M. *Commoners: Common Right, Enclosure, and Social Change in England, 1700–1820*. Cambridge: Cambridge University Press, 1993.

Nicholson, Mervyn. "The Eleventh Commandment: Sex and Spirit in Wollstonecraft and Malthus." *Journal of the History of Ideas* 51, no. 3 (1990): 401–421.

Oakleaf, David. "Graves, Richard (1715–1804), writer and translator." *DNB*. September 23, 2004. https://www.oxforddnb.com/view/10.1093/ref:odnb/9780198614128.001.0001/odnb-9780198614128-e-11313.

O'Brien, Karen. *Narratives of Enlightenment: Cosmopolitan History from Voltaire to Gibbon*. Cambridge: Cambridge University Press, 1997.

Overton, Mark. *Agricultural Revolution in England: The Transformation of the Agrarian Economy 1500–1750*. Cambridge: Cambridge University Press, 1996.

Pagden, Anthony. *European Encounters with the New World: From Renaissance to Romanticism*. New Haven: Yale University Press, 1993.

———. *The Fall of Natural Man: The American Indian and the Origins of Comparative Ethnology*. Cambridge: Cambridge University Press, 1982.

———. *Lords of All the World: Ideologies of Empire in Spain, Britain, and France c. 1500–1800*. New Haven: Yale University Press, 1995.

Patel, Raj. *Stuffed and Starved: The Hidden Battle for the World Food System*. New York: Melville House, 2012.

Paul, Tawny. *The Poverty of Disaster: Debt and Insecurity in Eighteenth-Century Britain*. Cambridge: Cambridge University Press, 2019.

Philp, Mark. "Godwin, William (1756–1836), philosopher and novelist." *DNB*. September 23, 2004. https://doi-org.ezproxy.cul.columbia.edu/10.1093/ref:odnb/10898.

Pluciennik, Mark. "Historical Frames of Reference for 'Hunter-Gatherers.'" In *The Oxford Handbook of the Archaeology and Anthropology of Hunter-Gatherers*, 55–68. Edited by Vicki Cummings, Peter Jordan, and Marek Zvelebil. Oxford: Oxford University Press, 2014.

Pluymers, Keith. *No Wood, No Kingdom: Political Ecology in the English Atlantic*. Philadelphia: University of Pennsylvania Press, 2021.

Pocock, J. G. A. "Barbarians and the Redefinition of Europe: A Study of Gibbon's Third Volume." In *The Anthropology of the Enlightenment*, 35–49. Edited by Larry Wolff and Marco Cipolloni. Stanford: Stanford University Press, 2007.

———. *Barbarism and Religion*. 6 vols. Cambridge: Cambridge University Press, 1999–2015.

———. "Gibbon and the Shepherds: The Stages of Society in the *Decline and Fall*." *History of European Ideas* 2, no. 3 (1981): 193–202.

Polanyi, Karl. *The Great Transformation: The Political and Economic Origins of Our Time*. Boston: Beacon Press, 1957.

Post, John D. *The Last Great Subsistence Crisis in the Western World*. Baltimore: Johns Hopkins University Press, 1977.

Poynter, J. M. *Society and Pauperism: English Ideas on Poor Relief, 1795–1834*. London: Routledge & Kegan Paul, 1969.

Prochaska, Frank. "English State Trials in the 1790s: A Case Study." *Journal of British Studies* 13, no. 1 (1973): 63–82.

Pullen, J. M. "Malthus' Theological Ideas and Their Influence on His Principle of Population." *History of Political Economy* 13, no. 1 (1981): 39–54.

Pullen, John, and Trevor Hughes, eds. *T. R. Malthus: The Unpublished Papers in the Collection of Kanto Gakuen University*. 2 vols. Cambridge: Cambridge University Press, 1997 and 2004.

Ritvo, Harriet. *The Animal Estate: The English and Other Creatures in the Victorian Age*. Cambridge, MA: Harvard University Press, 1987.

Robin, Libby, Sverker Sörlin, and Paul Warde. *The Future of Nature*. New Haven: Yale University Press, 2013.

Ross, Eric B. *The Malthus Factor: Poverty, Politics, and Population in Capitalist Development*. New York: Zed Books, 1998.

Rothschild, Emma. *Economic Sentiments: Adam Smith, Condorcet, and the Enlightenment*. Cambridge, MA: Harvard University Press, 2001.

Rubel, William. *Bread: A Global History*. London: Reaktion Books, 2011.

Schabas, Margaret. *The Natural Origins of Economics*. Chicago: University of Chicago Press, 2005.

Schwarz, Leonard. "Customs, Wages, and Workload During Industrialization." *Past and Present* 197 (2007): 143–175.

Scott, James C. *Against the Grain: A Deep History of the Earliest States*. New Haven: Yale University Press, 2017.

———. *Seeing Like a State: How Certain Schemes to Improve the Human Condition Have Failed*. New Haven: Yale University Press, 1998.

Secord, Anne. "Science in the Pub: Artisan Botanists in Early Nineteenth-Century Lancashire." *History of Science* 32, no. 3 (1994): 269–315.

Seed, Patricia. *Ceremonies of Possession in Europe's Conquest of the New World 1492–1640*. Cambridge: Cambridge University Press, 1995.

Sen, Amartya. *Poverty and Famines: An Essay on Entitlement and Deprivation.* Oxford: Clarendon Press, 1981.

Sharp, Buchanan. *Famine and Scarcity in Late Medieval and Early Modern England: The Regulation of Grain Marketing, 1256–1631.* Cambridge: Cambridge University Press, 2016.

Shaw, Brent D. " 'Eaters of Flesh, Drinkers of Milk': The Ancient Mediterranean Ideology of the Pastoral Nomad." *Ancient Society* 13/14 (1982/1983): 5–31.

Shryock, Andrew, and Daniel Lord Smail. *Deep History: The Architecture of Past and Present.* Berkeley: University of California Press, 2011.

Sjoholm, Barbara. "Lapponia." *Harvard Review* 29 (2005): 6–19.

Skousen, Mark. *The Making of Modern Economics: The Lives and Ideas of the Great Thinkers.* 2nd ed. Armonk, NY: M. E. Sharpe, 2009.

Smail, D. "In the Grip of Sacred History." *American Historical Review* 110, no. 5 (2005): 1337–1361.

Smith, Ruth L., and Deborah M. Valenze. "Mutuality and Marginality: Liberal Moral Theory and Working-Class Women in Nineteenth-Century England." *Signs: Journal of Women in Culture and Society* 13, no. 4 (1988): 277–298.

Smitten, Jeffrey R. "Robertson, William (1721–1793), historian and Church of Scotland minister." *DNB.* September 23, 2004. https://doi-org.ezproxy.cul.columbia.edu/10.1093/ref:odnb/23817.

Somers, Margaret R., and Fred Block. "From Poverty to Perversity: Ideas, Markets, and Institutions over 200 Years of Welfare Debate." *American Sociological Review* 70, no. 2 (2005): 260–287.

———. "In the Shadow of Speenhamland: Social Policy and the Old Poor Law." *Politics and Society* 31, no. 2 (2003): 283–323.

Stafford, James. *The Case of Ireland: Commerce, Empire, and the European Order, 1750–1848.* Cambridge: Cambridge University Press, 2022.

———. "Political Economy and the Reform of Empire in Ireland, 1776–1845." PhD diss., University of Cambridge, 2016.

Stedman Jones, Gareth. *An End to Poverty? A Historical Debate.* New York: Columbia University Press, 2004.

———. "Malthus, Nineteenth-Century Socialism, and Marx." *Historical Journal* 63, no. 1 (2020): 91-106.

Stephens, John Russell. "Dibdin, Thomas John (1771–1841), playwright and actor." *DNB.* September 23, 2004. https://www-oxforddnb-com.ezproxy.cul.columbia.edu/view/10.1093/ref:odnb/9780198614128.001.0001/odnb-9780198614128-e-7589.

Tan, Gillian G. "Pastoralists by Choice: Adaptations in Contemporary Pastoralism in Eastern Kham." In *Frontier Tibet: Patterns of Change in the Sino-Tibetan Borderlands,* 281–304. Edited by Stéphane Gros. Amsterdam: Amsterdam University Press, 2019.

Terrall, Mary. *The Man Who Flattened the Earth: Maupertuis and the Sciences in the Enlightenment*. Chicago: University of Chicago Press, 2002.

Thirsk, Joan. *Alternative Agriculture: A History from the Black Death to the Present Day*. Oxford: Oxford University Press, 1997.

———. *Food in Early Modern England*. London: Hambledon Continuum, 2006.

———. "Reply [to Jan de Vries]." Following "Policies for Retrenchment in Seventeenth-Century Europe: A Review Article." *Comparative Studies in Society and History* 22, no. 4 (1980): 637–638.

———. *The Rural Economy of England*. London: Hambledon Continuum, 1984.

Thirsk, Joan, ed. *The Agrarian History of England and Wales*. Vol. 5, part 2, *1640–1750: Agrarian Change*. Cambridge: Cambridge University Press, 1985.

Thomas, Keith. *Man and the Natural World: A History of the Modern Sensibility*. New York: Pantheon, 1983.

Thrush, Coll. *Indigenous London: Native Travelers at the Heart of Empire*. New Haven: Yale University Press, 2016.

Tree, Isabella. *Wilding: Returning Nature to Our Farm*. New York: New York Review Books, 2018.

Trentmann, Frank. *Free Trade Nation: Commerce, Consumption, and Civil Society in Modern Britain*. Oxford: Oxford University Press, 2008.

Tribe, Keith. "Professors Malthus and Jones: Political Economy at the East India College, 1806–1858." *European Journal of the History of Economic Thought* 2, no. 2 (1995): 333–335.

Tudge, Colin. *Neanderthals, Bandits, and Farmers: How Agriculture Really Began*. New Haven: Yale University Press, 1998.

Tyson, Gerald P. *Joseph Johnson: A Liberal Publisher*. Iowa City: University of Iowa Press, 1995.

Underdown, David. "The Chalk and the Cheese: Contrasts Among the English Clubmen." *Past and Present* 85 (1979): 25–48.

Uzgalis, William. "John Locke, Racism, Slavery, and Indian Lands." *Oxford Handbook of Philosophy and Race*, 21–30. Edited by Naomi Zack. New York: Oxford University Press, 2017.

Valenze, Deborah. "The Art of Women and the Business of Men: Women's Work and the Dairy Industry, c. 1740–1840." *Past and Present* 130 (1991): 142–169.

———. "Charity, Custom and Humanity: Changing Attitudes Towards the Poor in Eighteenth-Century England." In *Revival and Religion Since 1700: Essays for John Walsh*, 59–78. Edited by Jane Garnett and Colin Matthew. London: Bloomsbury Academic, 1993.

———. *The First Industrial Woman*. New York: Oxford University Press, 1995.

———. *Milk: A Local and Global History*. New Haven: Yale University Press, 2011.

———. "The Tortoise and the Hare: Thomas Robert Malthus as Natural Philosopher." In *An Essay on the Principle of Population: The 1803 Edition*, 497–515. Edited by Shannon C. Stimson. New Haven: Yale University Press, 2018.

Vernon, James. *Hunger: A Modern History*. Cambridge, MA: Harvard University Press, 2007.

Waal, Alex de. *Mass Starvation: The History and Future of Famine*. Cambridge: Polity, 2018.

Warde, Paul. *The Invention of Sustainability: Nature and Destiny, c. 1500–1870*. Cambridge: Cambridge University Press, 2018.

———. *Nature's End: History and the Environment*. Houndmills, Basingstoke: Palgrave Macmillan, 2009.

Waterman, A. M. C. *Revolution, Economics, and Religion: Christian Political Economy, 1798–1833*. Cambridge: Cambridge University Press, 1991.

Wheeler, Roxann. *The Complexion of Race: Categories of Difference in Eighteenth-Century British Culture*. Philadelphia: University of Pennsylvania Press, 2000.

Wickman, Thomas M. *Snowshoe Country: An Environmental and Cultural History of Winter in the Early American Northeast*. Cambridge: Cambridge University Press, 2018.

Wilson, Kathleen. *The Island Race: Englishness, Empire, and Gender in the Eighteenth Century*. London: Routledge, 2003.

———. "Print, People, and Culture in the Urban Renaissance." In *The Sense of the People: Politics, Culture, and Imperialism in England, 1715–1785*, 27–83. Cambridge: Cambridge University Press, 1995.

Winch, Donald. *Malthus*. Oxford: Oxford University Press, 1987.

———. "Mr. Gradgrind and Jerusalem." In *Economy, Polity, and Society: British Intellectual History, 1750–1950*, 243–266. Edited by Stefan Collini, Richard Whatmore, and Brian Young. Cambridge: Cambridge University Press, 2000.

———. *Riches and Poverty: An Intellectual History of Political Economy in Britain, 1750–1834*. Cambridge: Cambridge University Press, 1996.

Wolff, Larry. *Inventing Eastern Europe: The Map of Civilization on the Mind of the Enlightenment*. Stanford: Stanford University Press, 1994.

Wood, Paul B. "The Science of Man." In *Cultures of Natural History*, 204–205. Edited by N. Jardine, J. A. Secord, and E. C. Spary. Cambridge: Cambridge University Press, 1996.

Woods, R. I. "Review Article: Immortal Malthus." *Journal of Historical Geography* 14, no. 3 (1988): 298–300.

Wrigley, E. A. "Malthus's Model of a Pre-Industrial Economy." In *Malthus Past and Present*, 111–124. Edited by J. Dupâquier, A. Fauve-Chamoux, and E. Grebenik. London: Academic Press, 1983.

Wrigley, E. A., and Richard Smith. "Malthus and the Poor Law." *Historical Journal* 63, no. 1 (2020): 33–62.

Zeder, Melinda A. "Central Questions in the Domestication of Plants and Animals." *Evolutionary Anthropology* 15, no. 3 (2006): 105–117.

Zilberstein, Anya. *A Temperate Empire: Making Climate Change in Early America*. Oxford: Oxford University Press, 2016.

Index

Note: Illustrations are identified by italicized page numbers.